The Impact of Women in Public Office

Edited by Susan J. Carroll

INDIANA UNIVERSITY PRESS

Bloomington and Indianapolis

This book is a publication of

Indiana University Press

601 North Morton Street

Bloomington, IN 47404-3797 USA

http://iupress.indiana.edu

Telephone orders   800-842-6796
Fax orders   812-855-7931
Orders by e-mail   iuporder@indiana.edu

Library of Congress Cataloging-in-Publication Data

The impact of women in public office / edited by Susan J. Carroll.
p. cm.
Includes bibliographical references and index.
ISBN 0-253-34008-X (cloth : alk. paper) — ISBN 0-253-21488-2 (pbk. : alk. paper)
1. Women in politics—United States. I. Carroll, Susan J., date
HQ1236.5.U6 I524 2001
320'.082'0973—dc21
2001001680

1 2 3 4 5 06 05 04 03 02 01

TO THE MEMORY OF DIANE BLAIR

Contents

Contents

Acknowledgments

I am very grateful to the Charles H. Revson Foundation for their support of the research presented in this volume. Over the years the Revson Foundation has been a major sponsor of research conducted by the Center for American Women and Politics (CAWP), and without the generosity and encouragement of the Revson Foundation, scholars and political observers would certainly know far less about who the women in office are, how they got there, and what difference their presence makes.

In undertaking the major research initiative which led to this volume, one of CAWP's major goals was to stimulate research attention and scholarly interest in questions regarding the impact of women in public office. The scholarly work and the careers of the contributors to this volume are a testament to the fact that we at CAWP (and they as scholars) were successful in achieving that goal. Some of the contributors began this project as advanced graduate students or new Ph.D.s and have subsequently become major scholars in the field of women and politics. Others, who were already established scholars at the inception of this project, have grown older and grayer (some because of this project) but even more accomplished. All contributors are now well known for their work on women public officials and the difference the presence of women in office makes. Collectively, they and a few others have truly developed a whole new area of research on the impact of women in public office.

This project has taken a number of years to reach completion, and the contributors have shown enormous patience with long delays and too many requests for revisions. I thank them for hanging in there even

ix

when, I'm sure, they were convinced that this book would never be finished. I am constantly amazed and very grateful that they all still speak to me (although I'm sure if I ever even hint of editing another book, they will head for the hills with great haste)!

I also want to thank Joan Catapano, former Assistant Director and Associate Sponsoring Editor at Indiana University Press, for her unfailing interest, support, and patience. Michelle Saint-Germain, one of the few scholars in the country who knows as much about the subject matter of this book as the contributors, offered constructive feedback and helpful suggestions that far exceeded the responsibility of any reviewer. This is a much better volume because of Michelle's input.

I am grateful to all the current and former faculty and staff at the Center for American Women and Politics who contributed to the research project which formed the basis for this volume, especially my co-principal investigators Debra Dodson and Ruth B. Mandel, as well as Debbie Walsh, Kathy Kleeman, Lucy Baruch, and Ella Taylor. Finally, I want to thank the hundreds of public officials who took time from their busy schedules to participate in the various research projects described in this volume.

Introduction

Susan J. Carroll

Over the past three decades more and more women have won election to public office and obtained high-level appointive positions in government. Although women are still far from parity with men, the numbers of women holding office at most levels of government have increased incrementally over time.[1] For example, while the 1,670 women who serve in state legislatures across the United States in 2000 constitute only 22.5 percent of state legislators, the number of women serving in state legislatures increased from 344 in 1971 to 908 in 1981 to 1,368 in 1991 (Center for American Women and Politics 2000b).

The growing numbers of women serving in public office raise important questions about the political significance of gender. Barring significant changes in our system of electoral politics, the general trend of incremental increases in the numbers of women serving in public office is likely to continue well into the 21st century. As more and more women enter public office, it is critically important that we understand what the consequences are likely to be for both public policy and the political process.

Political scientists frequently distinguish between descriptive or numerical representation (i.e., the number of members of a particular group who hold office) and substantive representation (i.e., representation of group interests).[2] Most research on political women conducted throughout the 1970s and 1980s was concerned primarily with women's numerical representation and was aimed at understanding why so few women held public office (Diamond 1977; Githens and Prestage 1977; Carroll 1994; Darcy, Welch, and Clark 1994). This research focused on factors such as the attitudes of voters and party leaders, fund raising, gender-role socialization, the advantages of incumbency, and the nature of the electoral system. Because of this research, we now know a great deal about the obstacles women face when they seek public office and have a far better understanding of the reasons for women's historical and current numerical underrepresentation among public officials.

Although seldom explicitly addressed, the assumption that increasing the number of women in public office would make a difference in policy outcomes was implicit in much of this research. Researchers assumed that an increase in the number of women serving in public office would lead to better representation of women's interests—i.e., that there would be a relationship between numerical representation and substantive representation.

While researchers have long been interested in the question of whether increased numerical representation would lead to increased substantive representation, until recent years so few women were serving at most levels of office that it seemed premature to ask what difference their presence in office was making. So long as women were mere tokens struggling for survival in institutions unaccustomed to their presence, it seemed unlikely that women public officials would or could have much of a distinctive, gender-related impact. In recent years, however, women's numbers have increased to the point where women public officials are present in sufficient numbers at most levels of office that any distinctive impact which women are likely to have on public policy or the political process should begin to be evident. As a result, researchers have recently begun to explore the relationship between women's numerical representation and their substantive representation and to address the question of whether women's increased presence among public officials is making a difference. The studies included in this volume, which focus on women serving in different offices in varying locales, are among the first seriously to examine questions about the impact of women in public office.

Substantive Representation: What Is It That Women Might Represent?

The extent to which a relationship exists between numerical and substantive representation of women is an empirical question. However, there can be little doubt that the political arm of the feminist movement in the United States has viewed these forms of representation as inextricably intertwined. Advocacy organizations, such as the National Women's Political Caucus, and women's political action committees, such as EMILY's List and the Women's Campaign Fund, have argued for years that women have distinctive political interests and that the election of more women to public office would lead to greater representation of women's interests.

While many women in the general public still shy away from the label "feminist" and disagree with parts of the feminist agenda, today many more women seem to perceive their interests as somewhat different from those of men than was true two decades ago, largely as a result of the influence of the women's movement. The development of the so-called "gender gap" in public opinion and voting behavior over the past two decades is one indication that women increasingly see their political interests as distinct from those of men. In each of the presidential elections held between 1980 and 2000, 4 percent to 11 percent fewer women than men voted for the Republican candidate. In addition, the gender gap was evident in a majority of statewide races throughout the 1980s and 1990s, with women usually casting their votes disproportionately for Democratic candidates but occasionally giving their votes disproportionately to Republican candidates who appealed to women voters on the issues. Recent public opinion polls also have shown a gender gap on a variety of public policy issues. Compared with men, women in the general population are, for example: less militaristic on issues of war and peace, more often opposed to the death penalty, more likely to favor gun control, more likely to favor measures to protect the environment, more supportive of programs to help the economically disadvantaged, less critical of government, more critical of business, and more likely to favor laws to regulate and control various social vices (e.g., drugs, gambling, pornography) (Center for American Women and Politics 2000c).

Despite clear evidence of a gender gap in voting behavior and public opinion suggesting that women and men see their political interests somewhat differently, defining "women's interests," i.e., that which women public officials might distinctively represent, has become an increasingly difficult task in the 1990s. Both political developments and academic theorizing have called into question static and essentialized conceptions of the category "women" and of concepts such as "women's interests."

Of course, feminist activist organizations have long had policy agendas that represent one particular conception of women's interests. In recent years, however, feminist policy agendas have been called into question by nonwhite, non–middle class, non-heterosexual women who feel that the issues that most concern them often are not given priority by feminist organizations. Feminist policy agendas also have been challenged by the often very visible, politically conservative women who have attained office as part of the resurgence of right-wing politics in the United States during the 1980s and 1990s and who often express very different ideas about which public policy proposals best serve women's interests.

In the academy, feminist scholars also have waged an attack on static, uncomplicated conceptions of gender difference. Numerous scholars have argued that grand generalizations about differences between women and men tend to erase the experiences of nonwhite, non-heterosexual women and that the category "women" must be opened up and examined in order to reveal the great diversity that exists among those encompassed by the category (e.g., Spelman 1988; Phelan 1994; Mohanty 1991; hooks 1984). Some scholars, influenced by antifoundationalist, poststructural, or postmodern thinking, have also called into question the very idea that people have stable, fixed identities. They view identities as fluid, provisional, and contingent and believe that identity categories, such as the category "woman," are always exclusionary and serve to reify one difference while erasing and obscuring other differences (see, e.g., De Lauretis 1984; Butler 1992; Alcoff 1988; Scott 1986).

Given that the definition or even the very existence of "women's interests" is highly contested, is there an alternative way to talk about what women might bring to politics as they move into elective and appointive positions in increasing numbers? During the 1990s, especially during the 1992 election, women who ran for office frequently presented themselves and were viewed by others as representatives of "change" (Witt, Paget, and Matthews 1994; Cook, Thomas, and Wilcox 1994). This notion of women as "agents of change" is for the most part an even less well-defined idea than "women's interests" of what it is that women might represent in the political arena. However, at a minimum, the idea of women as agents of change seems to embody two components. First, it evokes the image of outsiders to the existing political establishment. As outsiders, women represent an alternative to "politics as usual"—bringing new ideas into the political arena, reaching out to different constituencies, or employing different ways of doing business. However, the idea of women as agents of change also seems to encompass an explicitly gendered dimension. Because women and men, even women and men of the same race or ethnicity and social class, are treated differently by society and have somewhat different responsibilities as a result of their gender, they may enter office with different sets of life experiences. Consequently, women may bring different perspectives and ideas to bear on public policy proposals. For example, they may more readily think about the impact that policies will have on their lives and the lives of other women as well as on the lives of children and the elderly, for whose care women in contemporary U.S. society still bear a disproportionate responsibility.

The various contributors to this volume do not share a single vision about what it is that women in office may distinctively represent or what gender-related impact, if any, women public officials are likely to have on public policy or the political process. Nevertheless, the contributors do share a belief that the empirical examination of evidence concerning women's attitudes, priorities, and actions as public officials can provide important insights about the extent and nature of any gender-related impact that women in public office might have. Ultimately, it is through research such as that presented in this volume that we will achieve an understanding of what women's increased presence among public officials means for both the political system and women's lives.

Important Influences on Gender-Related Impact

Evidence of gender-related impact is not likely to be evident in the same way for all women across all historical and political contexts. Skeptics often point to examples of political women, such as Margaret Thatcher or Indira Gandhi, whom they perceive as *not* having had a distinctive gender-related impact—women who, they argue, have acted "just like men." The existence of women leaders both abroad and in the United States whose actions appear unaffected by their gender directs our attention to the role that both differences among women and differences in political contexts may have in influencing women's impact on public policy and the political process.

Like women in the general population, women who hold public office are not monolithic. They differ not only from men but also among themselves in their backgrounds, their political ideologies, and their perceptions of their roles as public officeholders. Political scientists have generally thought of differences in backgrounds and ideologies as discrete variables whose effects could be separated, isolated, and measured. However, recent feminist theorizing has challenged this conceptualization, suggesting that race, class, gender, sexual orientation, and other such aspects of identity are mutually constitutive. In this view, the effects of race and gender, for example, cannot be isolated and separately measured (see, e.g., Higginbotham 1992; Glenn 1992). The experiences of African American women cannot be separated into those that are affected by gender and those that are affected by race; rather, the experiences of African American women are distinct from those of African American men, white women, and other women of color. Consequently, one would not expect African American women and white women, for example, to view and affect public policy in identical ways. Similarly, the impact of Republican women is likely to differ from that of Democratic women, and the impact of women who identify with feminism may be very different from the impact of women who do not. Variation among women in impact is to be expected, and the challenge for empirical scholars is to see whether there are patterns in the variation which can help us better understand what is likely to happen as more women of various types enter public office.

Similarly, the impact which women public officials have is likely to be strongly affected by context. Certain types of political situations are likely to be more or less conducive to the expression of gender differences in impact. Variation in impact can be expected, for example, to be affected by the extent to which the process for selecting officeholders is centralized or decentralized as well as by the values of those who do the selecting. Many people including party influentials, funders, and voters are involved in the selection of elected officials. In contrast, the selection of political appointees is more centralized. This gives those who select political appointees more potential for control over the types of women who become appointed officials; their values may lead them to choose women who will differ very little from their male colleagues or, perhaps in some cases, even to select women who are likely to try to have a gender-related impact.

Even though the values of selectors are less important in electoral politics because of the decentralized nature of the selection process, their values, nevertheless, may still have an effect. For example, compared with those women representing liberal constituencies, women elected by more conservative constituencies might differ in their impact, both in terms of what they might choose to do and in terms of what their constituents might permit them to do.

Characteristics of the institutions in which public officials serve may also affect the extent to which women in those institutions make a difference. Where institutional pressures, norms, or leadership discourage women from behaving differently from their male colleagues, women may be less likely to have a gender-related impact. Where women officeholders constitute a critical mass and are able to work together informally or are organized into a formal caucus, women may be more likely to make a difference.

The Project That Led to This Book

Most of the chapters in this volume are a product of a large, coordinated research project sponsored by the Center for American Women and Politics (CAWP) at Rutgers University and funded by the Charles H. Revson Foundation. Throughout its 25-year history CAWP has helped to set the agenda for research on women public officials and has conducted much path-breaking work aimed at understanding the status, problems, and contributions of women officeholders.[3]

In the 1970s CAWP commissioned the first systematic, in-depth study of women serving in public office, Jeane J. Kirkpatrick's *Political Woman* (1974), and conducted the first nationwide surveys of women serving in elective office at various levels of government, documenting their numbers, their backgrounds, and their perceptions (Johnson and Stanwick 1976; Johnson and Carroll 1978). In the 1980s CAWP directed its research attention toward answering one of the most critical questions about the representation of women in politics: the question why so few women hold public office either as elected officials or as political appointees at state and federal levels. During the early 1980s, CAWP conducted the most comprehensive research ever undertaken on women's routes into public office, examining the factors that inhibit and facilitate their entry into elective and appointive positions (Carroll and Strimling 1983; Carroll and Geiger-Parker 1993a: Carroll and Geiger-Parker 1983b).

For the past several years CAWP has turned its research attention to yet another critical question about women's representation in politics: the question of what difference, if any, women's presence among officeholders makes. Ideally this question could best be addressed through a large, representative, complexly designed, multimethod study of officeholders serving in various offices in various locales. Of course, such a study would be prohibitively expensive. Nevertheless, we at CAWP believed that we could generate strong and compelling evidence about women's impact with more modest resources by supporting several smaller-scale, original research projects which utilized a variety of methods and examined the possible impact of women officeholders in a number of very different circumstances.

In order to assess whether and how women public officials might be having a distinctive gender-related impact on public policy and political processes, the Center for American Women and Politics pursued a two-pronged research strategy. As one part of its strategy, CAWP undertook its own in-house project, a nationally representative study examining the impact of women state legislators on public policy and legislative institutions. The first and last chapters in this book, by Susan J. Carroll and Debra L. Dodson, respectively, present principal findings from this study.

As the second part of its research strategy, CAWP awarded a series of grants to scholars whose projects were selected in a national competition. With one exception,[4] the remaining chapters in this volume present results from various projects supported by these grants. These chapters focus on women public officials serving in a variety of different locales and contexts. The subjects of these chapters range from a single, prominent United States Senator who served in Congress from the early 1940s to the early 1970s, to local council members in one county, to women serving in top foreign policy posts in the United States State and Defense Departments, to women judges who preside in jurisdictions across the country. The studies employ a variety of research methods ranging from surveys to in-depth interviews to historical biography. Together, the studies in this volume provide the most comprehensive evidence available regarding the impact of women in public office.

Major Findings about the Impact of Women Public Officials

Considered as a whole, the chapters in this volume suggest several important conclusions about the impact of women public officials and the relationship between the increased numerical representation of women and their substantive representation. First, this volume offers considerable evidence that women public officials do have a gender-related impact on public policy and the political process that is evident to varying degrees in different officeholding contexts. The clearest and most consistent policy-related gender differences are evident in policies pertaining to women, children, and families. Strong evidence of gender differences in these policy areas is found among state legislators (see, e.g., the chapters by Susan J. Carroll, Sue Thomas and Susan Welch, and Debra L. Dodson). In addition, Janet K. Boles suggests that women among local council members are more active than their male colleagues on "women's issues," which they define more broadly than the men. Women public officials express more support than their male colleagues for various policy positions espoused by the contemporary feminist movement, but in addition, as Dodson demonstrates for state legislators, women appear more likely than men to translate their feminist policy attitudes into action. Boles, too, finds that women county and municipal council members are more likely than men to take leadership roles in raising women's issues and in establishing new programs related to these issues.

The research in this volume also suggests that gender differences among public officials are not limited to their impact on public policy. Several chapters present evidence of gender differences in the way public officials conduct political business. Some of the strongest evidence in this regard emerges in Lyn Kathlene's study of women and men in the Colorado House of Representatives. She finds a range of differences in women's and men's approaches to policy-making, with men exhibiting a more "instrumental" and women a more "contextual" orientation to politics. For example, women rely on a wider range of people and groups in formulating policy, approach issues from a broader and more interconnected perspective, and tend to use their positions as committee chairs to facilitate interaction among committee members and witnesses rather than to control and direct debate. Similarly, Susan Abrams Beck finds that both women and men serving on local councils agree that women are more responsive than men to their constituents and more persistent in their questioning, although men and women offer very different interpretations for these differences.

The studies in this volume also present substantial evidence that the impact of women public officials varies considerably across political environments. First, the studies in this volume suggest that gender differences in impact may be less evident at the local level than at the state level, perhaps because of the nature of local politics. Although both also find some evidence of gender differences, Susan Abrams Beck and Sue Tolleson-Rinehart find considerable evidence of similarities between women and men serving in local offices, especially in identifying the most important problems confronting their communities. Most of the possible explanations for why gender differences seem less evident at the local level have to do with the nature of local politics. As Beck notes, local officials mostly react to the issues put before them rather than initiate new projects, and the major issues that drive local politics in the county she studied—low taxes and high property values—are not issues where gender differences are likely to be evident. Sue Tolleson-Rinehart suggests that the context of local politics may make male leaders at the local level more likely to take on what are commonly perceived as female qualities, and this may be the reason for the lack of greater gender differences. Among the mayors she studied, the men as well as the women often express concern about issues traditionally thought to be associated with women's nurturing roles (e.g., education and social welfare), and the qualities of leadership they most value more often are qualities associated with femininity than masculinity.

Studies in this volume also suggest that certain political contexts are less women-friendly than others and that gender differences usually are less apparent in these more hostile environments. While gender differences may be less evident in local politics because qualities associated with femininity are prevalent among men as well as women, in other political environments male values and masculinity are so dominant that few hints of gender differences are able to emerge. For example, Nancy E. McGlen and Meredith Reid Sarkees discuss how the ethos of the United States Departments of State and Defense limit the ability of women in policy-making positions in those departments to influence foreign policy. The prevalence of traditional stereotypes of women in both departments and the importance attached to military background and training in the Department of Defense are two of the obstacles that restrict women's impact.

The historical context in which women serve can also influence their impact as well as the perception of their impact. Janann Sherman argues that Margaret Chase Smith's accomplishments on behalf of women must be viewed in the context of the times (1940–1973) during which she served in Congress. During most of her tenure Senator Smith was the only woman in an institution unaccustomed to the presence of women. In 1972, during Senator Smith's final re-election campaign, the president of the Maine chapter of the National Organization for Women, judging Smith by the standards of the newly emerging feminist movement, denounced her as an "elitist" who cared nothing for women's concerns. Yet, judged within the context of her times, Senator Smith's accomplishments appear quite remarkable. She managed to pave the way for other women by demonstrating that women could handle the demands of public office and to obtain some concrete legislative accomplishments for women, including the granting of permanent regular status for women in the military.

The number of women serving in public office and the extent to which women officeholders work together with each other and with women's organizations are other important features of the political context that may affect the impact of women public officials. Thomas and Welch suggest that the existence of a critical mass of supportive women colleagues and a women's caucus are critical factors affecting women's impact. They find that state legislatures where women are present in greater numbers, and especially where they work together collectively through a caucus, are more likely to focus legislative attention on and to pass legislation benefiting women, children, and families. While Thomas and Welch focus on intra-institutional organizing among women public officials, Boles suggests that women public officials' ties to outside women's groups also can be an important factor affecting the policy actions of women public officials. Although she finds that women's organizations in Milwaukee are not particularly active in interacting with women public officials, many women public officials would welcome input from these groups.

Finally, the research in this volume demonstrates that identification with feminism or identification with a particular racial or ethnic group can also affect the extent to which, and the ways in which, women public officials have an impact on public policy. Elaine Martin finds that self-identified feminists among women judges are much more likely than non-feminists to vote in a pro-woman fashion when presented with hypothetical cases. Similarly, Carroll finds feminist self-identification to be one of the personal characteristics most strongly related to women legislators' propensity to work on women's rights legislation, and Dodson observes that among state legislators, women who identify as feminists are more likely than both feminist men and non-feminist women to work on legislation aimed at helping women.

Just as identification with feminism seems to influence the impact of women in public office, so too does identification with a racial or ethnic group. Edith J. Barrett finds that African American women serving in state legislatures share a perspective and a policy agenda which are distinctive from the perspectives and agendas of both white women and African American men. Their shared agenda focuses on the issues of education, health care, economic development, and employment.

Organization of the Book

This book is divided into three sections. Part I focuses on the impact of women serving in public offices at the state and local levels and includes four chapters that provide evidence regarding the existence and nature of differences between women and men serving in public office. Susan J. Carroll's analysis of data from a nationwide telephone survey of women and men serving in state legislatures shows that women are more likely than men to work on legislation aimed at helping women and to have top-priority bills that focus on women's rights, health care, and the welfare of families and children. Based on an in-depth, multimethod study of Colorado state legislators, Lyn Kathlene identifies a number of differences in the way women and men view issues and operate in the legislature that suggest two distinctive orientations to politics and policy-making, which she identifies as "instrumentalism" and "contextualism."

At the local level, gender differences in impact appear more subtle. Susan Beck finds more similarities than differences in the views and actions of the women and men she interviewed who serve on municipal councils in suburban towns outside a major city. However, she suggests that women council members are less comfortable than their male colleagues with the existing model of politics and that the seeds of an alternative model can be found in their predispositions to respond to individual needs, strive for collegiality, and draw upon the experiences they bring with them into office. Janet Boles finds more evidence than does Beck of gender differences in her interviews with women and men who have served on county or municipal councils in Milwaukee, perhaps in part because gender-related issues are more likely to be part of the agenda in a larger municipality. Boles concludes that women are more active than men on women's issues, broadly defined, and in terms of representational roles they act more as feminist "trustees" in representing women's interests than as "delegates" for women's rights groups.

The essays in Part II of this volume illustrate how the political context can facilitate or inhibit the expression of possible gender differences, influence the impact of women public officials, and affect the interpretation that is applied to their behavior. Janann Sherman shows how the views, behavior, and influence of Senator Margaret Chase Smith were shaped by the expectations and constraints of both the era and the institution in which she served. Sherman also shows how the interpretation of Smith's behavior and contributions changed over time. As the political context changed with the emergence of the contemporary feminist movement in the late 1960s, Margaret Chase Smith, once greatly respected by women as a trailblazer who could lead the way to political equality, found herself denounced by activists in the women's movement as a warmonger who had betrayed women. In their study of women in top foreign policy–making positions, Nancy E. McGlen and Meredith Reid Sarkees find that only among career officials in the State Department do women express more moderate views than men on foreign policy; women career officials in the Defense Department and political appointees in both departments do not differ from men on many issues, and when they do differ, they tend to take more hard-line, conservative positions than the men. McGlen and Sarkees offer some possible explanations for their findings—gatekeeping, the political culture of the departments, and self-selection—all of which highlight the importance of the political environment. Like the other chapters in this section, Sue Tolleson-Rinehart's study of men and women mayors of major cities underscores the importance of political context. Finding few differences between the women and the men, she concludes that the nature of local politics may lead male leaders to be more like female leaders, thus reducing differences that might be apparent in a different context. Finally, Sue Thomas and Susan Welch find that women state legislators are most likely to make a difference in contexts where they are not mere tokens and where they are organized around women's concerns.

In showing that legislation dealing with women and families is given more attention in state legislatures with larger proportions of women and with women's caucuses—factors likely to promote identification with women and women's issues among women legislators—Welch and Thomas provide a natural transition to Part III of this book. The chapters in Part III demonstrate, among other things, the importance of certain aspects of identity politics, specifically racial identity and identification with other women and feminism, in influencing the impact of women in public office. The chapter by Edith J. Barrett suggests that both racial identity and gender identity affect the impact of African American women in public office, combining to form a distinctive black women's legislative identity. She finds that African American women among state legislators are more supportive than white Democratic women of policies that target the specific needs of women and share a more cohesive agenda than their white Democratic women colleagues. Elaine Martin finds that judges who self-identify with feminism are more likely than other judges to vote in a pro-woman fashion in hypothetical cases and suggests that judicial role theory needs to be revised to include feminism as well as more conventional judicial role orientations. Finally, Debra Dodson finds that both gender and feminism affect policy actions among state legislators; however, women state legislators who self-identify as feminists are more likely than non-feminist women or feminist men to express feminist policy attitudes and to have worked on legislation aimed at helping women.

Considered as a whole, this collection of essays makes important contributions to our understanding of the impact of women public officials on public policy and the political process. The research in this volume suggests that women's increased presence in public office often is making a difference, sometimes in more obvious and sometimes in more subtle ways, and that we may see even more evidence of gender differences in public policy and the way political business is conducted as women continue to move into office in increasing numbers and achieve more seniority and a greater number of positions of influence. The research in this volume also suggests that women's impact varies across political environments; clearly, no or very few gender differences are evident in some contexts while in other contexts gender differences are clearly apparent. Context does matter. So, too, do gender and racial identification. In fact, this volume offers strong evidence that African Americans and self-identified feminists are among the most supportive of all women public officials of policies targeted at helping women.

However, while this book does much to advance our understanding of the impact of women public officials, it also points to the need for more research. In particular, more research is needed that explores the possible impact of women public officials on seemingly nongendered policies and legislation in areas such as fiscal policy or transportation policy. Many questions remain about the extent to which there are gender differences in the ways public officials exercise leadership or relate to staff, colleagues, and constituents. We have much more to learn about how the impact of women public officials varies across offices, levels of government, and historical time periods. We also have much more to learn about how differences among women—for example, in race and ethnicity, sexual orientation, party, and ideology—may affect the impact they have as public officials.

Thus, in many ways this volume is merely an opening act in a much longer play. Nevertheless, we hope it is an opening act that will capture the interest of its audience and stimulate much new creative work on the impact of women in office and the ways in which gender influences political institutions and the policy-making process.

Notes

1. The main exception to this pattern is in Congress, where the number of women serving as representatives and senators fluctuated between 15 and 20 throughout the 1970s and seemed to remain stable around 23 to 25 throughout most of the 1980s. The number of women serving in Congress increased substantially after the 1992 elections, and since 1992 the number of women serving in Congress has increased incrementally with each successive election. In 2000, 56 women served in the United States House of Representatives and nine women served in the Senate. See Center for American Women and Politics 2000a.

2. See Pitkin 1967 for a discussion of various forms of representation. Also see Phillips 1995.

3. In 1999 CAWP changed its name from the Center for the American Woman and Politics to the Center for American Women and Politics. The

Introduction

former name is used throughout this volume for references to pre-1999 publications and materials.

4. The exception is the chapter by Edith Barrett, which was not one of the original grant-funded projects but was added to this volume because of its related themes and its ability to add to our understanding of the perspectives of African American women who serve in elected office.

References

Alcoff, Linda. 1988. "Cultural Feminism Versus Post-Structuralism." *Signs* 13: 405–436.

Butler, Judith. 1992. "Contingent Foundations: Feminism and the Question of 'Postmodernism.'" In *Feminism/Postmodernism*, ed. Linda J. Nicholson. New York: Routledge.

Carroll, Susan J. 1994. *Women as Candidates in American Politics.* 2nd ed. Bloomington: Indiana University Press.

Carroll, Susan J., and Wendy S. Strimling. 1983. *Women's Routes to Elective Office.* New Brunswick, N.J.: Center for the American Woman and Politics.

Carroll, Susan J., and Barbara Geiger-Parker. 1983a. *Women Appointed to the Carter Administration: A Comparison with Men.* New Brunswick, N.J.: Center for the American Woman and Politics.

Carroll, Susan J., and Barbara Geiger-Parker. 1983b. *Women Appointed to State Government: A Comparison with All State Appointees.* New Brunswick, N.J.: Center for the American Woman and Politics.

Center for American Women and Politics. 2000a. "Women in the U.S. Congress 2000." Fact Sheet.

Center for American Women and Politics. 2000b. "Women in State Legislatures 2000." Fact Sheet.

Center for American Women and Politics. 2000c. "The Gender Gap." Fact Sheet.

Cook, Elizabeth Adell, Sue Thomas, and Clyde Wilcox. 1994. *The Year of the Woman: Myths and Realities.* Boulder, Colo.: Westview.

Darcy, R., Susan Welch, and Janet Clark. 1994. *Women, Elections, and Representation.* 2nd ed. Lincoln: University of Nebraska Press.

De Lauretis, Teresa. 1984. *Alice Doesn't.* Bloomington: Indiana University Press.

Diamond, Irene. 1977. *Sex Roles in the State House.* New Haven: Yale University Press.

Githens, Marianne, and Jewel L. Prestage, eds. 1977. *A Portrait of Marginality: The Political Behavior of the American Woman.* New York: McKay.

Glenn, Evelyn Nakano. 1992. "From Servitude to Service Work: Historical Continuities in the Racial Division of Paid Reproductive Labor." *Signs* 18: 1–43.

Higginbotham, Evelyn Brooks. 1992. "African-American Women's History and the Metalanguage of Race." *Signs* 17: 251–74.

hooks, bell. 1984. *Feminist Theory: From Margin to Center.* Boston: South End Press.

Johnson, Marilyn, and Kathy Stanwick. 1976. *Profile of Women Holding Office.* New Brunswick, N.J.: Center for the American Woman and Politics.

Johnson, Marilyn, and Susan Carroll. 1978. *Profile of Women Holding Office II.* New Brunswick, N.J.: Center for the American Woman and Politics.

Kirkpatrick, Jeane J. 1974. *Political Woman.* New York: Basic Books.

Mohanty, Chandra Talpade. 1991. "Under Western Eyes: Feminist Scholarship and Colonial Discourses." In *Third World Women and the Politics of Feminism,* ed. Chandra Talpade Mohanty, Ann Russo, and Lourdes Torres. Bloomington: Indiana University Press.

Phelan, Shane. 1994. *Getting Specific: Postmodern Lesbian Politics.* Minneapolis: University of Minnesota Press.

Phillips, Anne. 1995. *The Politics of Presence.* Oxford: Oxford University Press.

Pitkin, Hanna Fenichel. 1967. *The Concept of Representation.* Berkeley: University of California Press.

Scott, Joan. 1986. "Gender: A Useful Category of Historical Analysis." *American Historical Review* 91: 1053–1075.

Spelman, Elizabeth V. 1988. *Inessential Woman: Problems of Exclusion in Feminist Thought.* Boston: Beacon.

Witt, Linda, Karen M. Paget, and Glenna Matthews. 1994. *Running as a Woman: Gender and Power in American Politics.* New York: Free Press.

PART I
THE IMPACT OF WOMEN IN
STATE AND LOCAL OFFICES

One

Representing Women
Women State Legislators as Agents of
Policy-Related Change

Susan J. Carroll

Over the past three decades, the Washington-based, mainstream arm of
the women's movement has advocated the election of larger numbers of
women to public office, arguing that our government does not suffi-
ciently represent women's perspectives and concerns. Most feminists
view the election of greater numbers of women as a *means* for social
change and not merely an *end* in itself. While feminist groups are interested in increasing the number of representatives who will "stand for"
women, they also want to elect women who will "act for" women by initiating and supporting feminist policies. Feminists assume that women
officials more often than men will be conscious of or responsive to
women's life experiences and their concerns and that women officials
will work to ensure that public policy adequately reflects those concerns. Thus the election of more women—i.e., increasing women's "descriptive" representation—is seen as an important strategy for achieving greater "acting for" or "substantive" representation for women.[1]

Feminist activists are not alone in expecting that there will be a relationship between "descriptive" and "substantive" representation. Social scientists have also hypothesized that the extent to which a group's
concerns are recognized and acted upon in the political process may
well be related to the number of political positions held by members of
the group. In one of the earliest books about the contemporary women's
movement, Kirsten Amundsen argued that there might well be a

> ... politically significant relationship between the proportion of
> representative positions a group can claim for itself and the degree

to which the needs and interests of that group are articulated and acted upon in political institutions. . . . The more group members are in decision-making positions, the better the chance the group has of fair and effective representation. (1971, p. 66)

More recently, Anne Phillips has theorized about the positive and negative aspects of descriptive representation, which she calls the "politics of presence." Eschewing arguments about an essentialist identity or universal experiences which all women share, Phillips insists that "the case for gender parity among our political representatives inevitably operates in a framework of probabilities rather than certainties" (1995, 82). She concludes:

Changing the gender composition of elected assemblies is largely an enabling condition . . . but it cannot present itself as a guarantee. It is, in some sense, a shot in the dark: far more likely to reach its target than when those shooting are predominantly male, but still open to all kinds of accident. (1995, 83)

Thus, Amundsen and Phillips, writing more than two decades apart, agree that increased descriptive representation does not *guarantee* increased substantive representation. However, both also agree that increased descriptive representation increases the probability and holds out the promise of enhanced substantive representation.

Clearly, as recent scholarship by feminist scholars, including many women of color, has poignantly argued (e.g., hooks 1981, 1984; Scott 1992; Spelman 1988; Butler 1992; Collins 1990), no experience is shared by all women in the same way, and gender differences in life experiences cannot and should not be reified or universalized. While women may have different experiences or interpret similar experiences in different ways, nevertheless there may be gendered dimensions to those experiences and interpretations. To the extent that women's life experiences and interpretations of those experiences differ from those of men with whom they share other social characteristics, women are likely to bring those differences into office with them. If and when these experiences and perspectives affect the types of policy initiatives women public officials put forth or the factors they consider when making decisions about the policy initiatives of others, they can be considered to be "acting for" women. For some women in some cases, this type of acting for women may promote feminist goals, thereby serving as the kind of "acting for" representation desired by feminist activists. In other cases this type of acting for women may be irrelevant or even counter to the agenda of feminist organizations (as it would be, for example, if a woman official brought her particular gendered experience as a mother to bear on a decision to restrict minors' access to abortion by requiring parental consent).

Ultimately, questions regarding the relationship between descriptive representation and substantive representation are empirical as well as theoretical. In this chapter I present some of the major findings from a survey of a nationally representative sample of women state legislators conducted by the Center for the American Woman and Politics in 1988. I focus on the question of whether women legislators do, in fact, act as agents of change within the legislatures in which they serve. I answer this question by examining legislators' perceptions regarding women's impact on public policy, their legislative priorities, and their involvement with women's rights legislation. I then attempt to identify some of the personal, intra-institutional, and extra-institutional factors that may affect the extent to which women legislators function as agents of change in the area of women's rights legislation. Throughout this chapter I adopt an explicitly feminist conception and standard for assessing whether women legislators are acting for women even while recognizing that women legislators could act for women in ways that may not be explicitly feminist.

Description of the Data Set

In the summer of 1988 under a grant from the Charles H. Revson Foundation, the Center for the American Woman and Politics conducted a nationwide survey of women and men serving as state legislators. Four samples of legislators were drawn: (1) the population of women state senators (n = 228); (2) a systematic sample of one-half of women state representatives (n = 474); (3) a systematic sample of male state senators, stratified by state and sampled in proportion to the number of women from each state in our sample of women state senators (n = 228); and (4) a systematic sample of male state representatives, stratified by state and sampled in proportion to the number of women in each state in our sample of women state representatives (n = 474).

A telephone interview lasting approximately one half-hour was attempted with each of the legislators, resulting in response rates of 86 percent for female senators; 87 percent for female representatives; 60 percent for male senators; and 73 percent for male representatives. Respondents did not differ significantly from all the legislators selected for any of the four samples in their party affiliation, the one variable for which we have data for all legislators.

Throughout this chapter, data are presented separately for state senators and state representatives. Like the United States Senate and House of Representatives, state senates and state houses are very different political institutions. The lower houses of state legislatures vary considerably in size and influence across the states, while state senates tend to be smaller and show less variation. Because of these differences, the upper and lower houses of the legislatures offer separate tests of each statistical relationship.

Legislators' Perceptions of Whether Women Make a Difference

Legislators' perceptions regarding the impact of women legislators provide one of the strongest indicators that women are viewed as agents of change in the legislative setting. In our survey we asked state legislators about their perceptions of how their legislatures had been affected as the number of women had increased in recent years. Table 1.1 shows the proportion of female and male legislators who believe that the increased presence of women had made "a lot" or "some" difference on various aspects of public policy and policymaking.

Both men and women legislators see perhaps the greatest impact of women legislators to be on legislation focusing on women. Women senators and representatives overwhelmingly perceive that the increased presence of women has affected both the extent to which legislators consider how legislation will affect women as a group and the number of bills passed dealing specifically with the problems faced by women. Despite significant gender differences in perceptions, more than seven of every ten men legislators agree that women have made a difference in both of these ways.

Somewhat smaller proportions of women and men—but still, with the exception of men senators, majorities of both genders—perceive women legislators to have made a difference in the extent to which the economically disadvantaged have access to the legislature and in expenditure priorities for the state (Table 1.1). Again, women legislators are significantly more likely than their male colleagues to see themselves as having had an impact. The fact that neither of these two items refers explicitly to women suggests that both men and women legislators see women's impact on public policy in the legislatures as extending beyond the realm of so-called women's issues.

There is less agreement within both genders about whether women have had an impact on the extent to which legislative business is conducted in public view, rather than behind closed doors. Among both state senators and state representatives, women are much more likely than men to perceive that the presence of women has resulted in more

Table 1.1 Proportions of Legislators Who Believe That Women's Increased
Presence in the Legislature Has Made a Difference on Various
Policy-Related Items

	Senate			House		
	Women %	Men %	tau$_c$ =	Women %	Men %	tau$_c$ =
The extent to which legislators consider how legislation will affect women as a group	85.4	71.8	.30*	85.3	74.4	.22*
The number of bills passed that deal specifically with the problems faced by women	86.2	70.8	.31*	87.7	77.7	.19*
The extent to which the economically disadvantaged have access to the legislature	77.6	48.5	.37*	79.5	61.2	.23*
Expenditure priorities for the state	79.8	53.3	.33*	74.3	62.0	.16*
The extent to which legislative business is conducted in public view rather than behind closed doors	57.5	20.9	.37*	57.2	34.7	.25*

n = 188–191 for women state senators, 132–135 for men state senators, 394–402 for women
state representatives, and 328–337 for men state representatives.

open public policy-making. Indeed, a majority of women believe that
the presence of women has led to more government "in the sunshine."

Nevertheless, the most compelling evidence in Table 1.1 may be
men's perceptions, rather than women's. Just as one might expect women
to overestimate their impact, one also might expect men to downplay
women's influence. Yet, on most of the items in Table 1.1, sizable
majorities of men believe that changes have occurred because of women.

Male senators are less likely than male representatives to perceive that the presence of women has made a difference, and yet on four of the five items, majorities or near-majorities of male senators believe that women have produced important policy-related changes.

Gender Differences in Top Legislative Priorities

An examination of the legislative priorities of legislators provides further evidence that many women are acting as agents of change in the legislative setting. We asked each legislator to describe the one bill that had been her or his personal top priority for the current legislative session.[2] We then coded these bills by content area and grouped them into 15 categories according to their major focus (women, children and family, environment, education, health care, tax and budget, insurance and business, labor, judiciary, state procedures, transportation, intergovernmental relations, elderly, other social services, and other).

The priorities of legislators are widely dispersed across these issue areas with no single area appearing to receive an unusually large amount of legislative attention. Nevertheless, statistically significant gender differences in legislative priorities are apparent in three content areas (Table 1.2).

First, women were significantly more likely than men to say that a bill focusing on women was their top legislative priority. Approximately one in ten women legislators mentioned legislation focusing on women's rights,[3] and their responses covered a wide spectrum of issues of particular concern to women including domestic violence, child care, equal rights, abortion, teen pregnancy, and parental leave. Consequently, on this measure of legislative activity, a small but notable minority of women legislators could be considered to be acting for women in a manner consistent with the goals of feminist organizations, and a larger proportion of women than men among legislators were acting for women in this fashion.

In our society women still share a disproportionate responsibility both for the rearing of children and for the care of those who because of illness or age cannot care for themselves. The legislative priorities of legislators reflect gender differences in responsibilities and concerns in these areas. Women senators and representatives were more likely than their male counterparts to place top priority on legislation dealing with families and children and with the provision and regulation of health care. Moreover, proportionately more women gave top priority to legislation on health care than to legislation in any other single content area.[4]

Table 1.2. Gender Differences in Proportions of Legislators with
Top-Priority Legislation in Three Issue Areas

	Senate			House		
	Women %	Men %	$tau_b =$	Women %	Men %	$tau_b =$
Women's rights	10.5	3.8	.12**	10.2	4.2	.11**
Health care	15.3	8.4	.10	13.7	6.0	.13*
Families and children[a]	3.2	0.0	.12***	4.0	0.9	.10**

n = 190 for women state senators, 131 for men state senators, 402 for women state representatives, and 335 for men state representatives.

*p < .001   **p < .01   ***p < .05

[a]This category is small because issues such as child care, parental leave, and teen pregnancy prevention, which are part of the agenda of many feminist organizations, were considered women's rights issues for purposes of this classification. Consequently, this category includes only issues (e.g., child abuse, foster care) which have not been as closely associated with the agenda of feminist advocacy groups.

Surprisingly, women were not more likely than men to have as their top priority a bill dealing with education, another area where women have traditionally borne disproportionate societal responsibility. In both the state houses ($tau_b = -.03$, not significant) and state senates ($tau_b = -.08$, not significant), women were slightly less likely than men to give priority to legislation on education.

Gender Differences in Work on Women's Rights Bills

An analysis of legislators' top priority bills for a single session is likely to underestimate the extent to which legislators are involved with legislation affecting women or, indeed, legislation in any given content area. A single legislative session is a mere snapshot in time, and legislators' top priorities may well vary from session to session. Over the course of several legislative sessions, one would expect to find much larger proportions of legislators giving priority to legislation focusing on women. Moreover, a legislator may devote time and energy to a variety of bills in addition to her or his top-priority bill during the course of one legislative session.

To develop a fuller assessment of the extent to which women legislators are involved with women's rights legislation, we asked each legislator whether she or he had worked on *any* legislation during the current session where the bill itself or specific provisions of the bill were intended to help women in particular. When a legislator replied affirmatively, we then asked her or him to describe in one sentence what specifically the bill did for women. To develop a measure of activity on women's rights bills, we excluded from the measure any legislator who replied affirmatively but could not describe what the bill did to help women. The few legislators who mentioned working on bills which seemed anti-feminist in intent also were excluded.[5]

Large and statistically significant gender differences are evident in the proportions of legislators in both upper and lower houses who worked on legislation to help women (Table 1.3). More than one-half of women representatives and almost two-thirds of women state senators acted for women by working on women's rights legislation, compared with just over one-third of their male colleagues.

Factors Influencing Women's Representation of Women

Who are the women legislators most likely to act as agents of change? What characteristics do they share? And what factors or conditions, both internal and external to the legislature itself, seem to enhance the likelihood that women legislators will act for women?

To begin to answer these questions, I examine the relationship between a variety of individual and political factors and the measure of whether a legislator had worked on any legislation during the current session where the bill itself or specific provisions of the bill were intended to help women in particular. While working on women's rights bills is only one of the ways in which women legislators may act as agents of change in the policymaking process, it is nevertheless a very important component of acting for women.

Personal Characteristics

Women officeholders are not monolithic in their concerns, their backgrounds, or their preferences. Consequently, several individual characteristics of the women legislators themselves, including their party affiliation, their political ideology, their identification with feminism, and their race, might be expected to affect the likelihood that women legislators would act for women.

Research has demonstrated that Democratic women are more likely

Table 1.3. Gender Differences in Proportions of Legislators Who
Worked on a Women's Rights Bill

	Senate			House		
	Women %	Men %	tau$_b$ =	Women %	Men %	tau$_b$ =
Worked on Women's Rights Bill	64.4	38.8	.26*	57.1	35.9	.21*

n = 191 for women state senators, 134 for men state senators, 399 for women state representatives, and 329 for men state representatives.
*p < .001

than Republican women to support liberal and feminist positions on public policy issues (Leader 1977; Johnson and Carroll 1978; Stanwick and Kleeman 1983; Dodson and Carroll 1991), leading one to expect Democratic women to be more likely than Republican women to act for women as well. Ideology and feminist self-identification are two other personal characteristics that might be important, with women who are liberals and who call themselves feminists more likely to act as advocates for women. Although relatively few women of color hold public office (Center for American Women and Politics 2000), previous research has found African American women to be more liberal and more feminist than their white counterparts, suggesting that African American women might be more likely than white women to work on women's rights bills (Carroll and Strimling 1983).[6]

The findings in Table 1.4 indicate that all these expectations are fulfilled. For both women state senators and state representatives, party, ideology, and feminist self-identification all show statistically significant relationships of moderate strength to the measure of whether a legislator had worked on women's rights bills. Women who identify as Democrats, liberals, or feminists are significantly more likely to have worked on women's rights bills than their women colleagues who are Republican, moderate or conservative, or non-feminist.

The relationship between race and working on women's rights bills is not as strong (and in the case of women state senators, not statistically significant), but it is nevertheless noteworthy. African American women legislators are more likely than their white colleagues to have worked on legislation targeted at women.

A comparison with men is most telling (Table 1.4). First, the rela-

Table 1.4. Proportions of Women and Men State Legislators with Various Personal Characteristics Who Worked on a Women's Rights Bill

	State Senate		State House	
	Women %	Men %	Women %	Men %
Party				
Democrat	74.5	44.9	65.2	38.8
Republican	50.6	32.8	46.2	32.9
tau$_b$=	.25**	.12	.19*	.06
Ideology				
Liberal	90.5	76.9	73.3	65.3
Moderate	65.3	43.1	56.3	33.3
Conservative	38.6	25.0	39.2	26.8
tau$_c$=	.37*	.29*	.26*	.23*
Self-identification				
Feminist	79.5	50.0	70.9	49.3
Non-feminist	51.0	36.7	44.9	32.9
tau$_b$=	.30*	.10	.26*	.14***
Race				
African American	83.3	50.0	85.7	45.5
White	62.8	37.0	55.9	35.7
tau$_b$=	.11	.03	.14**	.04

n = 183–188 for women state senators, 127–134 for men state senators, 385–399 for women state representatives, and 316–328 for men state representatives.
*$p < .001$ **$p < .01$ ***$p < .05$

tionships between these personal characteristics and working on women's rights bills tend to be weak for men and certainly weaker for men than for women in every case.

Second, for men, the only personal characteristic that shows even a moderate and statistically significant relationship to activity on women's rights bills is political ideology. Here it is clearly the relatively small number of men (9.5% of senators and 15.6% of representatives) who call themselves "liberals" who stand out. Three-fourths of liberal men state senators and two-thirds of liberal men state representatives worked on women's rights bills while their moderate and conservative male colleagues were much less active on women's rights legislation. Feminist self-identification also is significantly related to activity on women's rights legislation for male state representatives, although the relationship is not as strong as for political ideology.

Perhaps the most important conclusion to be drawn from the comparison with men is that within every category of each of the four personal characteristics (party, ideology, feminist self-identification, and race), women in both houses of the legislature are more likely than their male colleagues to have worked on women's rights bills. Conservative women are more likely than conservative men, Republican women are more likely than Republican men, non-feminist women are more likely than non-feminist men, and white women are more likely than white men to have worked on legislation focusing on women's rights. Consequently, gender seems to have an effect that transcends these other identity categories.

One additional finding from Table 1.4 is of particular significance. In both the state senates and the state houses, Republican women are not only more likely than Republican men but also slightly more likely than Democratic men to have worked on a women's rights bill. Thus, at least on this particular measure of acting for women, gender is somewhat more important than party.

Intra-institutional Factors

Although women may come into public office with different experiences and perspectives or with a stronger commitment to a feminist agenda than most men have, institutional pressures may work against the expression of those differences. As Drude Dahlerup has observed, "Women politicians must prove that they are just like (just as able as) male politicians, who in general have longer seniority and whose gender occupied the political arena long before women were allowed to participate" (1988, 279). Under certain circumstances women legislators may find themselves subject to institutional pressures to downplay their gender and to meet male norms and standards for behavior.

One might expect the pressure to conform to male norms to be greatest in legislatures where the proportion of women is small, especially when women lack a critical mass (Kanter 1977) and are not organized and do not meet as a group. Conversely, in legislatures where the proportion of women is greater and women meet regularly as a group, support for the expression of differences related to gender might be greater (see Thomas 1994; Thomas and Welch, this volume). One might also expect the professionalism of the legislature to affect the extent to which women feel free to act for women. Pressures to conform to male norms might be greater for women in more professional legislatures where norms of behavior are likely to be more clearly defined.

Consistent with the findings of Sue Thomas and Susan Welch (this volume) and Sue Thomas (1994), women legislators who reported that women in their legislative chamber met together as a group to discuss legislation that affects women were significantly more likely to work on women's rights bills than women in chambers where women did not meet. The meetings among women legislators took different forms. In some states women met through a formal women's caucus; in others, they met informally. Often the meetings were bipartisan; sometimes they were partisan. Nevertheless, regardless of the form they took, the meetings seem to have offered women legislators mutual support for working on women's rights legislation. Where women reported that women in their legislatures did not meet, they were less likely to be involved with legislation targeted at women (Table 1.5).

By contrast to this finding for women meeting together, the relationships between the two other intra-institutional variables and the dependent variable are contrary to initial expectations. For women state representatives, the proportion of women in the state house is negatively related, and the professionalism of the legislature is positively related, to working on legislation to help women (Table 1.5). These findings are counter to the expectation that women would feel more pressure to conform to male norms in legislatures with fewer women and higher levels of professionalism.

For women senators, the proportion of women serving in their legislative body appears to have no effect on their propensity to work on women's rights legislation. For women representatives, the likelihood that they will work on women's rights bills is roughly equal for those in chambers with low (less than 14%) and moderate (15–24%) proportions of women but falls off dramatically for those in state houses with 25 percent or more women. The pattern for women in state houses suggests that there may be a point at which women become such a sizable minority that the personal responsibility which individual women legislators feel to work on women's rights legislation diminishes. Because there are numerous other women to share the responsibility of acting for women, some women may turn their attention more toward other concerns.[7]

However, this cannot explain why the drop-off in activity apparent

Table 1.5. Proportions of Women Representatives and Senators
under Varying Intra-institutional and External Conditions Who
Worked on a Women's Rights Bill

		Senate %	House %
Intra-institutional Factors	Formal or Informal Caucus?		
	Yes	68.8	61.5
	No	51.1	40.2
	tau$_b$=	.16***	.17**
	% Women in Body		
	25 or more %	65.5	40.8
	15–24%	60.6	63.6
	0–14%	66.7	65.5
	tau$_c$=	−.04	−.18*
	Type of Legislature		
	Citizen	NA	48.1
	Semi-professional	NA	61.2
	Professional	NA	65.4
	tau$_c$=		−.14**
External Political Factors	Ideology of District		
	Liberal	100.0	82.5
	Moderate	66.0	56.5
	Conservative	50.8	50.0
	tau$_c$=	.26*	.16**
	Margin of Victory		
	No Opponent	87.5	63.9
	> 10%	62.7	57.2
	5–10%	47.6	56.3
	< 5%	65.4	53.8
	tau$_c$=	.14***	.06

16

Table 1.5. *Continued*

	Senate %	House %
Member of Women's Organization?		
Yes	69.9	63.7
No	47.9	39.3
$tau_b=$	.20**	.22*

n = 179–191 for women state senators and 381–399 for women state representatives.
*p < .001   **p < .01   ***p < .05

for state representatives does not occur for women state senators in legislative bodies with sizable proportions of women. The lack of drop-off in state senates suggests that the state house findings may also, in part, be the result of differences in the types of women who run for and are elected to state houses having larger and smaller proportions of women. For example, women representatives in state houses with larger proportions of women (25% or greater) are somewhat less likely (40.0%) than women representatives in state houses with smaller proportions of women (46.4%) to identify as feminists.

Differences in the types of women who are elected to state houses with larger and smaller proportions of women may also be the reason that women in more professional legislatures (as measured by annual salary) are more active on behalf of women's rights legislation than women in lower-paid, citizen legislatures.[8] The women serving in professional legislatures are much notably likely to self-identify as feminists (51.0%) than those serving in citizen legislatures (38.9%).

External Political Factors

Just as one might expect factors internal to the legislature to affect the extent to which women legislators work on women's rights bills, so too might one expect pressures and influences external to the legislature to play a role. For example, constituency characteristics might well affect the extent to which women act for women. Legislators from more liberal districts and those from "safe" districts, where their margin of victory in the last election was large or where they ran unopposed, might feel more freedom to advocate women's concerns, while those from more conservative or marginal districts might feel more constrained. Similarly, the extent to which women legislators act for women might be related to their external connections to women's networks that could provide support for actions on behalf of women. More specifically, one might expect women legislators who are members of feminist or other women's organizations to be more likely to work on women's rights bills.

Table 1.5 presents findings relevant to these hypotheses. There is a moderate and statistically significant relationship between legislators' perceptions of the dominant ideology of a majority of voters in their districts and their involvement with women's rights bills. In particular, women state senators and representatives from liberal districts are especially likely to work on women's rights legislation.

The evidence is mixed in terms of the relationship between margin of victory and activity on women's rights bills. For women state senators, the relationship is statistically significant with those from the safest districts (i.e., those who ran unopposed or who won by more than 10 percent of the vote) more likely to be involved with women's rights legislation than those who won by only 5 to 10 percent. Surprisingly, however, those women who won by less than 5 percent of the vote are as likely as those who won by more than 10 percent to work on women's rights bills. For women state representatives, unlike their senate counterparts, the proportions who worked on women's rights bills does not vary much across different margins of victory.

Finally, being a member of a women's organization[9] is moderately and significantly related to work on women's rights legislation for both women state senators and women state representatives (Table 1.5). Women who belong to at least one major women's organization are considerably more likely than those who are not members to have been involved with women's rights legislation.[10]

Discussion and Conclusions

This chapter has presented considerable evidence that many women state legislators are agents of policy-related change within the legislative bodies in which they serve. Women legislators have had an impact in a variety of ways. According to the perceptions of both male and female legislators, women have brought about changes in the extent to which the economically disadvantaged have access to the legislature, in expenditure priorities for the state, and perhaps in the extent to which legislative business is conducted in public view rather than behind closed doors. Women legislators also have given more priority than men to legislation on health care and the welfare of families and children.

However, perhaps women legislators' greatest impact as agents of change has been in acting for women on legislation to help women.

18

Large majorities of women and men serving in state legislatures agree that the increased presence of women legislators has made a difference in both the extent to which legislators consider how legislation will affect women as a group and the number of bills passed dealing specifically with the problems faced by women. Women legislators are more likely than their male colleagues to give top priority to legislation dealing with women's rights, and they are much more likely than men to work on women's rights bills.

The women who are most likely to act for women by working on women's rights legislation are Democrats, liberals, self-identified feminists, and African Americans. Nevertheless, women who are Republicans, moderates and conservatives, non-feminists, and white are more likely to work on women's rights legislation than men who share their characteristics. If similarly situated men are taken as the norm against which women's behavior is measured, then many women legislators of differing party affiliations, ideological perspectives, postures toward feminism, and races can be considered agents of change—agents who are more likely than their male counterparts to act for women.

Finally, the analysis in this chapter has also shown that factors both internal and external to the legislature can influence the extent to which women legislators actively work on women's rights legislation. One of the most important intra-institutional factors seems to be whether women legislators met together either through a formal legislative caucus or as an informal group to discuss legislation that affects women. Similarly, one of the most important external factors seems to be whether women legislators belong to women's organizations outside their legislatures. These internal and external women's groups may help to connect women legislators to other women in ways that make them more cognizant of women's concerns and the problems they face. These groups also may provide encouragement, support, and reinforcement for efforts that women legislators make on behalf of women. Consequently, creating and maintaining ties between women legislators and other women and women's groups, inside and outside the legislature, may be one of the strongest mechanisms for ensuring that women legislators continue to be agents of change who act for women.

Notes

I would like to thank Ella Taylor, who co-wrote a paper with me several years ago investigating some of the same questions this chapter investigates.

1. See Pitkin 1967 for a discussion of the distinctions among various conceptions of representation.

2. Because we interviewed respondents just a few months before the 1988 elections, most legislatures were at or near the end of a legislative session.

3. We excluded from this "women's rights" measure the tiny minority of the legislators (0.3% of all legislators) who had a women's issue as their top priority and appeared to be working on the issue from an anti-feminist perspective; almost all legislators working on women's issues were working to expand women's opportunities or to protect their rights. In determining whether legislators were working on women's issues from a feminist or an anti-feminist perspective, we examined not only their open-ended responses describing their top-priority bill but also responses to a follow-up question that asked whether they worked for or against the bill. The bills included in this "women's rights" category appeared to be consistent with the major policy goals of contemporary women's movement organizations such as the National Organization for Women (NOW), the National Women's Political Caucus (NWPC), and the former Women's Equity Action League (WEAL), as well as with the agenda for the future established by delegates elected to the government-sponsored National Women's Conference held in Houston, Texas, in November 1977 (see National Commission on the Observance of International Women's Year 1978).

4. This finding is consistent with another analysis of data from this study which found that women more often than men received appointments to committees dealing with health and human services and that women's assignments to these committees seem for the most part to be consistent with their preferences. See Carroll and Taylor 1989.

5. Only 1.2 percent of women legislators and 1.4 percent of men legislators had worked on bills which we classified as anti-feminist.

6. Because of the still very small number of women state legislators who are Latina, Asian American, or Native American, both Carroll and Strimling 1983 and the analysis in this chapter are limited for statistical reasons to an examination of African American women. As of 2000, only 48 Latinas, 17 Asian American women, and 12 Native American women served as state legislators, compared with 176 African American women.

7. Because there are more women to do the same amount of work, it does not necessarily follow that less is being done overall to help women in states with larger proportions of women legislators.

8. I considered the possibility that the relationship between professionalism of the legislature and the dependent variable might simply be a product of the greater amount of time that professional legislatures spend in session. More time in session might mean more time to work on legislation to benefit women. However, when days-in-session was substituted for salary as the measure of professionalism, there still was no significant positive relationship between professionalism of the legislature and work on women's rights legislation.

9. We asked only about memberships in the League of Women Voters, the American Association of University Women, Business and Professional

20

Women, the National Organization for Women, the Women's Political Caucus, and any other feminist group. To be classified as a member of a women's organization, a legislator had to indicate that she was a member of at least one of these groups.

10. For a much more detailed analysis and discussion, based on this data set, of the relationship between support from women's groups and work on women's rights legislation, see Carroll 1992.

References

Amundsen, Kirsten. 1971. *The Silenced Majority*. Englewood Cliffs, N.J.: Prentice-Hall.

Butler, Judith. 1992. "Contingent Foundations: Feminism and the Question of 'Postmodernism.'" In *Feminists Theorize the Political*, ed. Judith Butler and Joan W. Scott. New York: Routledge.

Carroll, Susan J., and Wendy S. Strimling. 1983. *Women's Routes to Elective Office*. New Brunswick, N.J.: Center for the American Woman and Politics.

Carroll, Susan J., and Ella Taylor. 1989. "Gender Differences in the Committee Assignments of State Legislators: Preferences or Discrimination?" Presented at the annual meeting of the Midwest Political Science Association, Chicago, Illinois.

Carroll, Susan J. 1992. "Women State Legislators, Women's Organizations, and the Representation of Women's Culture in the United States." In *Women Transforming Politics*, ed. Jill M. Bystydzienski. Bloomington: Indiana University Press.

Center for American Women and Politics. 2000. "Women of Color in Elective Office 2000." Fact Sheet.

Collins, Patricia Hill. 1990. *Black Feminist Thought*. New York: Routledge.

Dahlerup, Drude. 1988. "From a Small to a Large Minority: Women in Scandinavian Politics." *Scandinavian Political Studies* 11: 275–298.

Dodson, Debra L., and Susan J. Carroll. 1991. *Reshaping the Agenda: Women in State Legislatures*. New Brunswick, N.J.: Center for the American Woman and Politics.

hooks, bell. 1981. *Ain't I a Woman: Black Women and Feminism*. Boston: South End Press.

hooks, bell. 1984. *Feminist Theory: From Margin to Center*. Boston: South End Press.

Johnson, Marilyn, and Susan Carroll. 1978. "Profile of Women Holding Office, 1977." In *Women in Public Office: A Bibliographic Directory and Statistical Analysis*, compiled by Center for the American Woman and Politics. Metuchen, N.J.: Scarecrow Press.

Kanter, Rosabeth Moss. 1977. "Some Effects of Proportions on Group Life: Skewed Sex Ratios and Response to Token Women." *American Journal of Sociology* 82: 965–990.

Leader, Shelah Gilbert. 1977. "The Policy Impact of Elected Women Officials." In *The Impact of the Electoral Process,* ed. Louis Maisel and Joseph Cooper. Beverly Hills: Sage.

National Commission on the Observance of International Women's Year. 1978. *The Spirit of Houston: The First National Women's Conference, An Official Report to the President, the Congress, and the People of the United States.* Washington, D.C.: National Commission on the Observance of International Women's Year.

Phillips, Anne. 1995. *The Politics of Presence.* Oxford: Clarendon Press.

Pitkin, Hanna Fenichel. 1967. *The Concept of Representation.* Berkeley: University of California Press.

Scott, Joan W. 1992. "'Experience.'" In *Feminists Theorize the Political,* ed. Judith Butler and Joan W. Scott. New York: Routledge.

Spelman, Elizabeth V. 1988. *Inessential Woman.* Boston: Beacon.

Stanwick, Kathy A., and Katherine E. Kleeman. 1983. *Women Make a Difference.* New Brunswick, N.J.: Center for the American Woman and Politics.

Thomas, Sue. 1994. *How Women Legislate.* New York: Oxford University Press.

Two

Words That Matter

Women's Voice and Institutional Bias in
Public Policy Formation

Lyn Kathlene

Our understanding of legislative politics is informed by an array of diverse research extending from broad legal concepts of the institution to the details of individual congressional members in action. Most of the research has focused on the United States Congress. Much of what we know about our congressional members and legislative structures has been used to theorize and inform research on state legislatures and politicians. Yet despite the quantity, richness, and diversity of this research agenda, our theories and models are grounded in a common perspective: legislative politics as constructed by male politicians. What we have come to understand as politics in general is based mainly on the research of men, and predominantly white men.[1] We often presume that the politics of women or minorities will follow the same trajectory.[2] At the most, we concede that underrepresented groups will bring more sensitivity to issues particularly affecting their race or sex. But we fail to question adequately whether our understanding of legislative politics based on the experiences, attitudes, and behaviors of white male politicians is equally applicable to women and minorities.

Certain areas of legislative politics have been examined for minority and female impact. Campaigning, election studies, voting behavior, and personal surveying are the most common research efforts. Studies of political women paint a complicated and evolving picture of their policy priorities and political behavior. We know that women legislators are more ideologically liberal than their male counterparts (Dodson and Carroll 1991; Swers 1998; Welch 1985), are more likely than men to prioritize, champion, and sponsor women's and feminist issues (Dodson and Carroll 1991; Dodson et al. 1995; Gertzog 1995; Kathlene, Clarke, and Fox 1991; Saint-Germain 1989; Tamerius 1995; Thomas 1991, 1994; Thomas and Welch 1991; Carroll, this volume), and see themselves as representatives of women's special interests (Reingold 1992; Thomas 1997). Although voting behavior analyses have produced mixed results (see Norton 1997 for a discussion of the gender bias in roll-call voting tools), there is significant evidence that women are more likely to vote together on at least some "women's issues" bills (Burrell 1994; Dolan 1997; Swers 1998; Tatolovich and Schier 1993). As elected officials, women view themselves as more closely linked to their constituents (Bers 1978; Flammang 1985; Reingold 1992) and do more constituency work (Richardson and Freeman 1995). And within the policy-making arena, women endorse or use a more facilitative leadership style (Dodson and Carroll 1991; Flammang 1985; Kathlene 1994).

As women have become more numerous in our legislative bodies, many scholars suggest directly or indirectly that women's politics will change accordingly. That is, as women gain power and ascendance in the political domain, they will no longer behave as token members and women will gain the power and influence necessary to effect change (see, for example, Carroll 1984; Flammang 1985; Saint-Germain 1989). The question then is, will women mirror the politics of men, or will women apply a different set of expectations and attitudes that fundamentally challenge or change the legislative environment?

In attempting to address the question of women's impact, much of the research has been sensitive to, and theorizes about, the potential impact of gender differences arising from gender-related socialization. Ultimately, though, these gendered differences have been difficult to capture in traditional methodologies that measure political behavior through quantifying sex differences across discrete variables (Du Bois 1983; Kathlene 1990; Mies 1983). Thus, voting behavior, sponsorship of bills coded by issue area, committee assignments, and even the more context-sensitive priority lists generated by the legislators themselves only begin to scratch the surface of potential gender differences.

Even if women's bills are enacted at the same rate as men's, this is not enough information to conclude that men and women are treated equally in the legislative environment. It may be that women's bills receive more amendments and that those additions substantially change their intent or, more subtly, their approach to addressing the policy issue. If women's bills are subject to more transformation as they progress through the process, then the legislative institution, itself, is less accepting of (or more incompatible with) women's approaches. Thus, even if women "speak" with a different voice, and that voice translates into actual policy initiatives, few or none of these differences may be represented in the final law.

Important to this interpretation is the understanding that individuals with certain attitudinal approaches have created an entity that reflects the individual but, at the same time, transcends the individual (Ragins and Sundstrom 1989). Thus, in this country, white middle- and upper-class men historically have held the political, economic, and social power and therefore had the authority to define and create our institutions. Consequently, the distribution of power within organizations (see, e.g., Ragins and Sundstrom 1989; Sigel 1996), the formal rules and informal norms that guide daily operations (see, e.g., Acker 1992; Edelsky 1981; Ferguson 1984), and even the design of buildings, layout of interior spaces, and configuration of furniture (Kathlene 1995b; Spain 1992; Weisman 1992) are all gendered. Our legislatures, as much as any contemporary organization in the United States, because of their historical legacy as an exclusive male domain (Hearn 1992), represent an institutional entity that is gendered as masculine (see Duerst-Lahti and Kelly 1995). In practice, this means that the values, procedures, and expectations of behavior within the legislative environment conform and reward that which is masculinized and shun or marginalize that which is feminized. To the extent that a policy domain or a deliberative political process is marked by masculinized understandings or expectations, those members who do not (or are not expected to) conform to the masculinized norms are in danger of being marginalized and rendered ineffective.

Yet viewing the institution as all-powerful is unrealistic, too. There is a growing body of research that suggests that while women have not fundamentally changed the legislative institution, they have succeeded within the existing structure in promoting women, children, and family issues (e.g., Dolan 1997; Carroll 1990; Saint-Germain 1989; Thomas 1990; Swers 1998). Thus, women, in this case, are using existing institutional arrangements to promote their agenda without completely compromising their interests (Thomas 1991; 1994). Women have made an impact, and we must not lose sight of these achievements.

Given this important caveat, though, we also must not forget that institutions do serve the status quo and that any challenges to it, especially coming from a minority group (in this case a numerical minority), will have limited success (Duerst-Lahti and Kelly 1995; Kenney 1996; Thomas 1991; Yoder 1991). The potential of gender impact, then, is significantly decreased by the pervasiveness of a certain set of rules, norms, expectations, and stereotypes that are defined as proper and acceptable (Kenney 1996). It is the intersection of conflicts over untraditional approaches to policy-making and the response of the legislative institution that provides insight into understanding the importance of the resolution. How much is lost in the process of conforming? Perhaps substantively little is lost, perhaps a great deal.

Theoretical Construction of Gendered Voices

This research agenda is based on the premise that people have differing attitudinal orientations that provide the basis for how they process external stimuli. It assumes that people do hold different valuations or interpretations for the same events, the same people, and even the same information. Taking this reasoning to its limit, no two people will be alike. However, I am interested in understanding the differences between people by delineating some commonalities among groups of people. Here, I argue that men and women in Western culture[3] share a similar socialization and social reality based, in part, on biological sex. And these gender-related socialized norms have produced a set of gendered attitudes and, consequently, behaviors toward the social world.

Based on Carol Gilligan's (1982) findings of gender differences in moral decision-making, two general attitudinal constructs that represent different orientations to politics were developed for an earlier study (Kathlene 1989). Gilligan indicates that men tend to be more concerned with people's interfering with each other's rights, while women concern themselves with the possibility of omission, of not helping others when one could. Translating Gilligan's work into attitudes and behaviors relevant to the political arena, two constructs reflecting the broad themes of individualism versus interdependence were developed. The two distinctive orientations, labeled "instrumentalism" and "contextualism," represent the values, goals, and actions that would be involved during public policy formation.[4]

The influence of Gilligan's work cannot be overstated. It has generated a wealth of theorizing and testing in the social sciences, including gender studies in political science. At the same time, Gilligan's research has spurred much critical debate around such issues as her research methods and database, reliance on object-relations theory, dangerous or misconstrued stereotyping of men and women, and the lack of clear interpretative differentiation of the data (see, for example, Broughton 1983; Hockmeyer 1988; Kerber 1986; Kyte 1996; League 1993; Nails, O'Loughlin, and Walker 1983; Stack 1986). Nevertheless, even many of her critics acknowledge the conceptual and theoretical importance of her work (League 1993; Nails, O'Loughlin, and Walker 1983; Tronto 1987). And it is precisely these aspects of Gilligan's research, her conceptual and methodological insights, that can serve political science well.

Gilligan's work points toward several important research questions, epistemological stances and methodological considerations. First, Gilligan is not the first person to propose some version of *separateness* versus *connectedness* orientations related to sex,[5] although she departs from many past efforts by arguing for the strength (rather than the inferiority) of the proposed feminine relational orientation. It is possible that all these related theories are misconstrued, stemming from a patriarchal conception of men and women, but it is also possible that these theories tap into an existing aspect of human behavior because of the patriarchy that places an overwhelming emphasis on sex-socialization and gendered social realities. In addition, numerous feminist scholars dealing with questions of epistemology and methodology have argued for recognizing that women's social space (e.g., the paid and unpaid jobs women hold), class, race, ethnicity, sexual orientation, power relations, and so forth produce various standpoints from which women interpret the world (see, for example, Harding 1987, 1991; Hartsock 1983; Nielsen 1990; Fonow and Cook 1991; Reinharz 1992; Collins 1990). Gilligan's thesis fits well within standpoint theory as she argues that women have not been included in studies of moral development and that women's life experiences (or at least some life experiences) differ significantly enough from men's to question the accuracy of theories of "human" development that are based solely on men. Thus, Gilligan's work provides a framework for creating and testing questions of gender differences grounded in notions of a certain subset of standpoints, most notably those standpoints likely to be generated through the experience of being white and middle- or upper class during the 20th century in the United States (Nicholson 1994). Unquestionably, Gilligan's insights are, at best, applicable to only an exclusive and privileged group in society; however, it is precisely that group that makes up the great majority of elected officials in our state and national legislative bodies (Dolan and Ford 1997).

Gilligan does not initially provide empirical evidence of her thesis, as she notes both in her book (Gilligan 1982, 2–3) and later in replying to her critics (Gilligan 1986). Rather she asks her colleagues in psychology and other interested readers to "hear" how women's voices cannot accurately be reflected by Lawrence Kohlberg's (1981) six-stage morality development scale. Her important point is that women's responses have been coded as reaching only a midlevel development because women invoke language about relationships rather than "higher" notions of universal rights. But, as she demonstrates, the scale is unable to discern how this relational thinking differs from the notions imbedded in the scale. Thus, she points out two serious methodological limitations. One, psychological measurement scales developed to represent development theories based on one group of people may not be universally or even culturally valid. And two, acontextual coding of responses to match certain key words or ideas in a preconstructed measurement scale distorts or misses the important nuances constructed through words that reflect people's holistic thinking. All answers must fit somewhere within the scale's categories because it has become the interpretative framework. Thus, if some people do conceptualize problems differently (i.e., "speak in a different voice"), these conceptualizations are likely to be missed and coded incorrectly (Gilligan 1986; Johnson 1988). All of which brings us to the second important idea to be gleaned from Gilligan's work: Measurements that have been successful in describing various behaviors or attitudes of white men may provide a distorted picture of women (or minorities, see Stack 1986; or historical and cultural situatedness, see Nicholson 1994). We need to first "hear" from groups underrepresented in our development of theories and measurement instruments, rather than apply our exclusive theories and tools to their lives. Only then can we begin to more accurately understand and measure the impact of diversity.

These two lessons from Gilligan have direct application for the study of political elites. First, we need to frame questions of women's impact in politics around the broader notion of women's standpoint in society. There are many theories about the origins and resulting psychological and behavioral outcome of women's social reality; Gilligan provides one theory that is reasonable to test given the present descriptive characteristics of elected officials. Second, we must use methodologies congruent with the questions being asked. While many political studies of women refer to Gilligan's work as the impetus for testing differences between male and female political behavior, many research designs are unlikely to capture the differences Gilligan's work implies. Thus examining the voting behavior of men and women, while a worthy research project on partisan or ideological behavior, is not logically derived from Gilligan's notions of justice and care unless the research also examines the *content* (e.g., how is the problem defined, how will the problem be solved) of the bills. Studies of legislative issue areas, particularly those that look at women's or feminist issues, tap into a different notion of women's standpoint (i.e., women have a personal interest or experience in these issues), but gender difference in issue area is not represented in Gilligan's theory either.

Rather, because Gilligan argues that men tend to be more concerned with people's interfering with each other's rights, while women concern themselves with the possibility of omission, the political consequences of gendering are more apt to express themselves in terms of conceptualizing policy issues and interacting with people throughout the policy-making process. The attitudinal constructs, therefore, reflect a simplified set of complex gendered behavior applicable to the political domain. Men, I argue, tend to be more *instrumental* in their behavior and attitudes. Their dominant and relatively independent position and function in society have socialized them to view people as autonomous individuals (Gutmann 1970) in a hierarchical, competitive world (Parsons 1951). People are essentially self-centered and self-serving (Bakan 1966); therefore, knowledge that is subjective is suspect while objective knowledge is revered. The impersonal application of laws, rules, and norms is deemed "fair" and "objective" in a society where logical, analytical and abstract thinking are highly valued attributes (Bordo 1987). The view of persons as self-centered and in competition with one another leads to a strong adherence to the protection of individual rights in order to guarantee individual freedoms.

Women, on the other hand, approach the world from a more *contextual* viewpoint. Their subordinate and relatively dependent position and function in society have socialized them to view individuals in connection with one another and society (Dinnerstein 1976). People's lives are interdependent, based on a continuous web of relationships (Chodorow 1974). The world is not composed of distinct and separate spheres; thus women will not tend to view the world in terms of dichotomies. The public sphere is not separate from the private sphere. Subjective knowledge is not superior or necessarily distinct from objective knowledge (Belenky et al., 1986). Because women see individuals in terms of their symbiotic relationships to one another (Bakan 1966; Guttman 1970), women are more likely to be concerned with addressing the interrelated needs of individuals. Table 2.1 summarizes the values and approaches embedded in the attitudinal orientations.

The attitudinal constructs describe "ideal types" in a theoretical world of two dichotomies, which do not represent end points on a continuum but rather more accurately constitute two separate dimensions (Gilligan 1982; Johnson 1988; Lyons 1988). The most realistic description of a person in a given situation would probably consist of relying upon one orientation more than another or even utilizing some combination of attributes from the two constructs, whether by an individual's preference or through external pressure. People of both sexes, no doubt, rely on both instrumental and contextual approaches in their daily lives (Johnson 1988). Nevertheless, various psychological theories of gender

Table 2.1. Main Attributes of the Attitudinal Orientations

Instrumentalism	Contextualism
– views self as autonomous	– views self in connection with community/others
– human interactions are separate and competitive	– human interactions are part of a continuous web of relationships
– distinguishes between objective and subjective knowledge; favors objective	– integrates objective and subjective knowledge; believes both have "bias"
– main focus is protecting individual's rights	– main focus is addressing needs
– separates the public and private spheres	– sees the interaction between the public and private spheres

(Chodorow 1974; Dinnerstein 1976; Gilligan 1982; Gilligan, Ward and Taylor 1988; Miller 1976; Noddings 1984; Schaef 1981) purport that women tend to display contextual behavior more often than men, who are more likely to display instrumental behavior. And empirical research in communication and psychology has found support for the "connectedness versus separateness" theories of gendered views of behavior in the social world (see, for example, Carlson 1971, 1972; Finigan 1982; Gilligan, Ward, and Taylor 1988; Gilligan, Lyons and Hanmer 1990; Lang-Takac and Osterweil 1992; Turner 1992). Importantly, research has also found men are more bounded to the instrumental dimension while women are more likely to access both dimensions (Johnson et al. 1975; Johnston 1988). The questions that arise, then, are (1) whether people, based on their sex, tend to rely more on one approach than the other, especially in a *similar political context;* and (2) whether instrumental approaches, rather than contextual approaches, are more readily accepted within the masculinized legislative environment.

Construct Application and Hypotheses

The gender constructs move the analysis beyond the variable sex (which, though not inevitable, is typically undertheorized; see Duerst-Lahti and Kelly 1995) by enriching the entire research process from the conceptualization of the research design, to the selection of appropriate methodologies, to the interpretation of the data. Gender as applied in this research is the product of a two-step process: social and psychological *theories* of gender are translated into gendered *attitudes* applicable to politics which leads to hypotheses about political *behavior*. Once the gendered political behavior is defined, it can be empirically tested through the collection of appropriate data and the application of methodologies capable of discerning the types of gender differences highlighted by the constructs.

Specifically, the constructs represent the many psychological and social characteristics associated with masculinity and femininity, providing the researcher with a simplified framework of complex processes. By giving one label to each grouping of characteristics, we can discuss gender in reduced yet comprehensive terms. Second, the constructs theorize how these psychological and social differences would be manifested in the political arena. Building a theory of gendered political behavior clarifies the link between societal expectations and individual action in the political arena. Third, the constructs serve to interpret interview responses and observed behavior in committees. Given that the constructs are defined broadly in terms of autonomy versus interdependency, and specifically in terms of resulting attitudes and behaviors salient to the politics, gender differences in the data can be understood as part of a complex social web, not simply men versus women.

The interpretation of sex differences that are grounded in an applied gender framework suggest outcomes that go beyond the more simple, albeit important, hypotheses that are commonly tested in research on women in politics. Whether or not (1) feminist representatives will prioritize women's issues, or (2) women will have equal input in developing policy when they compose a certain proportion of elite politics, or (3) women will obtain equality of power when they gain similar positions in the political hierarchy, are only the tip of the iceberg when we apply more fully the implications of complex and deeply rooted effects of gendering.

Moreover, sex as it relates to gender proposes a set of far more complex and disturbing assumptions for political scholars to consider. It is important to consider how far-reaching this conceptualization of gendered attitudes and behavior may be for legislative policymaking. For example, given a women's world of interrelationships:

1. Women will have more difficulty researching and formulating policy because they will see a problem as affecting many people and groups, hence they will attempt to bring these actors into the policymaking process. While this may ultimately result in more comprehensive and sensitive policy, it also means that women will spend more time doing the "same job" as men. Either women will formulate fewer policies, or they will work longer hours.

2. The new groups or people women think should be heard when formulating policy will not be automatically or easily integrated into the process. The inclusion of new information sources probably will not be viewed as equally legitimate, knowledgeable, or relevant. Hence, women's attempt to integrate untraditional sources may be rejected or devalued by the male majority.

3. Women will conceptualize some policy issues in different terms. In explaining their position, the language they use will either be misunderstood (because the men have an alternative conceptualization) or will be discounted as tangential to the relevant policy problem and solution. Women will encounter resistance or even lose control of their conceptualization as the issue is redefined in traditional (masculine) terms.

4. Women will create more complex policies in an attempt to address the interrelated factors. Comprehensive bills receive more hearings because each specialized committee must consider the area of their expertise. More hearings result in more opportunities for a bill to be amended or killed.

5. Women will encourage discussion and alternative viewpoints. They will use positions of power and control to support other people's desire to participate in the process rather than to promote their own agenda through controlling discussion topics.

Each of the above hypotheses suggests that bringing women (or contextualized perspectives) into the political arena is not as simple as expecting new issue priorities to emerge out of the election of women. While women (maybe even particularly feminist women) will bring a heightened sensitivity and interest in women's issues, the gender differences between men and women (or instrumental and contextual perspectives) are far more profound. Women may approach women's issues not just more often but from an unconventional (contextual) standpoint that is not accepted by their male colleagues (or instrumentalists). If women define a "women's issue" as policy-relevant because they see the issue from a broader, contextualized perspective that includes public action, it may not be the "women's issue" that is being rejected but rather its conceptualization. Of course, this can be true for many policy areas, not just the so-called women's issues. And overcoming this institutionalized conceptual bias requires more than increasing the number of women (Kathlene 1995b; Kenney 1996). If women see the world as webs of interrelationships composed of a myriad of legitimate needs rather than competing claims of differing levels of importance, women will be more inclined to include men's conceptualization of the problem (as another equally legitimate concern) than vice versa (if men have elevated certain claims while dismissing others). Hence, women's approaches will be undermined or transformed in the legislative process.

A similar scenario can be sketched out for women's approach to decision-making, which emphasizes consensus rather than control. Women, and maybe even senior women in positions of power, will be less likely to use their power in ways we commonly associate with the word "power" (Kathlene 1994). However, time in the legislature may transform women's approaches as they become socialized to the institutional rules and norms and thus adopt masculine styles toward power and control. If institutional gendered (masculinized) socialization overpowers individual gendered socialization, then the hope that women might bring a different type of politics or even different priorities is also lessened. If their priorities are part of their social experiences, and these social experiences produce certain ways of viewing the world, the acceptance and incorporation of masculine-defined political behavior implies a rejection, or at least a subordination, of women's own worldview. In short, sex as understood in the gender framework produces a complicated and somewhat disturbing picture of legislative politics in western culture.

Database

In 1989, the state of Colorado ranked fifth among the fifty states in the number of women elected to state government (Center for the American Woman and Politics 1989). As occurs in most bicameral states, the number of women elected to the Colorado House exceeded their election to the Senate, both in actual numbers and percentage of the chamber, with 33 percent women (n = 22) seated in the House and 20 percent (n = 7) in the Senate. This project focuses exclusively on the Colorado House because of the greater number of women representatives.

To ascertain the attitudinal orientations that affect policy-making and the conditions under which the attitudes produce distinct legislative responses, personal interviews with the legislators were conducted to determine their attitudes and values regarding both the general legislative process and specific policy problems. The legislators' interviews provide a basis for comparing the individual perspectives of men and women and an examination of other salient factors that might produce differences in attitudinal orientations, such as party affiliation and terms in the legislature. The personal orientations revealed in the interviews were compared with the types of bills introduced in the 1989 session to determine whether the legislators were acting upon their value convictions.

All the bills introduced in the House (n = 360) were coded according to a variety of factors, including sex of the sponsor, issue area of the bill, committee assignments, and numerous committee outcomes. This legislation database allows an analysis of process differences based on sponsorship, issue area, or other possible factors that might elicit distinctive treatment as it moves through the legislative process.

Of the 360 bills introduced in the House during the 1989 session, sixty-eight (19%) were taped and transcribed, from the introduction by the sponsor of the bill in the first committee hearing through the final floor debate in the House. A large variety of bills were sampled to provide a basis for testing whether women legislators' attitudinal orientations influence more than just traditionally women- or feminist-oriented bills. The sample of selected bills was stratified by male and female sponsorship across eleven of the twelve issue areas.[6] Table 2.2 shows the distribution.

Eight of the ten standing committees in the Colorado legislature are represented through committee hearings of the 68 bills. The taped bills were compared with bills not taped by selection and outcome factors and showed no statistically significant differences in the sample distribution by sex, term of sponsor, party affiliation, fiscal impact, House committee hearing outcomes,[7] amendment action, House or Senate floor action, or governor action. Although women-sponsored bills were intentionally oversampled, the 68 bills appear to be fairly representative of all bills introduced in the House during 1989 across other salient features (for a detailed description of the database, see Kathlene 1991).

Gendered Approaches to Formulating Policy

Sources of Information Used

An important aspect of policy formulation is the initial research a legislator engages in before drafting a bill. Research involves the use of a variety of information sources that will influence and mold the proposed legislation. Sources can include people, such as constituents, fellow legislators, local politicians, staff personnel, professionals, citizens, and friends. Sources also can be items, such as previous research, reports, books, articles, laws in other states or countries, and so forth.

One indicator of a contextual versus instrumental approach to policy-

Table 2.2. Breakdown of Number of Bills Taped by
Issue Area and Sex of Sponsor

Issue	Men	Women	Total %
Business	4	1	5 (7%)
Civil Liberties	1	1	2 (3%)
Crime	4	4	8 (12%)
Education	2	4	6 (9%)
Environment	4	4	8 (12%)
Family/Children	4	4	8 (12%)
Health Care	4	6	10 (15%)
Legal	3	1	4 (6%)
Public Sector	6	4	10 (15%)
Social Services	2	1	3 (4%)
Tax	2	2	4 (6%)
Transportation	—	—	—
Totals	36 (53%)	32 (47%)	68 (100%)

making is the number and variety of sources a legislator uses to keep informed, in general, and to formulate a particular bill. More resources represent a contextual orientation, which recognizes the complexity of the environment and the need to integrate many sources of information in order to incorporate as many of the affected and interested people as possible. An instrumental approach relies more heavily on fewer information sources, most likely the ones that are viewed as more politically legitimate, more "objective." For example, experts will be highly valued. The use of fewer select resources arises from the notion that problems stem from separate and competitive claims; hence, reliance on people deemed most directly "knowledgeable" in the area of interest (but not necessarily those most affected).

In two separate sets of interviews with Colorado state legislators (Kathlene 1989, 1991), I found gender differences in the number and types of resources used to develop legislative bills. Table 2.3 reports resource range, mean, and mode (if any) of the number of responses, by sex, party identification, age, and freshman status in the legislature. A small sample t-test of sample means is used to determine if there are statistically significant differences within the categories.

In both sets of interviews, only sex is statistically significant. Party,

Table 2.3. Number of Different RESOURCES Reported by
Colorado Legislators When Developing Public Policies by Sex,
Party, Age, and Freshman Status

Interview Study 1: 1985 Legislative Session, n = 10					
Category	**N**	**Range**	**Mean**	**Mode**	**t**
Women	5	4–8	5.8	6	2.53**
Men	5	2–6	3.4	3	
Democrat	3	2–8	5.3	—	.75
Republican	7	3–6	4.3	3	
< 45 years old	5	3–8	4.8	3	.32
> 45 years old	5	2–6	5.4	6	
Freshman	5	2–8	5.0	6	.59
Second+ term	5	3–8	4.2	—	
Interview Study 2: 1989 Legislative Session, n = 20					
Category	**N**	**Range**	**Mean**	**Mode**	**t**
Women	8	4–10	6.9	7	1.85*
Men	12	2–8	5.4	4	
Democrat	8	2–10	6.4	7	.74
Republican	12	4–8	5.8	4	
< 45 years old	7	2–8	5.7	6	−.50
> 45 years old	13	4–10	6.2	7	
Freshman	4	5–7	6.3	7	.30
Second+ term	16	2–10	5.9	4	

**Statistically significant at p < .05.
*Statistically significant at p < .10.

generational age, and terms in the legislature do not differ significantly.
However, more interesting than a simple analysis of the number of resources mentioned is an examination of who, which groups, and what
types of informational sources are used. Table 2.4 lists six categories of
resource nouns legislators utilized when formulating bills.

Of the fifty-five different resources, only thirteen (24%) were mentioned by both women and men. These distinct vocabularies indicate
that women and men are relying on different resources when formulating policy, which suggests they may have different approaches to conceptualizing policy problems and researching solutions. For example,

Table 2.4. Six Categories of Resource Nouns Mentioned by Legislators, 1989 Session

Nouns Mentioned by Women & Men	Used by Women Only	Used by Men Only
1. General Population		
constituent(s,cy,cies) people	citizens (s)	advisers
	community	client
	country	consultants
	district	experts
	parents	industry
	world	some (one, body)
2. Political [Elected]		
DA (public defenders)	city council (men)	
	county commissioners	
	leaders	
	legislators	
	mayor (s)	
3. Political [Not Elected]		
groups (s)	private attorneys	police officers
lobbyist (s)	organizations	insurance
judges	social workers	commissioner
meeting (s)	legislative council (staff)	special interests
4. Government/Private Organizations		
department	public officials	agencies
NCSL	social services	
state (s)		
5. Personal Experience	husband	relatives
myself	personal experience	
6. Studies/Media	history	letters
articles	issue statements	policy
news/paper (s)	magazines	problems
	research	radio
		situations
		statute
		stuff
		television

men claim they became aware of policy problems more often through "experts" and political people with specialized knowledge. In contrast, women became aware of problems more through general information sources covering the full range of political geography, from their district to the world. Note that only women talked about receiving information from local and state political leaders. And even though both men and women spoke about their reliance on lobbyists, for women it was more an unfortunate fact of legislative life, while for men it was seen as a highly valued and essential resource. Moreover, an examination of resource usage by party affiliation revealed that men in both parties were more similar to one another than they were to their women counterparts. And women, be they Democrats or Republicans, used a wider variety of resources outside the legislative institution than the men in their own party.

Policy Study: Alternative Views of Crime

Do these orientations reflected in legislators' general approach to developing public policy apply to and affect their individual deliberations about specific policy problems and possible solutions? In a study examining how 47 legislators talked about the problem of crime (Kathlene 1995a), men tended to see criminals as autonomous individuals responsible for choosing a life of crime. Women, on the other hand, tended to see criminals as people interacting within the context of societal opportunities, most especially the lack of equal opportunities (i.e., access to healthy families, adequate education, economic prospects) and the lifelong processes that foster criminal behavior.

These gendered viewpoints on the origins of crime are directly related to their proposed policy solutions. Since men focus on the crime event, the policy questions they ponder are more narrowly defined, such as how to improve the administrative aspects of the criminal justice system or the prison system, how to keep criminals off the streets, or how to make criminals take responsibility for their behavior. Women's view of crime as a lifetime process led to broader policy questions such as how to prevent people from turning to a life of crime or how to make the criminal a functioning part of society after incarceration.

The crime and prison bills introduced in the 1989 Colorado session revealed these same gendered views. Men focused on legal proceedings (such as rules regarding new evidence in criminal court cases), expanding existing laws to include new crimes, and increasing penalties in existing criminal law. These crime bills with their legal focus (92%) and "get tough on crime" approach paralleled the men's discussion and policy recommendations in the interviews, which focused on the crime event. While women, too, sponsored legal changes (37%) such as stricter sentencing, that was not their overwhelming method. In fact, only women dealt with crime through prevention and intervention strategies —approaches that mirrored their discussion of the relationship between society and criminal behavior. What of success rates? Only 37 percent of women's crime bills became law, compared with 83 percent of the men's crime bills. In particular, all of the women's intervention and prevention bills were postponed indefinitely. While it may be pure sexism that prevented women's bills from becoming law, a more likely explanation stems from the second hypothesis: that women's contextual orientation resulted in a broader conception of crime, one that was at odds with the instrumental institutionalized discourse of the legislature. Hence, women's policy approaches are not understood or appreciated, seen at best as tangential to the problem at hand.

The interpretation of these attitudinal differences as gender-based was strengthened when other possible causal explanations were considered. Party affiliation played no role in explaining the differences in attitudinal orientations toward using and valuing information for policy development or crime problems. Democratic and Republican women were more similar to each other than men and women within either the Democratic Party or the Republican Party. The same was true for the men.

Gender and the Institutional Context

Gender and Policy Outcome Measures

The gendered approaches found in the interviews were then linked to the broader legislative context. Outcome measures, such as bill passage rates, were tested by sex. This common measurement of political effectiveness revealed that women were as successful as men in sponsoring bills that passed through the House and Senate and received the governor's signature, but the picture of legislative success was not that simple and clear-cut. For example, men and women initiated bills at different rates depending upon their terms in the legislature. First-term women sponsored fewer bills than their male counterparts, while seasoned women sponsored more bills than their male counterparts. In fact, it is the men's political behavior we associate with typical legislative behavior. We would expect to see legislators with longer tenure begin to drop off in their sponsorship of bills as they acquire positions of power. Positional power allows a person to influence state policy in more ways than simply sponsorship; thus, the extra duties associated with holding a legislative leadership position along with the additional power associated with the position leads men to sponsor fewer bills.

However, the same logic cannot be applied to women. That first-term women sponsor on average one-third fewer bills than first-term men may indicate that women are attempting to construct policy in a different, more time-consuming manner (see Kathlene, Clarke and Fox 1991). It also may indicate that lobbyists, governmental leaders, and bureaucrats do not seek out women as often as men to carry legislation. It may be that women need to be in the legislature longer to build these traditional ties, and that is one reason we see the seasoned women (three to five terms) carrying more bills. Given that women have had to spend more terms in the Colorado House before receiving leadership positions (Kathlene 1986, 1991), comparisons of seasoned legislators by sex may not be completely accurate with regard to acquiring legislative power. Hence, women who have spent two or three terms in the House may still be limited to bill sponsorship as the primary means for affecting state policy. The equal success rate of women- and men-sponsored bills is complicated by sex differences in initiation rates.

Beyond these statistical measurements of differences, the constructs suggest, and results from a conversational analysis found, that gender manifests itself in the political arena in even more complex ways. Indeed, an examination of how chairmen and chairwomen respond to witnesses and lead committee discussions suggests that even when women obtain the same power as men they will use it differently. Women's use of the chair to facilitate committee interaction among committee members and the witnesses without joining in the substantive debate themselves is in marked contrast to men's tendency to use their chair to control and direct committee debate along the lines of interest to them (Kathlene 1994). Thus we should not expect that women will mirror the behavior of men even when they achieve similar levels of power.

Gender and Legislative Treatment of Bills

In order to determine more precisely which bills are receiving differential treatment, a typology of bill treatment was developed. In order to classify bills together based upon the similarity of their legislative outcomes, all 360 bills that were introduced in the 1989 Colorado State House were analyzed through a statistical technique known as cluster analysis or numerical taxonomy (see Sokal 1974; Lorr 1983).

The two major advantages of cluster analysis over more traditional multivariate methods are its holistic, context-sensitive theoretical premises and its ability to classify cases based on many variables (Brunner 1986; Brunner et al. 1987). Cluster approaches the data unique case by unique case, each defined by all its variables, and compares how one case defined by N variables matches with the next case defined by N variables and so forth. It does not look for significant variables per se but rather partitions the data into clusters (usually called "types") where certain variables will emerge in one cluster as important but other variables will emerge in another cluster as important.

The cluster analysis revealed that women's bills received tougher legislative treatment, mainly because of multiple committee assignments. The number of committee assignments was highly significant with respect to the final action on the bill. Bills with more than one committee assignment in the House or Senate were more likely to be killed than bills assigned to a single committee in each chamber (House: chi = 12.2, p < .002; Senate: chi = 10.0, p < .007). Since women were more likely to sponsor bills that had a fiscal impact (chi = 4.5, p < .03), their bills were more likely to receive a standing committee assignment plus Appropriations assignment. Yet women had success rates similar to men's, which suggests two interesting trends: Women introduce legislation using tools with fiscal costs more than men (see Kathlene, Clarke, and Fox 1991); and women have to fight a harder and longer battle to get their legislation enacted at the same rate as men.

Interestingly, bills introduced by women, whether Republicans or Democrats, were more likely to cluster into the same type than men's bills. Men's bill types tended to be distinguished not only on the basis of sex but also on the basis of party and issue area. Hence we see Republican men's bills receiving different treatment than Democratic men's bills (e.g., first-term Republican men were typically successful while Democratic men had to be in their second term to have a similar success rate). In contrast, women's bills—be they Republican or Democratic, women's issues or business issues—were treated alike. The attitudinal constructs suggest that these gender treatment differences reflect more than simply the sex of the sponsor. Rather, the gendered treatment found in the cluster analysis highlights that the values, attitudes, and methods embedded in a sponsor's policy-making approaches are more aligned (if instrumental) or less aligned (if contextual) with the institutionalized status quo (masculinized) values and methods of the legislative environment (see Kathlene 1991 for details on the cluster analysis).

Gender and Policy Tool Preferences

The cluster analysis provides a macro-level examination of treatment differences based on gender. These "extra" committee hearings were not a result of overt sex discrimination but rather were intimately tied to the particular gendered approaches women used in their policy-making. Women's long-range view of legislative success, along with their broader resource base, provides the context for which women, more than men, sponsored comprehensive non-incremental bills. Coding each of the 68 taped bills by the policy tools used to accomplish its objectives, I found that women's approaches to policy mirrors the attitudes they expressed in the interviews. Women, more than men, were inclined to assume that the target population of a policy was already predisposed toward the policy goal and that people simply needed barriers removed or additional social supports to act appropriately. Men, on the other hand, were inclined to address policy goals through tools that assumed the targeted population needed to be coerced to act appropriately. Men used both incentives and disincentives to drive social policy. The belief that people need to be manipulated to behave differently is directly related to an *instrumental* view of human relationships, as separate and competitive and self-interested. The belief that people's behavior differs from the stated policy goal because of societal barriers is directly related to a *contextual* view of human relationships intertwined with each other and society. Thus, men and women interpreted and responded to problems based on different beliefs about human nature and society (Kathlene, Clarke, and Fox 1991).

Additionally, I discovered that women were more likely than men to sponsor complex non-incremental policy solutions—that is, bills that dealt with new areas for public legislation, new solutions to old problems, or new programs for the state. Men, on the other hand, were more likely than women to sponsor bills that modified existing laws or updated old laws. Table 2.5 provides the percentage breakdown of bill types by sex.

Although an analysis of all 360 bills found that women were not sponsoring legislation in particular issue areas that differed from the men's, that was not the case for non-incremental legislation. Here nearly half of the women-sponsored bills focused on education and family/children issues compared with only 13 percent of the men's non-incremental bills. The result was that women were initiating bills that addressed policy problems from a more comprehensive standpoint; their non-incremental policy efforts were mainly focused on a subset of so-

Table 2.5. Bill Types Sponsored by Men and Women in the 1989
Colorado Legislature

| | Percent Sponsored by | | |
Bill Type:	Men	Women	N
Non-Incremental	48.5	73.1	35.0
Modify Existing Law	45.5	23.1	21.0
Update Old Law	6.1	3.8	3.0
n =	33	26	59
chi-square = 6.38; p = .09			

called women's issues, the policy areas where women, because of their role in society, would hold a special interest and expertise.

In some respects, this is hardly surprising. Much of our interest in electing and observing women and minority representatives is based on the belief that they will be more attuned to issues affecting their groups. Given this sensitivity, we would expect women to demonstrate interest and expertise in "women's issues" that have been overlooked by traditionally male legislatures. My findings indicate that women's issues are being promoted in an important and particular way: as components of policy initiatives that see women's issues in new policy terms, rather than as incremental adjustments to old approaches. When examining all the issue areas of bills women and men sponsor, women's issues may not be overrepresented by women; but when viewed in terms of which legislators are promoting comprehensive non-incremental approaches to women's issues, it is the women who are making a difference for women.

Conclusion

This research project points out that gender impact goes well beyond the sponsorship of women's issues or even sponsorship itself. In fact, gendered attitudinal orientations can affect any issue area and can theoretically influence people who hold different attitudes. As some scholars have already noted, these different gendered approaches are already appearing, and not simply through the bills women sponsor (Gluck 1987; Saint-Germain 1989). Perhaps the more reflective and connected way of looking at our societal needs have begun to emerge indirectly through women's presence and pressure in government. As one Colorado Senator put it:

I think sitting next to [a male Senator] on the floor in the Senate is the best thing I ever did in my life because I can, he's on the Joint Budget Committee . . . sitting next to him and talking into his ear is probably the best thing I ever did. Because we can talk about handicapped children before the budget gets written; we can talk about AFDC-U before the budget gets written; and those places I've learned in six years where it's real important—it's not going to the microphone afterwards when it's too late; it's getting to know where the important spot is.

Women and men share many similar concerns and views of the world. However, in certain fundamental ways, women's perspective differs from men's. We should expect not only that women might serve traditionally female interests better than men but also that women may be providing a counterbalance to public policymaking in general. While some of the differences documented in this research may seem subtle, the implications of these differences are profound. For if most women do see and use a broader range of resources when formulating policy, then we should have both more sensitive policymaking and a broader definition of representative democracy. If women see society and the individual inextricably linked, then we should expect to see more comprehensive preventative policies rather than piecemeal reactionary policies. While my research cannot, at this point, say conclusively that these differences produce different legislative politics, the evidence thus far suggests that gendered attitudes do exist and are translated into the initial versions of bills.

Notes

1. Also, predominantly from the middle and upper socioeconomic strata of our society. However, this is less of a factor for this research because most politicians, be they male, female, white, or an ethnic minority, tend to be from a higher-than-average socioeconomic class.

2. Legislative research and political science in general are hardly the only fields to make these sweeping assumptions. For an extensive review of sex-blind research in the social sciences and a discussion of the resulting problems, see Eichler (1988).

3. Particularly, white non-Hispanic men and women from middle and upper classes.

4. For a detailed discussion of the constructs, see Kathlene 1989.

5. Separateness and connectedness constructs appear in "agentic" vs. "com-

munal" (Bakan 1966), "allocentric" vs. "autocentric" (Gutmann 1970),
"differentiated" vs. "united" (Frankenstein 1966), and "expressive" vs.
"instrumental" (Parsons 1951), to name a few. See Lang-Takac and Osterweil (1992) for a succinct overview of this literature.

6. Issue areas are not the same as standing committees, although the overlap
is substantial. Twelve issue areas are defined, whereas there were ten standing committees. Some committees, such as Health, Education, Welfare and
Institutions, presumably would hear three of the identified issue areas
(health care, education, and social services).

7. Except for the first committee assignment, where more of the taped bills
were postponed indefinitely. This probably was due to the high visibility
of a larger portion of the selected bills (visibility was one of the selection criteria used, see Kathlene 1991), which probably resulted in an over-
sampling of controversial bills.

References

Acker, Joan. 1992. "Gendering Organization Theory." In *Gendering Organizational Analysis*, ed. Albert J. Mills and Peta Tancred. Newbury Park, Calif.:
Sage.

Bakan, David. 1966. *The Quality of Human Existence*. Chicago: Rand-McNally.

Belenky, Mary Field, Blythe McVicker Clinchy, Nancy Rule Goldberger,
and Jill Mattuck Tarule. 1986. *Women's Ways of Knowing*. New York: Basic
Books.

Bers, Trudy H. 1978. "Local Political Elites: Men and Women on Boards of
Education." *Western Political Quarterly* 78: 381–391.

Bordo, Susan. 1987. "The Cartesian Masculinization of Thought." In *Sex and
Scientific Inquiry*, ed. Harding and O'Barr. Chicago: University of Chicago
Press.

Broughton, John M. 1983. "Women's Rationality and Men's Virtues: A Critique
of Gender Dualism in Gilligan's Theory of Moral Development." *Social Research* 50: 597–641.

Brunner, Ronald D. 1986. "Case-Wise Policy Information Systems: Redefining
Poverty." *Policy Sciences* 19: 97–125.

Brunner, Ronald D., J. Samuel Fitch, Janet Grassia, Lyn Kathlene, and
Kenneth R. Hammond. 1987. "Improving Data Utilization: The Case-Wise
Alternative." *Policy Sciences* 20: 365–394.

Burrell, Barbara C. 1994. *A Woman's Place Is in the House: Campaigning for
Congress in the Feminist Era*. Ann Arbor: University of Michigan Press.

Carlson, Rae. 1971. "Sex Differences in Ego Functioning: Exploratory Studies
of Agency and Communion." *Journal of Consulting and Clinical Psychology*
37: 270–271.

Carlson, Rae. 1972. "Understanding Women: Implications for Personality
Theory and Research." *Journal of Social Issues* 28: 17–32.

Carroll, Susan. 1984. "Women Candidates and Support for Feminist Concerns: The Closet Feminist Syndrome." *Western Political Quarterly* 37: 307–323.

Carroll, Susan. 1990. "Looking Back at the 1980s and Forward to the 1990s." *CAWP News & Notes* 7: 9–12.

Center for the American Woman and Politics. 1989. "Women in State Legislatures 1989." Fact Sheet.

Chodorow, Nancy. 1974. "Family Structure and Feminine Personality." In *Women, Culture and Society,* ed. Rosaldo and Lamphere. Stanford: Stanford University Press.

Collins, Patricia Hill. 1990. *Black Feminist Thought.* Boston: Unwin Hyman.

Dinnerstein, Dorothy. 1976. *The Mermaid and the Minotaur.* New York: Harper Colophon Books.

Dodson, Debra L., and Susan J. Carroll. 1991. *Reshaping the Agenda: Women in State Legislatures.* New Brunswick, N.J.: Center for the American Woman and Politics.

Dodson, Debra L., Susan J. Carroll, Ruth B. Mandel, Katherine E. Kleeman, Ronnee Schreiber, and Debra Liebowitz. 1995. *Voices, Views, Votes: The Impact of Women in the 103rd Congress.* New Brunswick, N.J.: Center for the American Woman and Politics.

Dolan, Julie. 1997. "Support for Women's Interests in the 103rd Congress: The Distinct Impact of Congressional Women. *Women & Politics* 18 (4): 81–94.

Dolan, Kathleen, and Lynne E. Ford. 1997. "Change and Continuity Among Women State Legislators: Evidence from Three Decades." *Political Research Quarterly* 50: 137–151.

Du Bois, Barbara. 1983. "Passionate Scholarship: Notes on Values, Knowing and Method in Feminist Social Science." In *Theories of Women's Studies,* ed. Bowles and Klein. Boston: Routledge & Kegan Paul.

Duerst-Lahti, Georgia, and Rita Mae Kelly, eds. 1995. *Gender Power, Leadership, and Governance.* Ann Arbor: University of Michigan Press.

Edelsky, C. 1981. "Who's Got the Floor?" *Language in Society* 10: 383–421.

Eichler, Margrit. 1988. *Nonsexist Research Methods.* Boston: Allen & Unwin.

Ferguson, Kathy. 1984. *The Feminist Case Against Bureaucracy.* Philadelphia: Temple University Press.

Finigan, Michael. 1982. "The Effects of Token Representation on Participation in Small Decision Making Groups." *Economic and Industrial Democracy* 3: 531–550.

Flammang, Janet A. 1985. "Female Officials in the Feminist Capital: The Case of Santa Clara County." *Western Political Quarterly* 38: 95–118.

Fonow, Mary Margaret, and Judith A. Cook. 1991. *Beyond Methodology: Feminist Scholarship as Lived Research.* Bloomington: Indiana University Press.

Frankenstein, C. 1966. *The Roots of Ego.* Baltimore: Williams and Wilkins.

Gertzog, Irwin N. 1995. *Congressional Women: Their Recruitment, Integration, and Behavior,* 2nd ed. Westport, Conn.: Praeger Publishers.

Gilligan, Carol. 1982. *In a Different Voice: Psychological Theory and Women's Development.* Cambridge, Mass.: Harvard University Press.

Gilligan, Carol. 1986. "Reply." *Signs* 11: 324–33.

Gilligan, Carol, Janie Victoria Ward, and Jill McLean Taylor. 1988. *Mapping the Moral Domain.* Cambridge, Mass.: Harvard University Press.

Gilligan, Carol, Nona P. Lyons, and Trudy J. Hanmer. 1990. *Making Connections.* Cambridge, Mass.: Harvard University Press.

Gluck, Hazel Frank. 1987. "The Difference." *State Government* 60: 223–26.

Gutmann, David. 1970. "Female Ego Styles and Generational Conflict." In *Feminine Personality and Conflict,* ed. Judith Bardwick, Elizabeth Douvan, Matina Horner, and David Gutmann. Belmont, Calif.: Brooks/Cole.

Harding, Sandra. 1987. "The Instability of the Analytical Categories of Feminist Theory." In *Sex and Scientific Inquiry,* ed. Harding and O'Barr. Chicago: University of Chicago Press.

Harding, Sandra. 1991. *Whose Science? Whose Knowledge? Thinking from Women's Lives.* Ithaca, N.Y.: Cornell University Press.

Hartsock, Nancy. 1983. *Money, Sex and Power: Toward a Feminist Historical Materialism.* New York: Longman.

Hearn, Jeff. 1992. *Men in the Public Eye: The Construction and Deconstruction of Public Men and Public Patriarchies.* New York: Routledge.

Hockmeyer, Anne. 1988. "Object Relations Theory and Feminism: Strange Bedfellows." *Frontiers* 10: 20–28.

Johnson, Miriam M. 1988. *Strong Mothers, Weak Wives.* Berkeley: University of California Press.

Johnson, Miriam M., Jean Stockard, Joan Acker, and Claudeen Naffziger. 1975. "Expressiveness Re-evaluated." *School Review* 83: 617–644.

Johnston, D. Kay. 1988. "Adolescents' Solutions to Dilemmas in Fables: Two Moral Orientations—Two Problem Solving Strategies." In *Mapping the Moral Domain,* ed. Gilligan, Ward, and Taylor. Cambridge, Mass.: Harvard University Press.

Kathlene, Lyn. 1986. "The Relative Success of Women Representatives in the Colorado State Legislature: Trends and Explanatory Factors." *Comparative State Politics Newsletter* 7: 12–17.

Kathlene, Lyn. 1989. "Uncovering the Political Impacts of Gender: An Exploratory Study." *Western Political Quarterly* 42: 397–421.

Kathlene, Lyn. 1990. "A New Approach to Understanding the Impact of Gender on the Legislative Process." In *Feminist Research Methods: Exemplary Readings in the Social Sciences,* ed. Joyce McCarl Nielsen. Boulder, Colo.: Westview Press.

Kathlene, Lyn. 1991. "Gender, Public Policy, and the Legislative Process: Delineating the Gendered Perspectives and Outcomes of Policymaking in the 1989 Colorado State House." Dissertation for the University of Colorado at Boulder.

Kathlene, Lyn. 1994. "Power and Influence in State Legislative Policymaking: The Interaction of Gender and Position in Committee Hearing Debates." *American Political Science Review* 88: 560–575.

Kathlene, Lyn. 1995a. "Alternative Views of Crime: Legislative Policymaking in Gendered Terms." *Journal of Politics* 57: 696–723.

Kathlene, Lyn. 1995b. "Position Power versus Gender Power: Who Holds the

Floor?" In *Gender Power, Leadership, and Governance,* ed. Georgia Duerst-Lahti and Rita Mae Kelly. Ann Arbor: University of Michigan Press.

Kathlene, Lyn, Susan E. Clarke, and Barbara A. Fox. 1991. "Ways Women Politicians Are Making a Difference." *In Gender and Policymaking: Studies of Women in Office,* ed. Debra L. Dodson. New Brunswick, N.J.: Center for the American Woman and Politics: 31–38.

Kenney, Sally J. 1996. "New Research on Gendered Political Institutions." *Political Research Quarterly* 49: 445–466.

Kerber, Linda. 1986. "Some Cautionary Words for Historians." *Signs* 11: 304–310.

Kyte, Richard. 1996. "Moral Reasoning as Perception: A Reading of Carol Gilligan." *Hypatia* 11 (3): 97–113.

Kohlberg, Lawrence. 1981. *The Philosophy of Moral Development.* San Francisco: Harper and Row.

Lang-Takac, Ester and Zahava Osterweil. 1992. "Separateness and Connectedness: Differences between the Genders." *Sex Roles* 27: 277–289.

League, Kathleen. 1993. "Individualism, Class, and the Situation of Care: An Essay on Carol Gilligan." *Journal of Social Philosophy* 24: 69–79.

Lorr, Maurice. 1983. *Cluster Analysis for Social Scientists.* San Francisco: Jossey-Bass Publishers.

Lyons, Nona Plessner. 1988. "Two Perspectives: On Self, Relationships, and Morality." In *Mapping the Moral Domain,* ed. Gilligan, Ward, and Taylor. Cambridge, Mass.: Harvard University Press.

Mies, Maria. 1983. "Towards a Methodology for Feminist Research." In *Theories of Women's Studies,* ed. Bowles and Klein. Boston: Routledge & Kegan Paul.

Miller, Jean Baker. 1976. *Toward a New Psychology of Women.* Boston: Beacon Press.

Nails, Debra, Mary Ann O'Loughlin, and James C. Walker, eds. 1983. "Women and Morality." Special issue of *Social Research* 50 (3).

Nicholson, Linda. 1994. "Interpreting Gender." *Signs* 20: 79–105.

Nielsen, Joyce McCarl, ed., 1990. *Feminist Research Methods: Exemplary Readings in the Social Sciences.* Boulder, Colo.: Westview Press.

Noddings, Nel. 1984. *Caring: A Feminine Approach to Ethics and Moral Education.* Berkeley: University of California Press.

Norton, Noelle H. 1997. "Analyzing Roll-Call Voting Tools for Content: Are Women's Issues Excluded from Legislative Research." *Women & Politics* 17 (4): 47–69.

Parsons, Talcott. 1951. *The Social System.* Glencoe, Ill.: Free Press.

Ragins, Bell Rose, and Eric Sundstrom. 1989. "Gender and Power in Organizations: A Longitudinal Perspective." *Psychological Bulletin* 105: 51–88.

Reingold, Beth. 1992. "Concepts of Representation among Female and Male State Legislators." *Legislative Studies Quarterly* 17: 509–537.

Reinharz, Shulamit. 1992. *Feminist Methods in Social Research.* New York: Oxford University Press.

Richardson, Lilliard E., Jr., and Patricia K. Freeman. 1995. "Gender Differences in Constituency Service Among State Legislators." *Political Research Quarterly* 48: 169–179.

Saint-Germain, Michelle A. 1989. "Does Their Difference Make a Difference? The Impact of Women on Public Policy in the Arizona Legislature." *Social Science Quarterly* 70: 956–968.

Schaef, Ann Wilson. 1981. *Women's Reality.* Minneapolis: Winston Press.

Sigel, Roberta S. 1996. *Ambition and Accommodation: How Women View Gender Relations.* Chicago: University of Chicago Press.

Sokal, R. R. 1974. "Classification: Purposes, Principles, Progress, Prospects." *Science* 185: 1115–1123.

Spain, Daphne. 1992. *Gendered Spaces.* Chapel Hill: University of North Carolina Press.

Stack, Carol B. 1986. "The Culture of Gender: Women and Men of Color." *Signs* 11: 321–324.

Swers, Michele L. 1998. "Are Women More Likely to Vote for Women's Issue Bills Than Their Male Colleagues?" *Legislative Studies Quarterly* 23: 435–448.

Tamerius, Karin L. 1995. "Sex, Gender, and Leadership in the Representation of Women." In *Gender Power, Leadership, and Governance,* ed. Georgia Duerst-Lahti and Rita Mae Kelly. Ann Arbor: University of Michigan Press.

Tatolovich, Raymond, and David Schier. 1993. "The Persistence of Ideological Cleavage in Voting on Abortion Legislation in the House of Representatives, 1973–1988." *American Politics Quarterly* 21: 125–139.

Thomas, Sue. 1990. "The Voting Patterns in the California Assembly: The Role of Gender." *Women & Politics* 9: 43–56.

Thomas, Sue. 1991. "Evaluating the Impact of Women Legislators on Political Policies and Processes: The Context of Success." Presented at the annual meeting of the Midwest Political Science Association, Chicago.

Thomas, Sue. 1994. *How Women Legislate.* New York: Oxford University Press.

Thomas, Sue. 1997. "Why Gender Matters: The Perceptions of Women Officeholders." *Women & Politics* 17 (1): 27–53.

Thomas, Sue, and Susan Welch. 1991. "The Impact of Gender on Activities and Priorities of State Legislators." *Western Political Quarterly* 44: 334–356.

Tronto, Joan. 1987. "Beyond Gender Difference to a Theory of Care." *Signs* 12: 644–663.

Turner, Lynn H. 1992. "An Analysis of Words Coined by Women and Men: Reflections on the Muted Group Theory and Gilligan's Model." *Women and Language* 15 (1): 21–26.

Weisman, Leslie Kanes. 1992. *Discrimination by Design: A Feminist Critique of the Man-Made Environment.* Chicago: University of Illinois Press.

Welch, Susan. 1985. "Are Women More Liberal Than Men in the U.S. Congress?" *Legislative Studies Quarterly* 10: 125–134.

Yoder, Janet. 1991. "Rethinking Tokenism: Looking Beyond the Numbers." *Gender and Society* 5: 178–193.

Three

Acting as Women
The Effects and Limitations of Gender
in Local Governance

Susan Abrams Beck

The struggle to open up the political world to women has been long and hard. The inclusion of women in the political world would, as John Stuart Mill put it in the mid-eighteenth century, ennoble them and society, doubling the resources available for human progress (Mill [1861] 1986, 88). The efforts to bring women into full political participation and into power have been based on the assumption that women would effect significant changes. On the local level, as the number of women has steadily grown, there has been what Janet Flammang has referred to as the "quiet revolution" (1985, 10), a slow but fundamental change in the substance and style of governance. This study focuses on the nature of that change, examining the impact women have had on routine policies, their role in introducing new concerns onto local agendas, and their effect on governance within the context of municipal government.

Previous research on local politics has generally addressed this question in terms of processes and substance. The procedural dimension is the extent to which women officeholders make contact with constituents, communicate and influence their colleagues, assume roles on the council, and so forth. The substantive dimension refers to the transformation of public policies to reflect the concerns of women. These analyses have revealed that the distinctions between men and women are seen in the roles they perceive and act on, although substantively little has changed. The model of a woman representative that has emerged is one who enters politics later in life than men, with an activist background in public service organizations (Lee 1976, 302; Stanwick and Kleeman

49

1983, 20–23). She sees herself more as a public servant than as a politician (Bers 1978, 385), perhaps as a product of her traditional caring role (Bers 1978; Johnson and Carroll 1978, 41). As a result, women politicians are more willing to listen and work for constituents (Flammang 1985; Johnson and Carroll 1978, 29a; Mezey 1978a, 498) and perceive that their constituents trust them more than men and expect more of them (Johnson and Carroll 1978, 40a–42a; Merritt 1980, 120–121). The practical aspects of this link to constituents are seen in the increased time that women devote to their public service, their availability, and their perception that they are better prepared and in general work harder (Johnson and Carroll 1978; Kanter 1977; Merritt 1980).

Merritt (1980) connects this delegate role to policy by noting that the suburban Chicago women officeholders she queried derived more satisfaction from achieving concrete end products, the logical consequence of their focus on reform and political action. This is in contrast to men, who expressed more satisfaction with the processes of government, such as negotiating. These distinctions remained even when her sample was controlled for working status, whereas distinctions of time and relationship with constituents were neutralized by employment.

Research on local representation makes the assumption that one of the constituencies women council members should be serving is what is usually referred to as the "feminist" constituency: women and men who have a certain agenda in mind, including policies on reproductive rights, pay equity and comparable worth, and public health issues. Thus, "acting for" women in a substantive way, not just fulfilling the descriptive representation by "standing for" them (Pitkin 1967), is an essential element of representation by women. In her examination of politicians in Hawaii and Connecticut, Mezey found that women's attitudes towards feminist policies were not more favorable than men's (1978b; 1978c). Moreover, she found the issue priorities of women and men to be almost perfectly correlated, as did Merritt (1980). Similarly, Donahue found that women on school boards, the institution with the greatest number of elected women, are not more likely to represent women or the disadvantaged. In contrast to politics at the state and national level, the effect of women was neutralized in the gender-equal environment of the school committees she examined (1997). However, those studies concentrate on women's policies as issues separate from the more traditional concerns of local governments. This study approaches questions about the impact of women by examining their role in the context of routine decisions, because the women's agenda is often remote from the consideration of local governments. Those matters are so often fought out elsewhere in the political system.

Local communities deal with the everyday concerns of women and men, taking responsibility for clean and safe streets, picking up the garbage, building parks. It is at this level that the average person is most likely to know their representatives and be familiar with the effects of their government's decisions. However, it is not the place where the most controversial women's issues are debated. For example, there are few municipalities gripped by the politics of abortion. This is especially true in small and medium-size communities but much less so in cities (see Boles, this volume; Appleton 1995) or surrounding counties (Flammang 1997) where the size of the population is more likely to require dealing with a decision such as the establishment of an abortion clinic. But if the more obvious cases are not deliberated, it is true that decisions made by local governors do affect women, such as the availability of child care or how they will deal with difficulties in their senior years. There may also be "women's" issues that have remained invisible, such as the unreported incidence of sexual assault among teens (Lefkowitz 1997). However, there are also the perennial considerations of budgeting, zoning, safety, and recreation that might be treated differently by women than by men. To what extent, then, as women have taken their places on local councils, have they addressed different concerns, approached the usual concerns differently, or conducted themselves differently in their new positions? In other words, what has been the impact of women on governance at the local level?

In understanding the effect of women on local governance, it is also important to examine the prevailing political culture. Not only do the concepts of liberalism shape the behavior of representatives, they shape the perceptions about the place of communities in the larger political scheme. A culture based on competitiveness and marketplace resolution of problems not only dominates the relationship between governors and the governed but also explains the competitiveness between communities. The capacity of women to transform local councils is inhibited by this prevailing culture in a way not typical of state or national affairs (Beck 1995). The female voice, which stresses connection and the effect of particular experiences on individuals, contrasts with the male view, based on rationality and individuals pursuing their own preferences (Diamond and Hartsock 1981, 718; Gilligan 1982). This affects the treatment of problems as they come before local councils.

Data Collection

To ascertain the answers to these questions, twenty-seven semistructured interviews were conducted in seven suburban towns outside a major American city.[1] Personal interviews were used because they permitted exploration of the particular political questions that were important in each community. A written formal questionnaire would be unable to tap the unique political cultures that existed. In advance of the interviews, research was conducted on each town's politics by reviewing news accounts for the previous five years, and council members were observed at public meetings. Then, in the interviews, the attitude and role of the council member in the development and shaping of an issue were discussed in much greater detail. This approach was required because often bills introduced or votes taken were not accurate indices of the prevailing politics. Council meetings are often *pro forma,* where limited discussion takes place, and decisions made before the meeting are ratified rather than deliberated. Thus there was no acceptable way to quantify the many modes of behavior and the subtleties of a very intimate kind of politics.

The towns ranged in size from 5,000 to 25,000 and included working-class, more middle-class, and very affluent communities. Every effort was made to select municipalities that reflected the ethnic and racial makeup of the region. The group consisted of fourteen men and thirteen women; sixteen Republicans and eleven Democrats. All the municipalities had council-mayor forms of government, used partisan ballots, and, except for one, had councils consisting of six members elected at large. The one exception had a single-member-district system. The county where the interviews were conducted has 19 percent of the council seats filled by women. Only councils with at least two women were considered for the interview set in order to avoid problems stemming from generalizations based on one token woman. Only one council had a majority of women.

The municipalities analyzed were all highly developed, with very little open space remaining. The affluent communities consisted of large suburban tracts dotted with very expensive homes and small, almost intimate commercial centers. The working-class communities tended to be near the central city, more commercial, with closer living. Some of the problems of welfare and homelessness spilled over into these towns, but only one had anything bordering on a serious problem. All were severely strained by the cost of municipal services, especially garbage collection and schools. Their police forces were paid, but with the exception of the poorest community, which was also the largest, the fire department was "voluntary." Council members usually served without pay, although in some towns they received small stipends, which rarely covered the expenses they incurred. Given this environment, it was expected that few differences would be found between men and women because, for the most part, their agendas were set for them. With business conducted at evening meetings and a calendar of obligations to fulfill, the chance for creative thinking was minimal. Moreover, politics in such municipalities was conducted among neighbors, which brought very strong socializing factors with it. Given these realities, it was hypothesized that governance with women participating would not look terribly different than when councils were exclusively male enclaves, and to the extent that women made a difference, those distinctions would be small, although potentially capable of being much more.

A Common Politics

On the whole, women and men council members were more alike than they were different. This was true in terms of their types, their priorities, the time they devoted to council work, and their positions, tenure, and partisanship. In other words, given the range of activities and decisions with which they were involved, there was little to distinguish councilwomen and councilmen.

In the early nineteenth century De Tocqueville ([1835] 1945, 42) described the townships of America as "the life and mainspring of American liberty," and indeed citizens who participate in local governance are the legatees of that tradition. These were devoted people, almost all of whom responded that their interest in town politics was "to do right" and undoubtedly tried their best to do just that. Men and women varied in their ability to accomplish that end, with both dividing into three groups: the ambitious, the competent, and the functionary.

The first group consisted of one woman and one man, who were both young and energetic and saw municipal politics as a temporary stepping-stone to higher office. The small numbers here are somewhat misleading, because there were some women over 50 who might have pursued higher office had they entered earlier. Indeed, one actually had tried for a mayoral nomination but had been denied. At the time of the interviews, however, this group consisted of only two members.

The predominant group was the "competents," able, hardworking individuals who brought commitment and caring to the tasks of governance. This group represented politics at its best, for it was here that the individual, in most cases without recompense, dedicated herself or himself to the community. Most of this group of women and men saw their role on the council as that of a facilitator, a person who brought good sense and hard questions to the issues before the council and then worked to move matters to decision. Most saw themselves as "above politics," as noted by one councilman:

I dislike partisan politics. I dislike the clubhouse politics. That is so manipulative. . . . I find myself, as a councilperson, being more one of trying to elevate and articulate a standard.

One councilwoman related that she had "bucked the system on more than one occasion . . . and stood up for what . . . was right." These individuals raised valuable questions because of their training, or sometimes just because of their good sense:

> I'm used to dealing with facts. . . . You have to do research. If you want to know the facts of a situation before you make a judgment you actually have to do the research yourself . . . and sort out what isn't fact and what's really fact. You have to talk to the financial people and get the data, sometimes you have to actually call the vendors and ask them what's included in their quotes. . . .

Both women and men contributed to this dialogue, and it was because of their general concern for responsible government that communities were able to thrive. It should be noted that often their honest commitment went unappreciated, if not actually attacked, but this point will be addressed in a later context.

The third group of council members consisted of functionaries, a euphemistic term used to describe a group of less able officials, both men and women, who often achieved nomination and election because of the political needs of a local party. Often municipal parties had difficulty recruiting candidates, and these individuals found that the opportunity was theirs. In one of the municipalities studied, the strong local boss kept certain functionaries in office as long as they continued to vote the "right" way and exhibit minimal independence. These individuals rarely brought insight to council deliberations, although they worked as hard as many of the others. They had little sense of their insufficiencies and, on the whole, behaved as good soldiers. Often they were given few responsibilities, although their official titles did not necessarily indicate that. They appeared to be on the outside looking in on decisions made by others. Attempts to pierce this veil were frustrated by others more able than they. This group was usually passive, pleased with the prestige that came with election to office but not in control or in full understanding of the direction that government takes.

Among all these groups there were no differences in the time women and men devoted to their jobs. The increased time available to some women who were not employed outside the home was balanced by time available to male retirees or others whose employment permitted them considerable latitude in handling their public responsibilities.[2]

The convergence between women and men in defining priority issues in their communities was also striking. Almost without exception, they pointed to the same thing: taxes, development, and the quality of life. They were all hostage to the tax rate, persistently seeking ways to keep it down, avoiding development whenever possible, and in general trying to freeze their communities in time. In essence, this meant making a concerted effort to exclude the poor, minorities, illegal aliens, or any other "undesirables" who might have changed the complexion of their towns. Working-class municipalities felt threatened by an exploding inner city; middle-class and affluent towns wanted to maintain their exclusivity, especially in light of the state law that demanded that they take on a greater role in providing affordable housing. This protectiveness was true for both the working-class and affluent towns and was the concept that informed almost all of their decisions. The effort to keep a community's "identity and character" in the face of people "who have just moved in" and "see opportunity to make a lot of money in a hurry" was the operating principle for both women and men. The desire to prevent change sometimes bumped up another important value, keeping taxes down. The members of councils wanted to avoid the wrath of the residents at all costs, and they were all aware that the quickest way to spur a revolt was to raise taxes. As one council member explained:

> People feel, oh God, another increase in taxes; my gas and electric are going up; this is going up. I don't think they can yell at the . . . utility company or even their own credit card. But they can reach out to the mayor and the Council and yell . . . that the taxes are going up.

These imperatives propelled them away from projects that put pressure on the tax rate and toward decisions that limited access to their towns. Suggestions for multifamily buildings or more flexible zoning laws that might have permitted single parents or seniors to find extra income were treated with suspicion. Where development had been permitted to creep in, the backlash had set in. Such proposals were seen as threatening to the town, imposing new burdens while contributing insufficiently to the revenue base. Residents of suburban condominiums were seen as the newcomers, whose lack of participation in the affairs of the town did little to endear them to the old-timers who sat on councils.

The last major similarity between men and women council members was in their perception of parties on the local level. Just as the economic-development issues were universal, there was very little to distinguish the parties in local terms. The choice of membership in one party or the other was often fairly arbitrary, with reports by several members of having been recruited by friends, being asked by both parties to run, or having thought of oneself as belonging to the opposite party at some earlier time. Even when a council member indicated that the difference between the parties lay in ideology, both parties claimed the same ideology: caring for the people, doing what's right, and spending with caution. Without exception the opposing party was blamed for irresponsible spending, bringing in too much development, making personnel decisions based on partisanship rather than merit. There was nothing distinct about their political cultures which might have made one party more receptive to women or men; there was no evidence of any class distinctions between the parties either, when just the council members were considered. Thus it was almost impossible to distinguish between the parties philosophically, with the practical result that each consistently blamed the other for overspending, overdeveloping, and catering to special interests. Predictably, these charges and countercharges emerged perennially as elections approached each November, but an observer of municipal politics was hard-pressed to ascertain who was a Republican or a Democrat on the basis of issue stands or statements. Both women and men, Republican and Democrat, hopped on the bandwagon to protect housing values, resist change, and promote themselves as the optimal managers and guardians of the public treasury.

Divergences: Men's View

The similarities between women and men council members were striking, but there were important differences as well. These distinctions emerged in their behavior, their conceptualizations about representation and politics, and their substantive contributions.

Both men and women agreed that councilwomen were more responsive to their constituents, but councilmen interpreted this attribute negatively, seeing women as too responsive to feelings and not analytic enough. "Women," claimed one councilman, "are not as detailed. They're generally more emotional and vote on emotion rather than on details and facts and figures. . . . They will react to the last few people [they've] spoken to rather than [to] more hard facts." Another argued that women "will avoid positions that will offend a group in town. They respond to feeling and people." And yet a third councilman stated that "women are more intuitive than men," which causes them to "get bogged down in affairs of the heart, individual cases, rather than being concerned about all the people." These "sympathy thoughts" were viewed negatively, because according to this view, emotionalism translated into poor public policy when programs were accepted or rejected because of constituent sentiment. For example, leaf ordinances that imposed a burden on seniors were opposed by women over the objections of their male colleagues, who argued that either fees or special bagging requirements were imperative because of escalating costs. Another example was cited by a councilman who was horrified to hear councilwomen arguing in support of an emergency appropriation for a homeless shelter that was not in the budget. To him "that violate[d] everything I know about budgeting . . . I wouldn't do that until I . . . [had] the appropriation." This adherence to the rules, what Carol Gilligan (1982) argues is the male voice, made them see the responsiveness of women as being unprofessional.

Men also saw other behavioral differences in women that they viewed negatively. One criticized women because

> they want to get on the phone with me and talk through an issue ad nauseam. . . . With women, they get very impatient with me. They want to talk it through. . . . You've got to be sensitive to their feelings. That's great. That's understandable. I don't want to be insensitive to them, but there's a point at which I think men are bigger risk-takers.

To this councilman, women threw obstacles in the way of decision making. Others agreed. One described as irksome the questioning of councilwomen:

> Years ago I didn't particularly care for women because their outlook or ideas sometimes come from a different angle. . . . They want everything explained to them. . . . Different questions that they ask sound silly to us. How come we're spending this money for this, or how come we're doing this? Why would you spend $500,000 [to] buy a truck when you can get one cheaper? But that's the kind of fire truck we want, one that has a ladder that goes up. They ask questions on why you're spending that much money —do you follow what I'm getting at? Women don't have the mechanical knowledge about trucks [and] automobiles.

The same idea was expressed by the councilman who objected to the "frustrated housewives" in politics who "have nothing to do all day . . . [but] go around looking for every little nit-picking thing in town . . . making a mountain out of a molehill." These comments were aspects of the female stereotype—talkative, nagging, arguing without knowledge —and are consistent with Mezey's findings that men see women as hyperemotional and overly concerned with trivia (1978a, 498).

For some, the distinctions between women and men were viewed more positively, stemming from the diversity women brought to the council. The "philosophy of woman" was how one councilman put it, although what such a philosophy entailed was not made clear. On the most elementary level, this presence elicited more "genteel" male behavior, such as less swearing. A more substantive contribution was offered by the example of women thinking about beautifying the downtown district with trees and less garish signs rather than just providing more parking spaces. In all, twelve of the fourteen men interviewed saw differences between men and women. Nine of those twelve made comments that were clearly negative, although some (four) of them evaluated women in positive terms as well. The question of attentiveness provides a good example of how some men juxtaposed the positive and negative. For some, the increased attention that men agreed that women gave to their council duties was seen as a bonus for the town and themselves. But others saw this devotion as a burden rather than a relief, leading to make-work that impeded the business at hand.

Divergences: Women's View

As might be expected, women perceived a different political reality, in terms of both what they brought to the council and what men brought. Whereas men saw the women's response to citizen's concerns as softhearted, women saw themselves as better representatives because of their responsiveness. Searching for additional money for a shelter, reducing or eliminating garbage fees or regulations, or supporting residents who objected to increased traffic headed for the garbage transfer station were what, in their view, their jobs were all about. To men these were decisions that women made with the heart and not the mind. Women interpreted this as a willingness to "listen, not look for the quick solution. Men were looking for the management solution." Put another way, women more often saw themselves as delegates, obliged to follow the direction of their constituents; men more often saw themselves as trustees, independent of citizen demands.

This interpretive divergence was also evident in how councilwomen saw their persistent questioning. They saw themselves as better prepared, more diligent, and more organized. They related how they were careful to do all their homework before a meeting, read all the minutes, and keep records on matters that needed follow-up attention. Women "go along very slowly, methodically, and they feel they have to be prepared, whereas men are more apt to wing it." Another saw herself as the monitor, keeping "a follow-up file, and I put things on paper. Then . . . in three months . . . I write another memo, you didn't answer my memo from two months ago. . . . I'm a nudge." And, in direct refutation of the hearts-over-minds theory exposited by the men, some argued that men "operated with less fact. . . . They get [in] a clutch and decide what to do and think that they have all the answers because they've come up with it somehow. When you start asking questions, it all falls apart."

These comments illustrate how councilwomen interpreted questioning as beneficial, whereas many of the men saw it as indicative of indecisiveness. This was a serious divergence and, for some women, led to a sense that councilwomen needed to be abler than their male peers to justify their questioning; in some cases, it led to inhibition on their part. One very experienced, competent councilwoman "always felt I'm under the gun here." Another also described this dual standard:

[A] woman has to prove herself where it's assumed that a man knows. . . . I think you have to be exceptional. . . . [M]y running mate . . . is a hands-dirty kind of guy. I don't think he's the brightest person. He's got the biggest heart, and I think he's a good councilperson. . . . If you had someone like that she never gets it. . . . You should always be a lady up there, always smiling. Men have more authority when they speak, not because they know more, but because they're more comfortable. Women are nervous because people say, "What does she know?"

These efforts and concerns reflected the "performance pressure" that Kanter (1977) describes token women taking on when they are in a minority situation.

Restraint that flowed from this duality resulted in a sense of discrimination. Of the thirteen women interviewed, eleven described some sort of discrimination, although not always in direct answer to the question on that subject. At one end of the spectrum this sense was quite minimal—the use of language such as "honey" and "dearie." For others, there were more serious offenses, such as being denied campaign assistance at re-election (technically outside council business, but not unrelated); finding out about decisions after they had been made; creating informal lines to authority to circumvent the woman who held the position of fire commissioner; publicly demeaning a councilwoman who had tried to express her concerns about the budget to a male colleague. One particularly frustrated woman described her sense of being on the outside, stating, "Nobody hears me." This discrimination did not spill over into the official committee assignments, nor were women given any additional workload, although, as noted, many felt obliged to take on that responsibility. What is clear is that almost all the women sensed that they were left out on some occasions.

What is important about these differences is not whether they were objectively true but that they were perceived as such. Women who "held back" because they feared intimidation, even subtly so, or women who took extra pains to be as "qualified" as they were able, or those who "felt" the concerns of their constituents, whether such a response was a positive or negative, changed the nature of the job. They were not behaving as the men did, and although these distinctions did not permeate everything the councils did, they molded behavior in significant ways.

There were also clear differences between women and men in the roads they took before assuming positions on their councils and, once having that experience, their reactions to it. The women had very different backgrounds than the men. Of the thirteen women interviewed, ten had long histories in community service, particularly on school boards, in PTAs, in the League of Women Voters or working on some particular cause, such as housing, the environment, or an unwanted supermarket. The three others came out of traditional party activity, working for the local organization (one replaced her husband upon his death). Of this latter group, two of the three were classified as part of the functionary group and the third was the single, young, ambitious councilwoman. Among the men, on the other hand, only one was drawn to politics through the vehicle of a cause. Their community experience was primarily within athletics, especially Little League or its equivalent, or the Boy Scouts. For those with experience in politics, it was heavily weighted towards traditional club work. Half the men received the nomination for council without any community experience, either through the party club or some other activity beyond athletics or Boy Scouts.

This divergence is not surprising, given the number of women who waited to enter public office until after their children were grown. Among the women, only two had children at home at the time they won election, although in one case the children were about to graduate high school. This pattern contrasted sharply with the men, 60 percent of whom entered office when their children were still at home.

Indeed, the women were well aware of how family considerations had influenced and continued to influence their political careers. Although the interview included no specific questions on family, every woman mentioned its importance. For those with children, their reference was to indicate how child-rearing obligations delayed their entry into politics. One woman delayed running for office because after years of community work, she thought her husband would think "enough already." Two women expressed regret that they had entered so late because higher office was now deemed to be out of consideration, although they would probably have pursued other posts had they begun earlier. "For me," one councilwoman confessed,

> I wish I had started a little sooner and been a little more ambitious on my own. I mean, it was always I was sitting back, and I had my family, and I was working, and I had a lot of other activities, and so I got on to this a little late.

Family pressures existed for all of them, even those without children. One councilwoman, a homemaker without children with long experience in community work, related that her husband thought that her political work was "just too much because you're out four nights a week." This pressure had deterred her from seeking the mayoralty. Another woman related how she had been "down at the firehouse one night for four hours, and my husband had a fit."

Thus, for women, political careers were delayed or, once begun, often constrained by family considerations. For men, there was barely a mention of family, except in the context of their pre-political community involvement with Little League or Boy Scouts or the one mention of the "understanding wife." The two exceptions were the councilman who had decided to defer a second attempt at a state legislative post in order to spend more time with his family and another who decided, "with his wife," not to seek a second term on the council. For men, family constraints were much less than they were for women, as others have also found (e.g., Johnson and Carroll 1978, 16a, 18a, 40a-43a; Mezey 1980, 62-63).

Not only do women often come to the council after their children are grown, but once in office, many of them find politics distasteful. Half the women interviewed said the thing they liked least about being in office was the politics, the "backstabbing." This "political junk," as one put it, involved the obligatory accusations that were launched at the opposing party on personnel questions, appointments, and tax rates. Nothing enraged them more than the charge that the other party was putting someone on some board just to give legitimacy to that person at election time, knowing full well that their party did exactly the same thing in the effort to establish the credibility of a candidate. Or being pressured to make a hiring or firing decision based on partisanship rather than competence. Or blaming the opponents for a tax increase, when in fact it was clear that mandated state programs were the cause of the additional costs. Or not being able to give credit for a good program or idea if its sponsor belonged to the opposing party. The nature of politics was appalling to some of them because they had a cooperative view of how councils should work. As one councilwoman expressed this distaste:

> Local politics [is] the kind of thing I don't like because . . . when you have someone that you're sitting next to on the council who happens to be of a different political party, and is going to run against someone from "your party," I find it very hard—I like this man and he's doing a good job, and I work well with him—to go out and not support him, no matter what party he [belongs to].

"Not working together" was the hardest thing about politics, and some even mentioned that it is what would propel them out of the political arena.

Men did not articulate this same displeasure. Their most common objection was to the complaints of "irate citizens" who were often the only ones to express themselves to the council. These "loudmouths" often made "unjust accusations" which these councilmen found disturbing. Women thought "it's great they come down, they're interested enough" to provide "public input." Rather than seeing them as citizen outbursts, they found them a positive expression of citizen concern.

Policy Distinctions

The substantive distinctions between women and men appeared within the context of the deep and broad consensus that existed on the major economic-development issues within municipalities. The differences that emerged were reflected in some specific efforts made to shape municipal ordinances, and a latent dimension was articulated by the women in their response to questions about some hypothetical public policies.

The suggestions made by councilwomen ranged over a wide array of programs, including instituting a municipal child care program; expanding a new library to take on community center functions; granting a permit to a women's shelter; reducing onerous garbage collection fees and eliminating bagging regulations; prohibiting motorcycles in parks; restricting the size and display of signs in commercial districts; and redefining "family" in the new master plan to include unrelated individuals. This list stood in contrast to the suggestions of councilmen, which included building town tennis courts; building a new soccer field; eliminating indoor garaging of garbage trucks to save money; erecting a veterans' monument; and introducing an innovative financing plan to get sidewalks built.

None of these proposals was central to municipal business; indeed,

most of them failed. But they reflect, when taken as a whole, the different experiences that women and men brought to council business and
thereby reflect the potential of having women in office.

This distinction was made even clearer by the responses to hypothetical issues. All interviewees were asked about their reactions to a
zoning ordinance that would permit homeowners to take in boarders
strictly to supplement income and not to share kitchen or other facilities
that would qualify as some sort of quasi-family unit, which the state
courts had held to be legal. The case was presented in order to address
the question of the single parent, left without adequate financial resources to continue mortgage payments after the departure of (usually)
her spouse. A second question asked whether the interviewee thought
the municipality had some responsibility to provide child care and, if
so, whether the council member had taken steps in that direction.

Surprisingly, the child care issue elicited a negative response from
both men and women. One councilwoman had taken it on as her *cause
célèbre*, but for the others, it was a problem to be addressed by the
schools or the recreation department in after-school soccer programs or
summer camps. They did not express any "demand" for such programs.
Only one council member, a man, argued against any such facilities
because a "woman's place is in the home." But it was not just the men
who did not see this as a municipal issue; the women were just as unre-
sponsive.

The issue of the boarders elicited a dramatically different reaction.
Only one woman was against it in principle, although it was illegal in
all but two towns. Women's reactions were almost universally sympathetic to the plight of the resident who needed the extra money, even to
the point of one admitting that although the practice was illegal, she
knew of it and elected to ignore it. Five men accepted the idea, not all
with enthusiasm. Councilmen objected to the effect of boarders on
property values; the "element" that would be brought into town; the
additional burden on municipal services without increased taxes; and,
for those towns in which they were illegal, the violations of the law.

Each of these municipalities was also adjusting to the state mandate
to fulfill its affordable housing obligations. The state had even set quotas
for every town. Many, indeed most, of the state municipalities have
fought the quotas, putting off adopting a plan as long as possible. Councilmen saw affordable housing policies "as a way that we can satisfy our
[obligation]," whereas councilwomen saw it as a way to offer options to
residents. One councilman who was the primary agent of implementing
the act in his town was "100 percent against the Act. . . . I only [devel-
oped a plan] because I felt it was in the best interest to [the town] to

reduce the impact. . . . ." For men, their actions were determined by the legal framework. Women, on the other hand, were sensitive to both the legal and compassionate dimension of the obligation (Beck 1995).

The Political Education of Women

This is a story still unfolding. What emerges is that the governance of these municipalities is not very different from what it would be without women on the councils. The broad strokes of taxes, development, and suburban life are painted with essentially the same brush. However, an important subtext is unfolding, one that requires close attention and cultivation. Women perceive and manage this political world in a manner that distinguishes them from their male colleagues, reaching out to constituents, occasionally adjusting policies to their view, certainly receptive to a new kind of politics. This conforms to Lyn Kathlene's descriptions of the differences between women and men at the state level, where men were dominant and autocratic in committee hearings but women acted as facilitators and were more democratic (see Kathlene, this volume, 1995). She argues that men think instrumentally and women think contextually. Men treat the individual autonomously, separated from others, whereas women see the individual connected to others, placing much more emphasis on responding to people's needs (see Kathlene, this volume, 1998). But as long as low taxes and high property values remain the *sine qua non* of municipal politics, women will continue to make decisions that do not fundamentally contrast with men's. Local policies will have to fit a standard that rejects inclusion, that attacks the opposition, that devalues thinking with the heart.

Women are often uncomfortable in this political world, and their instincts to respond to individual needs, reach out for collegiality, and call on their own experiences provide the seeds of an alternate model of politics. This is a politics that stresses cooperation, empathy, and openness over manipulation, efficiency, and exclusion, what Flammang refers to as a "moralist conception" of the political world, as opposed to the "marketplace theory" (1997, 207–208). This is not done through the agency of some feminist cause or through any organizational efforts of a women's caucus. It is politics done individually. It exists across party, ideology, age, and minority or majority status. However, this model is just that—a model—and one that will remain elusive until women are sensitized to the implications of playing by the old rules. Councilwomen on this level do not see the full range of the impact of local policies, but once those implications are pointed out to them, they are willing and able to recast them.

It is in their substantive suggestions about routine political decisions that the connection is established between constituency and policy. Their receptivity to constituents reflects a willingness to place the personal in a political context, to recognize that there is no natural division between the public and private (e.g., Okin 1989). Responding to an individual's plight is as rational to them as it appears irrational or trivial to their critics. Their perception of representation is not just to "act for" women but also to "act as" women, and this could have a fundamental impact on governance. For a councilwoman to be a delegate in this context, there has to be a broad definition of that concept, one that includes the way in which political business is done and public responsibilities are assessed. At times the substance of these decisions may be obviously related to the women's agenda—providing child care or granting a variance for a women's shelter, for example. More often, however, the substantive dimension is not that apparent. This is particularly evident in small towns. Research needs to be done to rethink the effect of routine decisions on citizens, and if councilwomen are to effect change, that research—on municipal consciousness-raising—must be disseminated to them.

For the most part, local representatives react to the issues put before them. They have little time and few resources to think out the context within which political problems are posed. Should greater efforts be made to change their consciousness, there is every indication that the impact of women in office, at least at the local level, is apt to grow. For the time being, however, women still play by the old rules, and business as usual continues to determine the direction of local governance. For change to occur, it will be necessary not only to elect women to office but also to make explicit what new directions that office can effect. This may require women's political mobilization to focus on local governance, particularly in small towns, as well as additional investigation of the engendered nature of local power. The liberal state is a powerful force, and for women to transform governance, there needs to be greater understanding of how their vision of politics can find a voice in the local context.

Notes

1. The quotes contained within are drawn from the interviews conducted in 1988 and 1989. Some small changes have been made in order to maintain confidentiality.

2. It is important to note that estimates about time as given in interviews

were probably grossly inaccurate. Most people had considerable difficulty in arriving at an estimate as to the number of hours they spent on duties each week or the number of constituent contacts they had. Their responsibilities are so variable that the figures they gave were obviously unreliable. In order to ascertain a true picture of the time and nature of their activities, a much more careful methodology would have to be used. For an example, see Margolis 1980.

References

Appleton, Lynn M. 1995. "The Gender Regimes of American Cities." In *Gender in Urban Research*, ed. Judith A. Garber and Robyne S. Turner. Thousand Oaks, Calif.: Sage.

Beck, Susan Abrams. 1995. "Gender and the Politics of Affordable Housing." In *Gender in Urban Research*, ed. Judith A. Garber and Robyne S. Turner. Thousand Oaks, Calif.: Sage.

Bers, Trudy Haffron. 1978. "Local Political Elites: Men and Women on Boards of Educations." *Western Political Quarterly* 31: 381–391.

De Tocqueville, Alexis. [1835] 1945. *Democracy in America*, vol.1. New York: Vintage Press.

Diamond, Irene, and Nancy Hartsock. 1981. "Beyond Interest in Politics: A Comment on Virginia Sapiro's 'When Are Interests Interesting?' The Problem of Political Representation of Women." *American Political Science Review* 85: 717–721.

Donahue, Jesse. 1997. "It Doesn't Matter: Some Cautionary Findings about Sex and Representation from School Committee Conversations." *Policy Studies Journal* 25: 630–647.

Flammang, Janet A. 1985. "Female Officials in the Feminist Capital: The Case of Santa Clara County." *Western Political Quarterly* 38: 95–118.

Flammang, Janet A. 1997. *Women's Political Voice: How Women Are Transforming the Practice and Study of Politics*. Philadelphia: Temple University Press.

Gilligan, Carol. 1982. *In a Different Voice*. Cambridge, Mass.: Harvard University Press.

Johnson, Marilyn, and Susan Carroll. 1978. *Profile of Women Holding Office II*. New Brunswick, N.J.: Center for the American Woman and Politics.

Kanter, Rosabeth Moss. 1977. "Some Effects of Proportions on Group Life: Skewed Sex Ratios and Responses to Token Women." *American Journal of Sociology* 82: 965–990.

Kathlene, Lyn. 1995. "Position Power Versus Gender Power: Who Holds the Floor." In *Gender Power, Leadership, and Governance*, ed. Georgia Duerst-Lahti and Rita Mae Kelly. Ann Arbor: University of Michigan Press.

Kathlene, Lyn. 1998. "In a Different Voice: Women and the Policy Process." In *Women and Elected Office: Past, Present and Future*, ed. Sue Thomas and Clyde Wilcox. New York: Oxford University Press.

Lee, Marcia. 1976. "Why Few Women Hold Public Office." *Political Science Quarterly* 91: 297–314.

Lefkowitz, Bernard. 1997. *Our Guys: The Glen Ridge Rape and the Secret Life of the Perfect Suburb.* Berkeley: University of California Press.

Margolis, Diane. 1980. "The Invisible Hands: Sex Roles and the Division of Labor in Two Local Political Parties." In *Women in Local Politics*, ed. Debra W. Stewart. Metuchen, N.J.: Scarecrow Press.

Merritt, Sharyne. 1980. "Sex Differences in Role Behavior and Policy Orientations of Suburban Officeholders: The Effects of Women's Employment." In *Women in Local Politics*, ed. Debra W. Stewart. Metuchen, N.J.: Scarecrow Press.

Mezey, Susan Gluck. 1978a. "Does Sex Make a Difference? A Case Study of Women in Politics." *Western Political Quarterly* 31: 492–501.

Mezey, Susan Gluck. 1978b. "Support for Women's Rights Policy: An Analysis of Local Politicians." *American Politics Quarterly* 6: 485–497.

Mezey, Susan Gluck. 1978c. "Women and Representation: The Case of Hawaii." *Journal of Politics* 40: 369–385.

Mezey, Susan Gluck. 1980. "The Effects of Sex on Recruitment: Connecticut Local Officials." In *Women in Local Politics*, ed. Debra W. Stewart. Metuchen, N.J.: Scarecrow Press.

Mill, John Stuart. [1861] 1986. *The Subjection of Women.* Buffalo, N.Y.: Prometheus Books.

Okin, Susan Moller. 1989. *Justice, Gender and the Family.* New York: Basic Books.

Pitkin, Hanna Fenichel. 1967. *The Concept of Representation.* Berkeley: University of California Press.

Stanwick, Kathy A., and Katherine E. Kleeman. 1983. *Women Make a Difference.* New Brunswick, N.J.: Center for the American Woman and Politics.

Four

Local Elected Women and Policy-Making
Movement Delegates or Feminist Trustees?

Janet K. Boles

The relationships between women and local politics are among the best established in the literature of women's studies. Because of an association with the home and family, it is within community politics that women have traditionally faced fewer cultural barriers and role conflicts. Local politics are "people" issues, where women are felt to have special expertise. Certain women's issues are most appropriately handled at the local level or lend themselves to participation by those familiar with local conditions (see Boneparth 1984; Flammang 1987). In a feminist movement dedicated to grassroots empowerment of women, local politics is the appropriate venue.

It is here that women enjoy greatest access to the political system. Bledsoe (1993, 46–47) has suggested several reasons: There are more female role models in local politics and thus the psychological barriers are lower; local issues are more salient for women; women, with their greater child care and family responsibilities, are less mobile; and local officeholding is less linked to the profession of law. Because of the preponderance of local offices—city, county, and special district—many times more female elected officials serve at the city and county levels than in state and national office. For example, there were 4,513 women serving as a mayor or city council member (or 20.9% of such positions) in 1994, as contrasted with 1,670 women in state legislatures in 2000 (Center for American Women and Politics 2000). In 1988, in the 47 states that have county governing boards, women held 8.9 percent of such seats (Center for the American Woman and Politics 1992). Because of the historic link between county government and rural services

68

such as road maintenance, women lag here. Surprisingly, there is a comparatively sparse women's studies literature on local politics and local elected women as compared with those on the national and state levels (but see Garber and Turner 1995). Most previous research has dealt with the personal characteristics of local elected women and the correlates (e.g., city size, charter type, electoral systems) of their election (MacManus and Bullock 1995).

Yet according to several surveys of elected officials, gender differences tend to decline with level of office. The gender gap on women's issues is smallest at the municipal level (Stanwick and Kleeman 1983). The higher the office held, the more feminist the female elected official (Mueller 1987). Even so, previous studies have found sizable levels of attitudinal and behavioral feminism among local elected women (Burns 1979; Carroll and Strimling 1983; Flammang 1985; Johnson and Carroll 1978; Merritt 1980; Mezey 1978; Mezey 1980; Stewart 1980b. For reviews of this literature see Antolini 1984; Darcy, Welch, and Clark 1994, 30–50; Flammang 1997, 239–45; Gelb and Gittell 1986). This study was designed to elucidate this seeming anomaly of large numbers of local elected women, a conducive setting for women's effective participation in politics, and the lowest level of feminist consciousness among female elected officials found within the U.S. political system.

Description of the Study

This study examines the impact of women officeholders by looking at the policy-making role of local legislators, male and female, in Milwaukee. The research focuses on changes in six policy areas of special interest to women: sexual assault, domestic violence, child care, displaced homemakers, library services for children, and childbirth in public hospitals.

The purpose here was to answer the following questions: Do male and female elected officials place different priorities on women's issues? Are there differences between male and female elected officials in providing leadership on these issues within local legislative bodies? And has the presence of women in local office affected in other ways the actions and operations of these institutions? Finally, if local female legislators do have a distinctive impact on legislation related to women's interests, are these officials acting as feminist trustees or as delegates from the women's movement? In particular, what role do women's policy networks play in the local decision-making process?

Milwaukee, the site for this study, provides a setting where women's political participation has been extensive and relatively effective. In

1998 there were ten (of twenty-five) female county supervisors; three (of seventeen) alderwomen on the Common Council; and three (of nine) female members of the Milwaukee School Board. These percentages meet or exceed the national average of female representation in that local office. If there is a "critical mass" in terms of numbers and proportions of female colleagues that is a requisite for a distinctive impact by female officeholders, then presumably Milwaukee meets that criterion.

Milwaukee-area women continue to support a wide variety of women's rights organizations. There are two chapters of the National Organization for Women (NOW) and local affiliates of the National Women's Political Caucus (NWPC) and 9to5. *The Milwaukee Area Women's Resource Directory* (1998) lists a number of groups and services relevant to this study, including three domestic violence shelters; an abuse hotline and task force on domestic violence; an older women's network; a sexual assault treatment center and two counseling services; a child care resource and referral group; and a nurse-midwifery service. Parallel groups exist on the state level as well: the Wisconsin Women's Network (with 90 member organizations) and coalitions on domestic violence, sexual assault, childbirth alternatives, and displaced homemakers.

Interviews were conducted in 1990 with the sixteen women who had served on the Milwaukee County Board of Supervisors or the Milwaukee Common Council since 1966. The same number of men, chosen from districts that closely resemble those represented by their female colleagues, were also interviewed. Although some attempt was made to include both veteran and newly elected officials, the average term for the male sample was twelve years, compared with eight years for female officeholders. Women continue to be comparative "new girls" in local politics.

In addition, thirteen city and county administrators or officials of community-based organizations holding government contracts to deliver services and fourteen leaders of women's organizations were interviewed. All were chosen because of their involvement with one of the six focal policy issues or their concern with women's rights generally.

Most interviews were conducted by the author in the office or home of the interviewee; most lasted 30–40 minutes; and all but six respondents allowed taping. Three interviews with former elected officials were conducted by telephone, and one took place in the author's office.

Activity on Women's Issues

In general, women officeholders reported activity on more and a broader range of women's issues than did men. Women placed a greater importance on these issues and were more likely to have provided leadership on the Board or Council when related policies were considered.

Initially, the local officials were asked to list any women's issues on which they had worked during their period of service. The mean number of issues on which men were active was 2.06; women, on average, reported activity on 3.69 issues. These figures reflect that women not only were active on more women's issues than were men, but they also defined a "women's issue" differently and more broadly. Whereas male respondents mentioned a total of eleven issues (three dealt with different dimensions of affirmative action), women officeholders recalled 27 different issues, including welfare payments, child support, women in local jails, family recreation programs, homeless families, AIDS, and gay rights.

The role of male and female officeholders on the six focal issues— sexual assault, domestic violence, child care, displaced homemakers, library services for children, and childbirth in public hospitals—was studied in three ways. Each indicated in writing the extent to which that issue had been of special importance to him or her. All were also asked to recall whether those issues had been addressed by the Board or Council during their period of service. Finally, each was questioned about policy outcomes and those colleagues who were most actively involved on each issue.

Although, in practice, both the city and county governments have some programs in each policy area, it is a common perception that one level of local government is "more" responsible for a particular service than is the other. For example, county government in Wisconsin is the primary administrator of social services, including what was then Milwaukee County's only public hospital (but the city's Health Department provides means-tested pre- and post-natal care). Local libraries are a part of municipal government (but the County Federated Library System assures an open borrowing policy for all residents).

To allow for any officeholders who might consider "important" only those issues closely associated with her or his own level of government, respondents were given the option "not a Council/Board issue" in reporting their priorities on the six women's issues. As Table 4.1 indicates, women in city and county office placed a higher level of importance on all six issues than did their male colleagues. This also remains true after those "opting out" of the ranking are dropped from the analysis, even though women were less likely to perceive these issues as "not my job." (Fifteen percent of all responses from women were of this type, compared with 29 percent for men.)

There was no similarly clear-cut pattern differentiating the ability of

Table 4.1. The Priorities of Milwaukee Legislators on Women's Issues

Issue	Common Council		County Board	
	Men	Women	Men	Women
Day Care	2.44	1.89	2.00	1.14
Domestic Violence	2.33	2.22	1.86	1.14
Sexual Assault	2.33	1.67	1.86	1.29
Displaced Homemakers	4.00	2.89	2.86	1.86
Children's Library Services	3.22	2.44	4.29	3.14
Childbirth in Public Hospitals	4.00	3.00	2.43	1.86

All figures are mean scores: 1 = high/top priority; 2 = important but not a top priority; 3 = some importance; 4 = not at all important; 5 = not a Common Council/County Board issue.

male and female officeholders to recall examples of policy-making on the six issues.[1] On three of the issues (day care, domestic violence, and sexual assault), there were high levels of awareness of activity among local legislators. Only on the three remaining issue areas did alderwomen (children's library services and displaced-homemaker programs) and female supervisors (childbirth in public hospitals) exhibit markedly greater knowledge of policy-making.

Women officeholders have played an important but not dominant role in shaping policy on day care, domestic violence, and sexual assault. This was confirmed in interviews with urban administrators. Ten (of thirteen administrators) recalled direct contacts with elected officials on one of these policies. And although roughly equal numbers of male (n = 9) and female (n = 10) officials were mentioned at least once by a bureaucrat, contacts from women (regarding one of the six issues) made up a larger percentage (63%) of the total responses. This is particularly striking in that women constitute a much smaller percentage of elected officials.

It is in qualitative terms, however, that women's leadership on these issues differs most from that of men. Rarely did men volunteer information beyond the policy adopted (e.g., the formation of the Task Force on Sexual Assault and Domestic Violence as a part of city government, the establishment of a sexual assault counseling unit within the District Attorney's office). For several women on the Board or Council, however, the politics of each decision was recalled in vivid and full detail: the funding of the first women's shelter in Milwaukee, despite a motion by a male colleague to deny the request ("I looked at the alderman and said, 'Could I ask you to withdraw your motion before we may need a home for a battered man?' At which point, he did withdraw his motion"); the negotiations with the Chief of Police to establish a special sexual assault unit ("he was backed into a corner by the city's Finance Committee, who held his purse strings . . . he did have to do certain things"); an expanded prosecution unit in the District Attorney's office to handle a greater number of domestic violence cases arising from a new local mandatory arrest policy ("many of your colleagues are attorneys . . . and many of these attorneys feel that it's going to reflect badly on some of their clients if all of a sudden they wind up getting arrested . . . it was held in committee and held in committee . . . ").

Women were more likely to take the lead in initially raising the issue and in establishing new programs and bureaucracies. In the area of day care, for example, women coordinated the first day care needs assessment in both city and county government. Women were key to the establishment of an on-site day care center in the County Courthouse, an (unsuccessful) attempt to open a center in City Hall, and an after-school latchkey program offered through the County Parks System. Male legislators were active in other important but more technical ways: manipulating the committee system to get a day care proposal on the agenda; establishing a voucher system for day care services in the community and a payroll deduction for county employees; expanding the supply of private day care through granting zoning variances; and (unsuccessfully) requiring developers to provide space for day care in exchange for a building permit.

A core group of three female legislators was viewed as leaders on all three visible issues, which would seem to indicate a general advocacy position on behalf of women's issues. Male leaders often played a leadership role on only one issue as a part of some other official position (i.e., Council President, Board Chair, or chair of the Finance, Public Safety, or Judiciary Committee). Exceptions here were men who linked their activity with district interests (e.g., funding for a shelter or day care center) or a general concern for social services. Female officials were somewhat more aware of available grants and services for displaced homemakers. Two of the women had also served as advisers to displaced homemakers' organizations.

Children's library services were also more salient to female legislators. Two related the issue to their own backgrounds as professional educators; two others noted their service on the Library Board, including one (the acknowledged leader) who reported regular meetings with children's librarians to plan the summer reading program. Four others gave examples of their efforts to expand or preserve branch library services in their districts. Interestingly, only one man acted as district ombudsman on library services; the only other specific policy noted (by two men) was the audiovisual library maintained for school use by the County Public Museum—a service the Board eliminated from the 1990 budget.

Childbirth in public hospitals was associated with a number of maternal and infant policies by both men and women. Women again had a higher awareness and a broader knowledge base. For example, two female supervisors knew that the Board had just authorized the modernization of County Hospital's obstetrics unit to include birthing rooms and a more family-oriented style of childbirth. And only women reported personal involvement here in blocking a required drug test for pregnant women receiving welfare ("all that means is that women who are doing cocaine are going to have their babies at home; they're not going to get prenatal care"); dealing with teen pregnancy and associated insurance problems; preserving midwife services at a hospital serving a poor neighborhood; and canceling county prenatal care contracts with those providers not informing their clients about their eligibility for WIC food supplements.

The Impact of Women in
Local Elected Office

It is possible that merely posing a question concerning whether women in local elected office have had an impact introduces a bias for reporting change. In fact, the responses to this question correspond closely with the findings already presented. Twelve male and fourteen female officials suggested one or more ways that women had made a difference. And even those who disagreed did so because of the (correctly) perceived ideological diversity among the women. They did not deny that some women as individuals had brought about change, only that women as a group had done so.

As the more objective data on levels of activity, knowledgeability, and leadership on women's issues also revealed, both male and female officeholders credit women with raising women's issues (including the need for nonsexist language) and bringing a different viewpoint to policymaking. And male officials in particular believed that their female col-

Table 4.2. The Impact of Women in Local Elected Offices

Reason given for:	Men %	Women %
An impact		
Women bring a different viewpoint	37.5	25.0
Women raise women's issues	56.3	62.5
Men are more sensitive to women's issues	37.5	18.8
Non-sexist language adopted	12.5	31.3
Women stick together	–0–	12.5
Serve as role models/make body representative	12.5	12.5
Women "better" (work harder, more humanist, brighter, better educated)	–0–	12.5
General conduct of meeting (more polite less profanity)	12.5	6.3
Less "good old boy" networking	12.5	–0–
Women are more aggressive	6.3	–0–
Women are more liberal	12.5	–0–
No impact		
People are people	12.5	–0–
Women come from very different political bases/ideologies	12.5	12.5
Women are not more liberal on social issues/ don't have different interests	6.3	–0–
	n = 16	n = 16

leagues had sensitized men on the Board and Council to the policy needs of women. (See Table 4.2.)

The Representative Role of
Local Elected Women

The classic typology of representative roles is threefold: (1) the *trustee,* who acts as a free agent, basing decisions on personal judgments of what will best serve the interests of the constituency; (2) the *delegate,* who consults constituents or depends on specific instructions as a premise for decisions; and (3) *the politico*, who assumes both of the above roles, serially or simultaneously (see Eulau, Wahlke, and Abramowitz 1978). Although the politico role is generally conceded to be the dominant one within American politics, studies of local elected women (Antolini 1984; Beck 1991; Bledsoe 1993) have found strong support for the delegate role as well.

As Fenno (1978) has noted, a representative's "constituency" may variously be defined as: (1) a geographical constituency (the primary social or economic groups in an electoral district); (2) a re-election constituency (voters); (3) a loyalist constituency (workers and activists); or (4) a personal constituency (those bound to the official by emotional ties). It is possible that local elected women make a unique contribution because of their identification with women and women's issues. This identification could be reflected through their participation in an informal or formal women's caucus in the local legislature or within a government association. Alternatively, it might consist of a women's policy network, where local female officials nurture ties with one or more local women's rights organizations.

Welch and Bledsoe (1988), in their study of city council members, found that women were more likely than men to acknowledge campaign support of neighborhood and single-issue groups (especially those left of center, including feminist ones.) Further, Carroll and Strimling (1983, 124) report that 13 percent of female county commission members and 8 percent of city councilwomen (but no men) mention a desire to represent women or women's issues as a major reason for seeking office.

Studies conducted before or during the mid-1970s found that relatively few women candidates or officeholders reported holding memberships in feminist groups, basing their campaigns or agendas (once in office) on women's issues, or even frequently conferring with their female colleagues about women's issues (Carroll 1985; Johnson and Carroll 1978; Mezey 1978). Low numbers and fears of adverse reaction from male colleagues sometimes prevented a formal women's caucus from forming (Mueller 1984). Existing associations of elected women often were reluctant to organize for women, preferring instead to maintain internal unity by avoiding partisan or controversial policy issues (Margolis 1986; Strimling 1983; but see Dodson and Carroll 1991, 34–35). Even so, by 1983, many female elected officials belonged to some explicitly feminist organization (Carroll and Strimling 1983, 87–89; see also Dodson and Carroll 1991, 21–23.) Fully 29 percent of county board women and 7 percent of city councilwomen were members of at least one feminist organization in 1981. Similarly, 22 percent of female county commissioners and 11 percent of councilwomen were affiliated with a group of other female officials.

Women's Caucuses

As Mueller (1984) has observed of women in state legislatures, in the absence of a formal women's caucus, ad hoc coalitions of women may emerge around issues. Table 4.3 suggests that this pattern also applies in Milwaukee.

Interestingly, men overestimate the extent of formal caucusing and underestimate informal cooperative activities on women's issues as reported by their female colleagues. Issues on which women have worked together include sexual harassment, day care, sexual assault, minority women's issues, and the environment. And the three women most frequently mentioned as being leaders on women's issues are (correctly) perceived by their colleagues as working together. As one alderman put it:

> At times it [an informal women's caucus] has surfaced whereby irrespective of ideological position . . . women have gotten their acts together and said, "No, we can't cave in. We're going to take a stand on this. Let's go out and get the votes." They have been an effective force, not on a great number of issues, but at times it has surfaced. This is most likely on issues that have an impact on women per se.

There is no women's caucus for female elected officials in the Milwaukee area (although one supervisor had tried to organize one and another had plans to do so but became too busy once in office). Nor are women uniformly incorporated into Women Officials in the National Association of Counties (WON) or Women in Municipal Government (a section of the National League of Cities). Three supervisors are members of WON, but only one is active in the group. And even though several alderwomen were aware of the NLC group, only one (arguably the most traditional member) had joined. Another had been a member of both groups but dropped out in dissatisfaction.

A Local Women's Policy Network

It is possible that the information networks upon which local female officials rely vary in important ways from those of men. A question concerning attendance at any conferences dealing with the six focal is-

Table 4.3. Cooperative Relations Between Women in Milwaukee
Legislatures

Question	Men %	Women %
Have women on the Council/Board ever met together to discuss policy that affects women?		
Yes	25	—
No	56	94
Don't know/no response	19	—
Only one woman	—	6
Have women on the Council/Board ever worked together on policy that affects women?		
Yes	19	44
Some women only	13	25
No	50	19
Don't know/no response	19	6
Only one woman	—	6

sues did suggest a difference in the information networks of men and women. Not only were women more likely to have attended such a meeting, the sponsor was also more likely to be a women's organization.

Of greater interest is the possible existence of a local "women's policy network," a term used by activists and feminist scholars to describe feminist strategies within government (Ferree and Hess 1985, 151–152; Fraser 1983, 138–139; Freeman 1975, 221–229; Gelb and Klein 1988, 8–9; Gelb and Palley 1987, 203–204; Hartmann 1989, 99–103; Spalter-Roth and Schreiber 1995). The concept of a "policy network" refers to a constellation of expert or interested groups and individuals, public and private, forming around a policy area. The workings of a policy system are characterized by continuous interchanges among members at every stage of the policy process, from agenda building to implementation. From the perspective of the interest group, membership in such a policy system offers "insider" status. Ready access to elected officials, managers, and sympathetic bureaucrats can provide information on new regulations, policy shifts, and effective strategies (Heclo 1978; Walker 1981).

Women are well situated to become a part of an emerging local policy network. Local feminist groups are pervasive: NOW had 511 local chapters as of 1995, and the NWPC had more than 300 local caucuses. In

Table 4.4. The Role of Women's Rights Organizations
in Local Politics

Question	Men %	Women %
Does a women's policy network exist in Milwaukee?		
Yes	50	44
No	25	50
Don't know/no response	25	6
How frequently do women's groups contact you?		
Frequently	6	19
Sometimes	19	25
Infrequently	56	50
Never	12	6
Don't know/no response	6	—
Do you ever contact women's groups?		
Yes	38	38
No	50	50
Don't know/no response	12	12

addition, women have often gained direct representation in government through local commissions on the status of women. The number of such commissions doubled between 1975 and 1980 (Stewart 1980a), and by 1990 there were 204 active local commissions (U.S. Department of Labor 1990). Ideally, these commissions serve to institutionalize both the women's movement and women's participation in policy decisions.

Although women officials in Milwaukee were not asked about their group affiliations, several spontaneously noted their memberships in the League of Women Voters (six); the NWPC (four); the Wisconsin Women's Network (three); and two local women's groups, the Black Women's Network (three) and the Woman to Woman Conference (three). Yet despite these personal ties with local women's rights organizations, women were no more aware of a women's policy network than their male colleagues, nor were they more likely to initiate contacts with women's organizations. (See Table 4.4.) Women were, however, somewhat more likely to recall being contacted by women's groups.

Again, differences between men and women officials in their relations with women's groups showed up most strongly in the open-ended responses. For the most part, men responded to the questions in a factual and objective manner: who belongs to the women's policy network, what sorts of issues are involved, the groups most commonly heard from or contacted. Women were more likely to be evaluative of networks generally and their (not always positive) experiences with Milwaukee groups:

Do we have such a network in Milwaukee? No, but we are going to have. I have in the past contacted women's groups (to lobby on women's issues) and they just flat out said, "Well, we're not into doing those sorts of things." And I said, "Look, I am not asking you to put on a skirt and lipstick, I am asking you to make a phone call." (A female supervisor)

Without it (the women's policy network), I'd have been dead in the water, absolutely. Public office is a "we" job; it's not a "me" job. You cannot do it without others. (An alderwoman)

In a women's policy network, you end up talking in a different vein. You see issues and you see what other women are concerned about. It's kind of bolstering. It keeps you focused. (A female supervisor)

Underlying many of the comments of female officeholders was a frustration that women's groups weren't more active in Board and Council politics and on the most important issues of today:

The Wisconsin Women's Network is the only group that even comes close (to being influential) and they usually focus their efforts at the state level . . . the (local) groups just sort of seem to be dying on the vine. . . . What we have are a lot of social service agencies that are run by feminists and have some sort of feminist outlook. (A female supervisor)

Right now, they (women's groups) seem to be a little dormant, you know, on the wane. (An alderwoman)

I see a great deal of potential energy being wasted (by women's groups) on the fringes, and that disturbs me, and I think it disturbs a lot of other women. (A female supervisor)

What is strongly suggested here is that at least some female officials are quite positive about networking with women, supportive of women's issues, and interested in and involved with the feminist movement. At the same time, they are disappointed with the low level of activity and the priorities of local women's groups.

Interviews with urban administrators and women's group leaders both confirmed and clarified the role of women's organizations in Milwaukee politics as seen by female officials. Local women's groups, especially those pursuing multiple policy goals such as NOW and NWPC, were active in state politics and could easily list several female state legislators with whom they were regularly in contact. What is found on the local level are issue-specific policy networks (see Boles 1994). Well-developed policy networks have formed around day care, domestic violence, sexual assault, and displaced homemakers.[2] And although state and national (single-issue) groups are part of these issue-specific networks, the key actors are drawn from local advocacy groups, women-run services, and urban bureaucracies responsible for delivering, funding, or regulating each policy. These networks are characterized by close and frequent contacts, interlocking directorates, co-production, and mutual support and respect. Task forces, advisory committees, and group boards have overlapping memberships. Advocacy groups provide in-service training for bureaucrats and lobby for these agencies' budgets before the Common Council and County Board. Bureaucrats help to raise private donations for advocacy groups and women-run services and refer clients to or directly contract with these organizations for services such as hotlines, shelters, health care, and counseling. And although virtually all group leaders reported some contacts with local elected officials (and contacts with female elected officials constituted a slight majority of such responses), fewer details or evaluative comments concerning these relationships were volunteered, in sharp contrast with responses concerning bureaucratic ones. Urban politics is widely viewed as uniquely bureaucratic politics (e.g., Peterson 1981; Yates 1977), and local women's policy networks have adapted to this "different" political setting.

Discussion and Conclusions

With certain qualifications, the importance of having women officials in strategic decision-making positions was again confirmed. Female elected officials in Milwaukee have clearly made a difference for women. Over the ten to twenty years that women's issues have been on local agendas, a relatively small number of female officials have disproportionately provided strong and consistent leadership on these issues. Although not every woman played a leadership role, ten of the sixteen women to serve in local public office since 1966 were recalled by one or more colleagues as having been a leader on at least one of the six policy areas considered in this study. As a group, women officials were active on more and a broader range of women's issues and placed a higher priority on them.

Women's leadership is also qualitatively different from that of men. Women are more active in agenda building and the design of major new policy programs. Men are more likely to advance the women's agenda through incrementally changing existing programs or by using bureaucratic procedures such as zoning and contracting. But whereas men appear to provide leadership as a part of some other role—as district advocate, legislative leader, or committee chair, or out of welfare liberalism generally—the representative role of female officials is less straightforward.

The influence of a formal caucus of female supervisors, alderwomen, or elected women in Milwaukee or nationally does not underpin these distinctive roles. Instead, women rely on informal cooperative relations as each issue arises.

Nor is there sufficient evidence of female officials' participation in a local women's policy network to support an instructed delegate role. These women do maintain closer ties to local women's groups in terms of conference attendance, formal memberships in such groups, and group-initiated contacts. And many were very positive about women's networks. But women officials, like their male colleagues, were quite divided concerning the exact nature of such a network in Milwaukee. This uncertainty appeared to be linked with a rather low level of activity and visibility of women's groups in local legislative politics, as well as some perceived problems of agenda-setting and strategic effectiveness.

Fortunately for women, Milwaukee elected women act on their own initiative as feminist trustees to represent women's interests. This role is rooted in both the nature of urban representation generally and the character of local feminist groups today. From the San Francisco Bay Study, conducted in the late 1960s, to the most recent studies of urban elected officials, local legislators have been found to adopt a trustee representative focus (see Heilig and Mundt 1984; Welch and Bledsoe 1988; Zisk 1973). As a result, elected representatives resolve most issues on the basis of their independent judgments, even though these decisions generally tend to be consistent with the preferences of affected citizens (see Schumaker 1991, 173). In the case of local elected women, feminist concerns can be addressed by these friendly allies within city and county government with only minimal contacts between representative and issue constituency.

In contrast to the legislative policy-making that dominates on the national and state levels, however, the primary responsibility of city and county governments is the delivery of services within their own jurisdictions. Therefore, in seeking to advance the feminist agenda on the local level, feminist groups rationally have concentrated on bureaucracies and the service-delivery system. And here again, local female officials play a role as advocates for women before the bureaucracy.

In summary, local elected women in Milwaukee, acting as feminist trustees, have served as internal catalysts for change by raising women's issues, sensitizing their male colleagues and urban administrators to these issues, and bringing those officials into active or passive support of concrete policies. Many may also be willing, but underutilized, delegates for local women's rights groups who support these same issues.

Notes

The author gratefully acknowledges the financial support of the Center for American Women and Politics, a unit of the Eagleton Institute of Politics at Rutgers University; the American Political Science Association; and the Bradley Institute for Democracy and Public Values, the Institute for Family Studies, and the Graduate School, all of Marquette University. This chapter reflects the views of the author and not necessarily those of any grantor. Thanks also go to Josephine Morstatter, Mary Agnes Murphy, and Genevieve Weston for their assistance.

1. It should be noted that two alderwomen completed their terms before most of those issues were addressed locally. In addition, one alderwoman and one female supervisor were in their first year of service at the time of the interview.

2. No genuine policy network exits around childbirth or children's library services. However, each has a core support group with some bureaucratic allies or contacts.

References

Antolini, Denise. 1984. "Women in Local Government: An Overview." In *Political Women*, ed. Janet A. Flammang. Beverly Hills: Sage.

Beck, Susan Abrams. 1991. "Rethinking Municipal Governance: Gender Distinctions on Local Councils." In *Gender and Policymaking*, ed. Debra L. Dodson. New Brunswick, N.J.: Center for the American Woman and Politics.

Bledsoe, Timothy. 1993. *Careers in City Politics*. Pittsburgh: University of Pittsburgh Press.

Boles, Janet K. 1994. "Local Feminist Policy Networks in the Contemporary American Interest Group System." *Policy Sciences* 27: 161–178.

Boneparth, Ellen. 1984. "Resources and Constraints on Women in the Policy-making Process: State and Local Arenas." In *Political Women*, ed. Janet A. Flammang. Beverly Hills: Sage.

Burns, Ruth Ann. 1979. *Women in Municipal Management*. New Brunswick, N.J.: Center for the American Woman and Politics.

84

Carroll, Susan J. 1985. *Women as Candidates in American Politics.* Bloomington: Indiana University Press.

Carroll, Susan J., and Wendy S. Strimling. 1983. *Women's Routes to Elective Office.* New Brunswick, N.J.: Center for the American Woman and Politics.

Center for American Women and Politics. 2000. "Women in Elective Office 2000." Fact Sheet. New Brunswick, N.J.: Center for American Women and Politics.

Center for the American Woman and Politics. 1992. "Women in Elective Office 1992." Fact Sheet. New Brunswick, N.J.: Center for the American Woman and Politics.

Darcy, R., Susan Welch, and Janet Clark. 1994. *Women, Elections and Representation.* 2nd ed., revised. Lincoln: University of Nebraska Press.

Dodson, Debra L., and Susan J. Carroll. 1991. *Reshaping the* Agenda: *Women in State Legislatures.* New Brunswick, N.J.: Center for the American Woman and Politics.

Eulau, Heinz, and John C. Wahlke, with Alan Abramowitz. 1978. "The Role of the Representative." In *The Politics of Representation,* ed. Heinz Eulau and John C. Wahlke. Beverly Hills: Sage.

Fenno, Richard F. 1978. *Home Style.* Boston: Little, Brown.

Ferree, Myra Marx, and Beth B. Hess. 1985. *Controversy and Coalition: The New Feminist Movement.* Boston: Twayne.

Flammang, Janet A. 1985. "Female Officials in the Feminist Capital: The Case of Santa Clara County." *Western Political* Quarterly 38: 94–118.

Flammang, Janet A. 1987. "Women Made a Difference: Comparable Worth in San Jose." In *The Women's Movements of the United States and Western Europe,* ed. Mary Fainsod Katzenstein and Carol McClurg Mueller. Philadelphia: Temple University Press.

Flammang, Janet A. 1997. *Women's Political Voice.* Philadelphia: Temple University Press.

Fraser, Arvonne S. 1983. "Insiders and Outsiders: Women in the Political Arena." In *Women in Washington,* ed. Irene Tinker. Beverly Hills: Sage.

Freeman, Jo. 1975. *The Politics of Women's Liberation.* New York: Longman.

Garber, Judith A., and Robyne S. Turner, eds. 1995. *Gender in Urban Research.* Thousand Oaks, Calif.: Sage.

Gelb, Joyce, and Marilyn Gittell. 1986. "Seeking Equality: The Role of Activist Women in Cities." In *The Egalitarian City,* ed. Janet K. Boles. New York: Praeger.

Gelb, Joyce, and Marian Lief Palley. 1987. *Women and Public Policies.* 2nd ed. Princeton, N.J.: Princeton University Press.

Gelb, Joyce, and Ethel Klein. 1988. *Women's Movements: Organizing for Change.* Washington, D.C.: American Political Science Association.

Hartmann, Susan M. 1989. *From Margin to Mainstream: American Women and Politics since 1960.* New York: Knopf.

Heclo, Hugh. 1978. "Issue Networks and the Executive Establishment." In *The New American Political System,* ed. Anthony King. Washington, D.C.: American Enterprise Institute.

Heilig, Peggy, and Robert J. Mundt. 1984. *Your Voice at City Hall.* Albany: State University of New York Press.

Johnson, Marilyn, and Susan Carroll. 1978. "Statistical Report: Profile of Women Holding Public Office, 1977." In *Women in Public Office: A Biographical Directory and Statistical Analysis,* ed. Kathy Stanwick and Marilyn Johnson. Metuchen, N.J.: Scarecrow.

MacManus, Susan A., and Charles S. Bullock III. 1995. "Electing Women to Local Office." In *Gender in Urban Research,* ed. Judith A. Garber and Robyne S. Turner. Thousand Oaks, Calif.: Sage.

Margolis, Diane Rothbard. 1986. "Bargaining, Negotiating and Their Social Contexts: The Case of Organizations of Women in the Public Service." In *Women and Politics: Activism, Attitudes, and Office-Holding,* ed. Gwen Moore and Glenna Spitze. Greenwich, Conn.: JAI Press.

Merritt, Sharyne. 1980. "Sex Differences in Role Behavior and Policy Orientations of Suburban Officeholders: The Effect of Women's Employment." In *Women in Local Politics,* ed. Debra W. Stewart. Metuchen, N.J.: Scarecrow.

Mezey, Susan Gluck. 1978. "Support for Women's Rights Policy: An Analysis of Local Politicians." *American Politics Quarterly* 6: 485–497.

Mezey, Susan Gluck. 1980. "Perceptions of Women's Rights on Local Councils in Connecticut." In *Women in Local Politics,* ed. Debra W. Stewart. Metuchen, N.J.: Scarecrow.

Milwaukee Area Women's Resource Directory. 1998. 10th ed. Milwaukee: Center for Women's Studies, University of Wisconsin–Milwaukee.

Mueller, Carol. 1984. "Women's Organizational Strategies in State Legislatures." In *Political Women,* ed. Janet A. Flammang. Beverly Hills: Sage.

Mueller, Carol. 1987. "Collective Consciousness, Identity Transformation and the Rise of Women in Public Office in the United States." In *The Women's Movements of the United States and Western Europe,* ed. Mary Fainsod Katzenstein and Carol McClurg Mueller. Philadelphia: Temple University Press.

Peterson, Paul E. 1981. *City Limits.* Chicago: University of Chicago Press.

Schumaker, Paul. 1991. *Critical Pluralism, Democratic Performance, and Community Power.* Lawrence: University Press of Kansas.

Spalter-Roth, Roberta, and Ronnee Schreiber. 1995. "Outsider Issues and Insider Tactics: Strategic Tensions in the Women's Policy Network During the 1980s." In *Feminist Organizations,* ed. Myra Marx Ferree and Patricia Yancy Martin. Philadelphia: Temple University Press.

Stanwick, Kathy A., and Katherine E. Kleeman. 1983. *Women Make a Difference.* New Brunswick, N.J.: Center for the American Woman and Politics.

Stewart, Debra W. 1980a. "Commissions on the Status of Women and Building a Local Policy Agenda." In *Women in Local Politics,* ed. Debra W. Stewart. Metuchen, N.J.: Scarecrow.

Stewart, Debra W. 1980b. *The Women's Movement in Community Politics in the U.S.* New York: Pergamon.

Strimling, Wendy S. 1983. *Elected Women Organize Statewide Associations.* New Brunswick, N.J.: Center for the American Woman and Politics.

U.S. Department of Labor. Women's Bureau. 1990. "Commissions, Committees, and Councils on the Status of Women." Washington, D.C.

Walker, Jack L. 1981. "The Diffusion of Knowledge, Policy Communities and Agenda Setting: The Relationship of Knowledge and Power." In *New Strategic Perspective on Social Policy*, ed. John E. Tropman, Milan J. Dluhy, and Roger M. Lind. New York: Pergamon.

Welch, Susan, and Timothy Bledsoe. 1988. *Urban Reform and Its Consequences: A Study in Representation*. Chicago: University of Chicago Press.

Yates, Douglas. 1977. *The Ungovernable City*. Cambridge, Mass.: MIT Press.

Zisk, Betty H. 1973. *Local Interest Politics: A One-Way Street*. Indianapolis: Bobbs-Merrill.

PART II

THE IMPORTANCE OF POLITICAL CONTEXT

Five

"Senator-at-Large for America's Women"

Margaret Chase Smith and the Paradox of Gender Affinity

Janann Sherman

Until very recently, few women—and the number is still minuscule—have had the opportunity to make a significant impact on American politics. And fewer still have climbed as high in the male hierarchy of government as Senator Margaret Chase Smith. Smith was the first woman to earn a seat in both the United States House of Representatives and the United States Senate. For all but six of her twenty-four years as a senator, she served as the only woman among ninety-five, later ninety-nine, men. Her thirty-three-year tenure in Congress, 1940 to 1973, spanned the administrations of six presidents, the prosecution of three wars, and the evolution of marked changes in the roles of women.

While working in a hostile male environment, Margaret Smith, a self-professed non-feminist woman, managed to balance her conflicting roles of woman and legislator. She attained power in the highest levels of government without upsetting gender stereotypes but at the same time found ways to assert a woman's point of view. Because Smith was both a shaper and a product of her culture, placing her within her time and period of history reveals her extraordinary accomplishments and the promise they implied for other women.

A Barrier Breached

The halls of Congress rang with female voices on the opening day of the 81st Congress, January 3, 1949. As the newly elected, and only woman, United States Senator entered the Senate chamber, the gallery broke into spontaneous applause. Senator Margaret Chase Smith's decisive victory generated great excitement and anticipation. Scores of women had traveled to Washington—by auto cavalcade, by plane, and by two specially chartered trains—to celebrate the entry of one of their own into that most exclusive men's club in the world. "It seemed to me," wrote reporter May Craig, "that all the women in the world were there" (*PPH*, 6 January 1949).

The "Tribute Train" carried representatives of the National Federation of Business and Professional Women's Clubs (NFBPW) from across the country who had organized a huge gala luncheon to honor Smith and the eight other women of the 81st Congress.[1] Speaking before the assembled five hundred men and women, including top government and military officials, Smith (1949) extolled the significance of her success. Hers was "a victory," she said, "for all women, for it smashed the unwritten tradition that the Senate is no place for a woman." Her achievement clearly demonstrated that "ability and proved performance, rather than sex, are the best standards for political selection."

The women aboard the second train could not have agreed more. Nearly one hundred delegates of the Multi-Party Committee on Women, representing more than thirty-six state and national women's organizations, arrived aboard the "Women for Public Office Special."[2] Led by Judge Lucy Somerville Howorth, this group came armed with a specific program for training women in public service, lobbying for appointive positions, and encouraging bipartisan gender solidarity. The Multi-Party Committee intended to harness the energy and optimism surrounding Smith's victory to launch a million-dollar campaign to promote women for public office. "The powder was there," Howorth said, "and this seemed to be the spark it was waiting for." Senator Smith was, she said, a "shining example of the purposes the Multi-Party Committee hopes to accomplish" because Smith had won her high position on the basis of her own ability yet recognized that women needed one another in order to correct the inequities of American democracy. Women would have to band together across party lines, Howorth asserted, and women's organizations should lead the assault (Howorth Papers).[3]

In January 1949, activist women were stirred with enthusiastic expectation—parity was just around the corner. Margaret Smith had breached the barrier of the Senate, and she promised she would continue to speak out for women in her new capacity. While noting that her first duty was to the people of Maine, Smith assured her women listeners that she would "gladly accept the unofficial responsibility of being Senator-at-large for America's women . . . to be a voice of America's women on the floor of the Senate and in committees." Smith hastily noted, however, that she believed there was little difference between the sexes on the major issues. The subjects of greatest interest to women, world peace and domestic security, she insisted, were also of great interest to men. "Men and women are no different on this point" (Smith 1949).

Men and women were no different on many points, Smith avowed, at least not those that had any relevance for political involvement. "Women are people," she frequently proclaimed, and they should be treated the same as men. Suffrage had been won; it was up to the women themselves to make effective use of their public responsibilities. "Citizenship is without sex," Smith insisted. "It makes no distinction between the rights and responsibilities of men and women" (Smith 1946).

Smith's cohort in the women's organizations concurred. After noting that 1948 was the hundredth anniversary of the women's rights meeting at Seneca Falls, which launched the suffrage movement, NFBPW President Dr. K. Frances Scott observed that, unlike their earlier sisters, today's women could no longer blame men for injustice and inequality. Scott urged women to "cease hiding their talents and take their places in government on equal terms with men" (Smith Papers). From now on women's achievements would be measured in individual terms; the public world was a world of the strong and the able. Economic independence and political access had become the new frontiers for women.

Political Apprenticeship

While there was no organized "women's movement" in this period, to a limited extent some women, particularly business and professional women, found a voice to interpret their discontent and frustration through single-sex organizations such as the NFBPW. When the promises of suffrage did not elevate women to political power, the NFBPW began to self-consciously prepare women for elective and appointive office. Their increasing emphasis on the active political participation of women was justified by the particular talents that these women could bring to the political sphere, including organizing and leadership skills, a perspective that "differed from that of men, and from women who find their first interest in home life" (Sargent 1979), and an ability to "use the word 'political' without squirming" (Howorth Papers). *Independent Woman*, the aptly named official voice of the NFBPW, functioned as a training manual for active female citizenship. Expressly committed to improving and mobilizing federation women, it kept its readership informed in great detail of the happenings in the federal government, whether or not they related directly to women; taught women how to succeed in the male world of business and the profes-sions; and urged women to realize and act upon their responsibilities as citizens, including the ultimate goal of that citizenship, political office. Although avowedly nonpartisan, women's clubs emphasized the impor-tance of the economic elevation of women and lobbied for broadened rights and responsibilities in the public realm, demanding for women a sexless equality, a citizen's right to freedom and liberty within a demo-cratic society (Bowman and White 1946).

Margaret Smith shared her peer group's belief in an individual's right to self-determination, and she was a vigorous advocate for that ethic. Active in the NFBPW since she organized her hometown chapter in her early twenties, Smith later served as president of the state organi-zation. She frequently expressed her allegiance and credited them with her political socialization. "The BPW is largely responsible for putting me in the Senate," she said, because her work with that organization "taught me the very touchstones of political success," attributes such as efficiency, cooperation, tact, and leadership (Smith 1949).[4]

Smith and her cohort of women achievers pejoratively dismissed as "feminists" women who sought special favors. Feminism was associ-ated with rebellion, disharmony, and unreasonable hostility toward men (Cott 1987). "I have studiously avoided being a feminist," Smith (1949, 1972) often stated,

I have been particularly conscious of, and perhaps sensitive to, the general criticism that women selfishly seek equal rights without agreeing to give up those feminine privileges and niceties which are in direct conflict with the rights sought.

Feminist demands, then, were inappropriate. In order to take their rightful places in public society, women must educate themselves, culti-vate achievement, and, above all, work together for the betterment of all women.

Why So Few

The debate about why so few women held public office intensified after Margaret Smith's election. Several theories formulated by women's groups laid much of the blame on women: (1) Women do not support women because they do not see other women as suitable leaders or as appropriate advocates for their viewpoints; (2) women think of politics as dirty and unsuited for women's participation; and (3) women do not understand politics—they need education in organizing and utilizing their latent voting power to further a woman's agenda. Women active in the political arena, however, recognized the structural restraints imposed by male politicians reluctant to share political fruits with women. Although women had recently been granted equality in numbers on party state committees, for example, many of the women saw themselves as marginalized, consulted only on matters pertaining to women and, though acceptable in the precincts, were considered out of place in policy-making. When male leaders were forced to apportion power, they often named token, and frequently unqualified, women to minor but highly visible positions (*CSM*, 30 October 1948).

There were two main reasons why there were not more women in public office, Margaret Smith believed: "The reasons are (1) men, and (2) women—men because they vigorously oppose women holding public office—and women because they haven't stood together and exercised their power of the majority voting power."

Smith exhorted women to get in there and fight for their rightful places as she had:

Some claim the availability of leadership to women has been unfairly limited. I have no sympathy with this view because it is only those who "make the breaks" that "get the breaks." In other words, to increase the availability of leadership, we must by our own actions create and force that increased availability. (Smith 1946)

If men were unwilling to surrender positions of power to women, then women had but one choice: to unify and make themselves so strong that male politicians could not ignore them. Women would have to force their way in, expecting no chivalry and giving no quarter.

Making the Breaks

Smith's biography resembles the classic American success story, with a few gendered twists. Born the eldest of six to a barber and his wife, three years before the beginning of the twentieth century, Margaret Chase grew up in the small mill town of Skowhegan, Maine. She got her first job at thirteen, when she was "tall enough to reach the shelves" in the local five-and-ten. After finishing high school she worked at a succession of jobs, each one better—having more status or salary—than the one before. After nine weeks as a rural schoolteacher, she worked in the telephone company office. Her next job was as jill-of-all-trades for the local newspaper, until she was hired as office manager at the town's largest textile mill. At the same time, she was active in women's club activities, including the NFBPW, and in state and local political organizations. She spent six years as the Somerset County representative on the Republican Party State Committee.

At 32, she quit her job and married Clyde H. Smith, an exceptionally successful state and local politician, who had never lost an election in 48 tries. Margaret's political apprenticeship began with their courtship. "Mostly," she said, "we went campaigning." In the sparsely settled state of Maine, campaigning meant traveling to scattered hamlets and meeting individually with voters. When Clyde Smith ran successfully for Congress from Maine's Second District in 1936 and again in 1938, Margaret Smith drove the car, kept track of Clyde's contacts, answered his mail, and dealt with the press. While he stayed on the job in Washington, she made frequent trips back to Maine, accepting speaking engagements as his emissary and acting as liaison with his constituents. She recalled, "I did everything for his office short of going to the committee room or to the floor of the House to vote" (Interview, 8 January 1987).

The day before he died following a series of heart attacks, Congressman Clyde Smith dictated a press release acknowledging his illness and the uncertainty of his future in politics. He asked his friends and supporters to

> support the candidate of my choice, my wife and my partner in public life, Margaret Chase Smith. I know of no one else who has the full knowledge of my ideas and plans or is as well qualified as she is to carry on these ideas and my unfinished work for my district. (Smith Papers)

Clyde Smith died a few hours later. The press release ran side by side with his obituary (*PPH*, 8 April 1940).

Despite Clyde's deathbed plea, his new widow did not find his notable friends and supporters to be friends of hers. Several of his more prominent Republican colleagues were forthright in telling her that they aspired to replace Clyde Smith in Congress. Other members of the Maine Republican Party hierarchy gave her their grudging support but specified that she would have it only for the completion of the eight months left in Clyde Smith's unexpired term. The Republican Party would support another candidate, she was told, for the 77th Congress (Interview, 8 January 1987).

Forced to rely upon her own political resources, Margaret Smith successfully fought two uphill battles in the five months after her husband's death to win a regular seat in the House of Representatives. One Republican ran against her for the unexpired term; four chose to oppose her in the primary for the full term. In Republican Maine, primary wins were tantamount to victory. In each case, she won with large majorities: 91 percent in the initial primary and 64 percent over her four opponents in the second (Smith Papers).

Margaret Smith had earned her extraordinary popularity. During her ten-year apprenticeship with Clyde Smith, she had acquired considerable political assets, including a positive public image, an acquaintance with important state and party political leaders, an intimate knowledge of her constituent's concerns, and a clear understanding of the demands and rewards of public office (Gertzog 1984). Together she and Clyde had carefully built a power base in rural Maine that almost automatically became hers when he died. "My base was so solid," she said, "and those people knew me so well they would send me on to others. That is how I got going" (Interview, 26 July 1989).

The Smith Approach

Once in office, Margaret Chase Smith set herself two primary goals: to stay on the job in Washington and to keep close to the people in her district. This required almost superhuman effort. She did not miss a single roll call vote from 1955 to 1968, 2,941 consecutive votes, a record that stood for twenty years. In addition, at least once a month she covered her entire district, geographically the second-largest in the country at that time, "setting up shop" in Grange halls and post offices to meet with constituents about their concerns. In effect, she never ceased campaigning. Smith answered every letter the day it came, and her staff worked nearly full time at constituency service, responding to voters' concerns and running interference with the federal bureaucracy on their behalf. Her constituents knew that if a pension check didn't come through, they could get in touch with "Margaret" and she would do something about it (Interview, 16 March 1987).

In addition to letters and conversations, Smith maintained her personalized communication through a weekly column in local papers. *Washington and You* was a folksy letter home, often referring to visitors from Maine and specific requests. It contained, as well, educational discourses on the workings of various branches of government, yearnings for Maine from afar, and reassurances that all was being done to aid particular Maine concerns (Smith Papers).

Margaret Chase Smith's proudest possession was her reputation for attending to the smallest details of her constituents' concerns. She once confessed:

> My constituents are my friends, my family, my future. I have no family of my own, no hobbies; my job is my life. . . . I [often] wonder why I work so hard. And then, I will walk down to the town

square and shake some hands and hear my name called out; and I will know why all over again. (Markel 1964)

Smith's personal, interactive style with her constituency was an important factor in her success. So was her straightforward New England approach to politics, including an ability to communicate a deeply shared commitment to the Yankee ethic of hard work, integrity, moderation, independence, fair play, and equality of opportunity. This combination proved sufficient time after time to overcome formidable opposition, lack of party endorsement, and inadequate funding to win with large electoral margins.

Risking It All

In 1948, Margaret Smith surrendered her secure seat in the House to run for the Senate against great odds. First, no other woman had run on her own for the Senate without first having been appointed to the post. Second, she was without the resources of the GOP machine in Maine, which was dividing its spoils between her two strongest opponents: the sitting governor and a well-liked former governor. Third, she had been ideologically inconsistent vis-à-vis the Republican Party throughout her eight and one-half years in the House.

Maine commentators gave Smith credit for an adequate job in the House, but the Senate was an entirely different matter. "The little lady from Skowhegan is simply over-reaching herself in trying for the Senate," they said (*PST,* 10 December 1947). "The little lady . . . has simply stepped out of her class. . . . The Senate is big league stuff, the glittering prize. . . . Nobody in Maine gets into the Senate without a political machine, fat campaign funds, the right business connections and the help of the powers that be. Margaret hasn't got any of those things" (Beverly Smith 1948).

While eager to contend that these trying times called for male leadership, the Republican Party, aware that women constituted 64 percent of Maine's registered voters, were wary of alienating the "women's vote." They decided to fight fire with fire. All three of her opponents used their wives and women employees to stump the state for them and held many large, well-attended meetings and debates before women's clubs. As a result, commented political analyst Edward D. Talberth, Smith's candidacy produced political activity on the part of Maine women unmatched since they had attained the suffrage (*PST,* 7 March 1948).

Margaret Smith was forthright in acknowledging her gender, but she denied its relevance. "I am proud," she told her radio audience on the eve of the primary,

> of being a woman, but I want it distinctly understood that I am not soliciting support because I am a woman. I solicit your support wholly on the basis of my record of eight years in Congress. (Smith 1948)

However, when Smith found herself the victim of a "whispering campaign" that the Senate was "no place for a woman," she turned it on its head. She announced that while she had consciously avoided making her gender an issue in the campaign, her opposition had done so. This effort, she said, constituted "a direct challenge to every woman in Maine." She turned that phrase to a rallying cry for all subsequent campaign speeches and ads (Smith Papers).

Her opponents' displeasure with her femaleness and her willingness to exploit it was exacerbated by her reputation for taking each measure on its merits and voting with her own closely held convictions. Smith (1948) characterized herself as a "moderate," which she defined as "somewhat more Liberal, and somewhat less Conservative, than one in the past category of 'middle-of-the-road.'" The perception that she did not blindly follow party ideology angered Maine's GOP while making her enormously popular with voters. One political commentator (*BC*, 22 June 1948) praised Smith as an exemplar of "intelligent liberalism," a progressive voice who had not "made a fetish of party regularity" and who had consistently demonstrated "the courage of her convictions." Another Maine editorial (*KJ*, 24 June 1948) insisted that "Mrs. Smith is not too liberal for the state of Maine. She acts, walks and votes like a Yankee, with that typical independence on which Maine folks place a premium."

Smith's strong stand on military defense, an area of expertise she developed during the war, pleased liberals and conservatives alike. What particularly nettled her conservative opponents was her liberal voting record on labor and social welfare programs. *The New York Times* flatly observed that "if she had been born in any other state except Maine she'd be a Democrat. . . . She has a mind of her own and uses it" (20 May 1948). Considered a friend of labor, and consistently sympathetic to old-age legislation and aid to working mothers, her position exposed her to substantial criticism from the right but applause from her working-class constituency. Indeed, since many political insiders were unsure that a Democratic candidate would be a challenge ideologically, there was serious debate among Maine Democratic Party leaders about endorsing Margaret Smith in the primaries themselves (*PPH*, 31

July 1947; *LJ*, 14 June 1947). Such a move would give her a second chance at the seat in the general election if one of the machine-backed Republicans were to defeat her in the primary. In addition, since many Maine Democrats registered as Republicans in order to have a voice in the primary, a move to endorse Smith would deliver that Democratic bloc to her and swing the primary her way (*PST*, 15 June 1947). Although the discussion went nowhere, its very existence indicated her appeal across the political spectrum. Moreover, Smith shrewdly pitted her all-volunteer campaign against her opponents' money and machine politics and made much of her insistence upon staying on the job in Washington, coming home to campaign only on weekends.

Out of desperation, her conservative opponents initiated a vicious smear campaign which linked her voting record with that of an avowed communist, American Labor Party Representative Vito Marcantonio of New York (Smith Papers).[5] The tactic backfired. In early June, too late for her opponents to respond to her, Smith broadcast a statewide radio address refuting the smear sheets point by point and demonstrating that her supposedly ultraliberal votes matched up with those of a number of her conservative colleagues. She spoke eloquently of herself as "a symbol of a 'grassroots' protest against political machines, money politics and smears." "I want to win," Smith told her radio audience the night before the primary,

> for that 18-year-old girl in Portland who sent me a one-dollar contribution. . . . for that Worumbo Mill worker. . . . for that Spanish War veteran. . . . for that housewife of Bath. . . . for that granger of York County. . . . for that Aroostook woman farmer. . . . for that longshoreman. . . . I want to win for these typical independent Republicans and hundreds of other rank-and-file Republicans who have refused to sell their votes, who have courageously resisted political intimidation, who have denounced and fought smears—and who have put their hearts and souls into my campaign because they were convinced that I was their symbol of protest against such things. (Smith 1948)

Margaret Smith's victory was stunning: she won 63,786 votes, a margin of 4,675 votes over the combined totals of her three opponents, winning 14 of Maine's 16 counties and 15 of 21 cities (Brunelle 1978).

"Senatorette"

Margaret Chase Smith had arrived. Hard work and serious attention to duty had yielded her a place in the most exclusive men's club in the world. Never again, wrote Washington columnist Ruth Millett (*WS*, 1 October 1948), would it be quite so hard for a woman to battle her way to the Senate alone. Within a few short years, Millett predicted, few would remark on a woman's election to the Senate. The national media, fascinated with the possibilities, debated how soon it would be before women had parity in Congress. Most agreed twenty years would be more than sufficient time for women to achieve the experience and the numerical strength. Indeed, Smith's very ordinariness seemed cause for optimism. She had won without money, without powerful backers, without advanced education or specialized training. If intelligence, integrity, and a desire to serve were all that was necessary, then there was no reason more women could not aspire to do the same (*WP*, 8 June 1949).

While Smith's achievement was duly celebrated, the public discourse set the limits for her new role, and it often led to contradictory messages. Margaret Smith occupied two seemingly incompatible roles: woman and senator. Debate over how to address a female senator, let alone how best to describe this particular one, occupied many column inches. Senatorette or Senatrix? Was she "glamorous" or "plain," "feminine" or "sensible"? In this unexplored territory, commentary, particularly by women, took on a "yes, but" quality. For example, Josephine Ripley assured readers that Smith was "definitely the feminine type . . . yet she is effective and competent as a politician" (*CSM*, 8 March 1949). Smith's increased access to power seemed to require reassurances that she still responded to the world as a traditional woman. She wisely cooperated with media efforts to polish her image with a domestic cloth, posing for pictures in stereotypical female occupations: cooking, ironing, typing, sweeping, primping before a mirror, talking on the telephone. Smith engaged in the same discourse when she described government as homemaking writ large, demonstrably appropriate for women's interest and influence. The home, she said, "is the most fundamental form of government," in which women

> legislate the rules of the home; they execute and enforce the rules of the home; and they interpret the rules of the home. . . . The home, then, should not be severed from the government. In fact, there has been too little of the home in the government and too much government in the home. The most obvious and natural way to reverse this trend is to put more of the home governors in the government—and that means women. (Smith 1948)

While Smith recognized that most women would not make the same choices she had, she found women's apathy and indifference to the political process infuriating. Moreover, because she believed so strongly in the American dream of individual self-fulfillment, she assumed that women's failure to attain parity was as much their fault as a function of male obstructionism.

> The dearth of women in public service can be attributable to women themselves for lack of interest and aggressiveness—and the will to public careers. . . . women themselves are guilty of such political inertia as not to overcome the opposition of men. (Smith 1948).

Juxtaposing herself against this portrait of self-indulgent, weak-willed, disinterested women, Smith attributed her success to working "awfully hard," campaigning affirmatively, doing her homework, and fighting "like a man" for what she believed in (Interview, 18 January 1989).

Learning Woman's Place in Congress

Margaret Chase Smith had broken the barrier for all women and, in the bargain, acquired for herself a national constituency of women. But the bequest was an ambivalent one. On the one hand, she had accepted the mandate to act as Senator-at-large for women; on the other, she was aware of the political risks involved in identifying with women. She could not afford, as a politician, to align herself with one-half of her constituency when the powerful half was threatened by that allegiance. Her task as a legislator was to speak for a subgroup, but that subgroup was Maine, not women. Moreover, she risked alienating her colleagues by any acknowledgment of affiliation with women and their concerns. Stepping carefully, Smith balanced on a tightrope between genders— not too masculine, not too feminine—while steadfastly maintaining that her sex was irrelevant.

This awkward balancing of gender was hardly unique to Smith; nor was it a recent development. Women in male-dominated professions, as well as the six other women representatives she joined in 1940, had long struggled with finding a middle course.[6] The difficulty was in conveying a sort of gender neutrality. Most women then in public life, including Margaret Smith, repeatedly referred to themselves as human beings, not just women. It seemed axiomatic to them that "women are people" so "women deserve equal rights" (Ware 1981). These assertions, though, were quickly followed by a denial of feminism. A slippery and loaded term, feminism had long been associated with radical suffragist women whose militant actions smacked of sex-antagonism (Cott 1987). The movement's anger and single-minded zeal seemed selfish and unreasonable to women who believed in the virtues and rewards of individual achievement. "I definitely resent being called a feminist," Smith affirmed. "A woman's viewpoint should be objective and free of any emphasis on feminine interests" (Smith Papers).

Despite their denials of allegiance, congresswomen were invariably lumped together in the popular press where the public perception of them was shaped by powerful imagery of women in the home. Their views on national issues were infrequently solicited while an extraordinary amount of space was devoted to descriptions of dress and physical attractiveness, womanly attributes, and assurances of domesticity. Less flattering conceptions of women also flourished in 1940s characterizations of a "petticoat contingent" completely absorbed by fashion competitions and smoldering catfights. Though writers attested that "most of the petticoat tribe ask only to be treated like men," these same reporters assured that that would seldom happen (*NYWT*, 6 January 1945). At once demonstrating conflicting conceptions of political women and catering to them, Representative Bolton dropped a note to gossip columnist George E. Sokolsky describing her friend and colleague, Margaret Smith: "A hard worker and a fine investigator, she gives evidence of judgment and sincerity, of tolerance and understanding. . . . In addition to this she is charming and attractive and the men buzz around her like bees" (Smith Papers).

Given the importance of collegial networks in the functioning of Congress, and the likelihood that they were isolated from those formed among the men, it would seem probable that the women would associate with one another for their mutual benefit (Oleszek 1984; Baker 1980). Nonetheless, they did not. Individual friendships, such as that between Margaret Smith and Frances Bolton, blossomed and endured, but alliances as women were anathema. The very idea of a women's bloc in Congress brought a sharp response from Mary Norton, who emphatically stated that she sincerely hoped that day would never come. "Nothing would indicate our weakness more" (*WS*, 5 January 1945). Smith, too, believed women should always "avoid any tendency to . . . stand as one sex against another" (*LJ*, 23 June 1941). Moreover, female members frequently denied that any common cause existed. Their interests and their constituencies, they asserted, were as varied and unique as those of male members of Congress. "We women represent all the people of our district just as the men do" (*NYWT*, 6 January 1945). Constantly drawn into the debate on women's issues, their rejoinder was to define them broadly: No political or social issue existed that was not the legitimate concern of women. What's more, congresswomen argued, their sex was unrelated to their occupations as lawmakers. Reflecting this common theme, Representative Gracie Pfost declared, "I really don't think being a woman in politics is different from being a man. After all, elections are based on the issues, and any capable woman can develop an understanding of the issues, can present them, and can win at the polls" (Porter 1943). Yet Mary Norton's widely repeated remark, "I'm no lady. I'm a member of Congress," often taken to indicate the women's resistance to gender pigeonholing, at the same time seemed to acknowledge that the two roles were incompatible.[7]

When she began her congressional career, Margaret Smith was denied Clyde Smith's relatively powerful seat on the Labor Committee, in part because she was a freshman and in part because she was a woman. (Although Labor was an attractive assignment sometimes sought by more senior members, Clyde Smith assumed that position as a freshman). Since some committee seats were much better places to begin a climb to leadership than others, male leaders who desired to restrict women's participation imposed a gendered division of political labor in Congress, channeling women into certain clearly bounded fields considered to be of interest to women, such as health and education (Duverger 1955). Smith's first assignments were to Education, Invalid Pensions, and Post Offices and Roads. It would take three years of building up her personal contacts and credibility to earn a more prestigious seat. When her opportunity came, she chose for herself a "hard" issue, an issue with strength—defense—which, by its very nature, allowed her to create an image of forceful leadership.

The fortuitous circumstance of wartime significantly enhanced this strategy. World War II transformed the American economy, led to unprecedented governmental intervention into the private lives of men and women, and profoundly disrupted social arrangements. At least temporarily, the nation's need for woman-power elevated the female worker's primacy as a citizen and contributor to the war effort. While scholars continue to debate the liberating potential of wartime for women and whether it fostered enduring or transitory progress, for Congresswoman Smith, wartime brought a new legitimacy to women in the public sphere and increasing consideration to their representation in government (Chafe 1972; Anderson 1981; Campbell 1984).

Naval Affairs

After three years in the House, at the height of World War II, Smith managed an assignment to the House Naval Affairs Committee. She was awarded this seat on the basis of a longtime interest in a strong national defense dating from her personal experiences with World War I and, perhaps more importantly, because it was politically expedient for the leadership to reward "the ladies" for their war work. At the same time that Smith was named to Naval Affairs, Clare Boothe Luce was assigned to the Military Affairs Committee. Minority Leader Joe Martin explained that

In singling out the women members for these assignments, the committee was guided by the realization that the women of the country take an important part in the war effort.

Since "in both the Army and Navy thousands of women are performing splendid services," Republicans believed it was desirable to give the women a voice on the military committees (*WP*, 19 January 1943).

For Margaret Smith, the goal was to appear ladylike but tough enough to handle the hard issues. Defense turned out to be the perfect attention-getter. And in Smith's hands, it turned out to be double-gendered. That is, a strong national defense was both a strong, therefore masculine, ideology projecting seriousness and firmness of purpose and a feminine plea for safety, preservation, and protection. Smith's public statements equated a strong national defense and a firm foreign policy with the maintenance of peace and domestic security. "I have voted for every measure for national defense," she stated, "not because I want our boys to go to war, but because adequate preparedness means peace. . . . We must protect ourselves against invasion" (Smith Papers).

A significant portion of Smith's work on the House Naval Affairs Committee had to do with women, notably military women. During a tour of hospital facilities in the Pacific during the war, she found the conditions under which the nurses worked to be "appalling," but worse was their insecurity: If they got sick or hurt as a result of such duty, they were simply sent home. Alarmed by this gross unfairness, Smith subsequently worked on a series of measures over three years resulting in regular status for Army and Navy nurses—that is, positions commensurate with men in rank, pay, and authority.

When Smith attempted to expand that effort to regular status for all women in the military, she encountered significantly stronger resistance. Despite repeated testimony by top-ranking officers of all the services that they needed to retain women in the regular forces, service committees in Congress insisted upon holding women to reserve status only. As the only insider favoring regular status, Smith made skillful use of her single vote and access to the press. When the House Armed Services Committee (formed by the merger of Naval Affairs and Military Affairs in 1947) reported out the bill limiting women to the reserves (without benefits or status, while using them indefinitely in active service) at 26 to 1, her lone "no" vote prevented the bill's swift passage. Her stubborn stand forced the issue to a floor debate where she argued that if the military needed the women they must grant them regular status, since any other arrangement was clearly discriminatory. With all members' positions a matter of public record, her committee colleagues ultimately failed to prevail, and legislation granting regular status to all women in the military passed in 1948 (Sherman 1990). Smith's complex fight in the face of powerful opposition earned her political wings, proving her acumen in managing legislation with the best of them. By the time she reached the Senate, Margaret Smith had gained a reputation as a woman who could play hardball.

Senator-at-Large

The debut of Senator Smith sharpened a growing interest in political participation among women. Since the nonpartisan League of Women Voters evolved from the National American Woman Suffrage Association in 1920, organized women expressed considerable ambivalence about direct participation in partisan politics. But in the postwar years, at least one major women's organization, the NFBPW, swallowed its aversion and moved from "encouragement" and blanket endorsements of "qualified women" to recommending specific women for specific posts (Rawalt 1979). Women's organizations also became more skillful in pressure-group politics on behalf of important legislation in the late 1940s, pushing housing bills, federal aid to education, and the extension of minimum wages and maximum-hour provisions to service workers (*NYT*, 3 January 1949). Despite their growing sense of legitimacy in the political arena, however, debates continued over appropriate methods. For example, Mary Donlon, chair of the New York State Workmen's Compensation Board, urged women to educate, not agitate:

> Organized women's groups have two major alternatives of purpose. They can become pressure groups, spearheading a woman's bloc. That is not an attractive or useful destiny. Or they can function to educate women for and graduate them into politics and government. That is both useful and attractive. (*CT*, April 1949)

All this activity coupled with reports of women's economic importance and numerical superiority raised the threatening specter of burgeoning political clout. Women were said to control 60 percent, or as much as 85 percent, of the nation's wealth. Women bought 80 percent of consumer goods, inherited 80 percent of the nation's life insurance, controlled 47 percent of corporate stock and owned 65 percent of all saving accounts (*CSM*, 12 June 1948). Perhaps more threatening to traditional power arrangements were the statistics reported by Senator Howard McGrath, chairman of the Democratic National Committee, that in the next election year there could be 2 million more women voters than men. Should women chose to vote in a bloc, he warned,

> We would find ourselves addressing the occupant of the White House as Madame President. We would have 32 gentlewomen in the U.S. Senate. . . . our entire House of Representatives would be composed of women. . . . There would be 33 women governors . . . even the dog catchers would wear skirts. (*CSM*, 8 March 1948)

Such potential strength required some accommodation. Male leaders of both parties supported Equal Rights Amendment planks in their platforms, and both began to appoint token women to positions of apparent power. At the 1940 Democratic Convention, women were admitted to the Platform Committee on equal terms with men; the Republicans did the same in 1944. By the 1948 conventions about 10 percent of the delegates were women, and both conventions chose women for officers that year. Reporting on these measures, syndicated columnist George Dixon, who habitually referred to women as "dolls," began to fret about the "tremendous and comparatively sudden influx of women into politics" (*WP*, 19 September 1948). Women participants were not fooled. They realized their positions were window dressing and did not constitute a restructuring of the political community. Eleanor Roosevelt pointed out that

> shortly before election time the men of both political parties always make this appeal to women. In between times, however, the ideas women may have on how women are best organized, and how their interests are best kept alive in political questions, are a matter of very little concern to the men officials of either party. (*NYWT*, 1 November 1948)

Smith for Something

Among the Republicans, Margaret Chase Smith became the catalyst for an escalating effort to secure the elusive "women's vote." At a pre-inauguration dinner in her honor, Robert "Mr. Republican" Taft, lamenting his party's recent humiliating defeat, hailed the new Senator as the "Joan of Arc who may lead the Republican Party to victory" (*PPH*, 20 January 1949). In March, Broadway columnist Dorothy Kilgallen broke the story that a number of top-ranking Republicans were "dead serious" about promoting Margaret Smith for the vice presidency in order to capitalize on her "political sex appeal" and her ability to give the party the "jazzing up" it needed; by June, Smith allegedly had enough delegates lined up to ensure her the vice presidential nomination in 1952 (*WTH,* 26 March 1949; 5 June 1949). Columnist Jack Lait added more details, describing "a secret confab" in New York between the GOP hierarchy and Smith to cement her candidacy in an "attempt to stampede the feminine voters" (*NYM,* 7 September 1949).

Rumors of vice presidential possibilities escalated into presidential fantasies. Imagine a woman president. . . . Would she require a "lady Secret Service"? Would she have the presidential plane redecorated in chartreuse and pink? Would romance bloom in the White House between the President and Vice President? And if so, who then would be the real President? (*WTH,* 19 June 1949). Smith had fun with it all, too. When NBC commentator Robert Trout asked her, "What would you do, Senator Smith, if you woke up some morning and found yourself in the White House?" she replied, "I think I'd go right to Mrs. Truman, apologize, and go right home" (Smith Papers).

Despite the levity of the public discussion, or perhaps because of it, interest in women in politics, and in the nation's highest office, seemed to be intensifying. The latest Gallup Poll reported that 48 percent of voters were willing to support a qualified woman for president; the percentage had climbed from 33 percent in 1937 (Gallup 1972). What was significant about Smith's possibilities, observed a Maine daily, was that "hard-headed pols" were considering the matter. "Whatever the outcome of this discussion, it is a real tribute to the political acumen and the demonstrated ability of Mrs. Smith" (*BDN,* 10 October 1949). May Craig figured it could go either way. Her friend was "a liberal in a Republican Party whose leaders are reactionary. That may put the kibosh on her candidacy for vice president—or it may induce the leaders to try to sweeten their ticket with liberal Margaret Smith" (*PPH,* 22 April 1950).

Finally even Maine's senior Senator, Owen Brewster, who had vigorously supported her opponent during the campaign and had been saying behind her back that Mrs. Smith had been a New Dealer ever since she first came to Washington, clambered aboard the "Smith-for-Something" bandwagon, telling reporters that the new Senator "would make a very attractive candidate on the national Republican ticket" and assuring them that he spoke not of Mrs. Smith's "physical charm alone, but also her demonstrated capacity to get votes" (*NYT,* 12 November 1949). Esteem that Senator Taft had earlier expressed seemed, in light of the current discussion, portentous. Put on the spot by reporters, he somewhat reluctantly conceded that Senator Smith would make an ideal candidate for Vice President, although, he hastily added, he knew of no efforts toward that goal (*PST*, 10 April 1949). The press ran with it: Taft and Smith would balance conservative and progressive, business and labor, male and female, "ability and magnetism" (*WS*, 19 April 1950).

Smith added spark to the speculation when she remarked during a radio address that she believed women should fight for a spot on the national tickets of both parties and that the "party that nominates a woman for vice president or president will win the 1952 election." Since Smith was the Grand Old Party's exemplary woman and vote-getter extraordinaire, her quick disclaimer that she was not seeking such a seat for herself, but would fight for other qualified women candidates, was largely ignored (Smith Papers). Despite all the talk, Smith was politically wise enough to know that she had no chance of being taken seriously for such a post. After five straight losses, Republicans might be desperate for a change, but not that desperate. Smith knew, for example, that she had little to offer the GOP ticket other than her gender, which she rightly believed was not enough. The "women's vote" was too ephemeral to count on and likely to be won by less drastic means. In addition, Smith had few electoral votes to deliver; Maine would vote Republican in any case. While she might appeal to the more progressive wing of the party, they were a decided minority and, especially as the Cold War intensified, represented the insurgency, not the leadership.

Margaret Smith's response to everyone who asked about her aspirations was to note that by entertaining the notion she had disqualified herself, and, although she was flattered—"In that way, perhaps, I'm more woman than senator" (Smith Papers)—she was simply not interested in having any other duty than representing the people of Maine in the Senate. Nonetheless, she took advantage of her access to the public forum to press her GOP colleagues to actively demonstrate their commitment to gender equality and to urge her female listeners to seize the moment. Merit alone would not eliminate inequality, she said, so women must make more effective use of their "majority voting power," not to gain any "special privileges" for women but to counter "the silent ban by men against electing and appointing women to public office just because they are women" (Smith Papers).

The ERA Conundrum

Unwilling to surrender partisan advantage to the Republicans, Democrats scrutinized their rosters for a prospective woman Senator of their own. India Edwards, vice chairwoman of the Democratic National Committee, petitioned major women's organizations that had supported

Smith to endorse Helen Gahagan Douglas in her Senate bid in California. Both NFBPW President Dr. K. Frances Scott and Mrs. J. Blair Buck, president of the General Federation of Women's Clubs, acknowledged that while their organizations were supposed to be non-partisan, they had actively supported Smith's candidacy, not on the basis of party but because she was a woman. On this basis, Edwards pressed them to do the same for Douglas (*WP*, 26 November 1949).

The situation quickly became more complex when it was revealed that Helen Douglas had opposed the ERA, a stand which both of her male opponents and the California BPW, along with other national women's groups, supported. This raised the complicated question of whether women would, or should, support other women, regardless of party affiliation. The California BPW's answer was no (*SFC*, 9 January 1950). Douglas lost her race for the Senate to Richard Nixon in what would later be described as one of the dirtiest campaigns in American history. Tarring her with the brush of leftist ideology as well as gender, Nixon repeatedly referred to Douglas as the "pink lady," an attribution to her supposed Communist sympathies. Coming at the height of Cold War hysteria, such a combination was devastating (Scobie 1992).

How significant the BPW endorsement might have been is questionable, but it spoke to the very heart of "the women's vote"—whether women, espousing a variety of perspectives and opinions, also possessed a gender solidarity of sufficient strength to overcome differences to speak with a unified voice. Divisions among women seemed most apparent in the odyssey of the Equal Rights Amendment. Women were irrevocably split between those with a passion for equality and those who believed legislation must recognize the cultural impositions women face in American society, and the line was closely drawn along class lines. Women who supported the ERA, like Smith, were mostly upper- and middle-class business and professional women, who placed their emphasis on personal freedom and accomplishment, values relevant to women who aspired to compete equally with men in public arenas. They contended that protective legislation, any legislation that distinguished between the sexes, did more harm than good. Those opposed to the ERA, by and large working-class women, had no intention of surrendering the hard-fought gains provided them in protective legislation for some abstract notion of equality (Cott 1987; Harrison 1988).

An equal rights amendment had been proposed in every Congress since 1923. Efforts on its behalf were intensified during the war years, when recognition of women's contributions was acute. Margaret Smith was the first Congresswoman to endorse the ERA in 1943, and in 1945, Smith teamed with Edith Nourse Rogers to cosponsor the bill, the first women to take that initiative. In nearly every Congress until she left office in 1973, Smith cosponsored the amendment. The Equal Rights Amendment was entirely consistent with Smith's belief in strict equality for all people. The ERA, she argued on the Senate floor, "is not a petticoat measure.

> It is a measure designed to give fuller meaning and expression to the traditional American way of life. . . . I am in favor of the Equal Rights Amendment to the Constitution. . . . neither race, nor color, nor creed, nor sex must be permitted to be the basis for agitation for special rights and special treatment under the guise of . . . equality. (*Congressional Record*, 23 January 1950)

Repeatedly, legislators found the measure easy to shelve with the argument that women themselves could not agree on its merit.

Title VII

The closest approximation that women now have to legislation granting them equal rights is Title VII, a simple phrase that hitched a ride on the Civil Rights Act of 1964. During the debate in the House of Representatives on the Equal Employment Provision of the Civil Rights Act—Title VII—Judge Howard Smith, Democrat from Virginia, proposed that the word "sex" be added to the phrase that barred discrimination in employment on the basis of race, creed, color, and national origin. It is widely assumed that he did so for the express purpose of making the provision so controversial that it would probably be defeated. It had the opposite effect, however, in that, once the word was there, few were willing to take the political risk of speaking out in opposition to women to remove it. Others resisted denying to white women what would be granted to black men if the Civil Rights Bill passed. Hence the bill, including the sex provision in Title VII, passed the House and moved to the Senate (Whalen and Whalen 1985).

Margaret Smith's intervention in the progress of this legislation during informal negotiations in the Senate changed the course of women's history. At the regular luncheon meeting of the Republican Conference, Senate Minority Leader Everett Dirksen announced his intention to propose 40 amendments to Title VII in order to weaken federal control over its provisions and stated unequivocally that the sex stipulation would have to go. The sole woman Senator confronted Dirksen: "Do you mean to say that you are going to state on the floor of the Senate that the Republican Policy Committee voted to strike the word 'sex' and have it known around the country that the Republican Party is opposed to women?" (Interview, 30 August 1989). Loath to risk the political consequences she so clearly delineated, Dirksen decided not to pursue the matter further. The amendment stood.

The importance of Smith's colleagues' willingness to take her seriously cannot be overstated. The United States Senate was a closed society with firmly established norms and an intolerance for mavericks. Leadership was diffuse, and power required cooperation (Matthews 1960; White 1968; Baker 1980). What kind of a woman was acceptable to her colleagues? Her mentor on the Naval Affairs Committee, Chairman Carl Vinson, wrote that "while Mrs. Smith retains her charming femininity . . . she never insists upon feminine prerogatives or privileges. She is an exceptional woman—but she is an extremely effective champion of National Security before she is a woman" (Smith Papers). Smith earned her legitimacy through large electoral margins, experience, and seniority. She took the lead in narrow areas where she had a certain level of expertise, as she did in military defense matters, or where she felt a certain level of passion, as in her consistent denunciation of injustice and extremism, most forcefully demonstrated by her Declaration of Conscience speech in 1950 against the depredations of her colleague Senator Joseph McCarthy (Smith 1972).

Gendered Political Dangers

In taking on the role of Senator-at-large, Smith became entangled in opposing demands, working for women while trying to distance herself from gender considerations in Congress. She was caught between a denial and an affirmation as a representative of women, either one of which was politically dangerous. How dangerous became apparent when a new generation of activist women began what would later be termed the women's movement. The seeds of hope for genuine equality, fertilized with generous portions of frustration and disappointment, blossomed in the 1960s into a radical movement of women who demanded more than a legislative guarantee of legal equality. These young women, impatient with the conservative approach, dismayed by the individualistic explanations and self-blame of the earlier generation, demanded a recognition of women's cultural and social responsibilities as well as legal restrictions. They proposed a sophisticated and complex reformulation of cultural values which, while including equal rights, went well beyond them to articulate a radical challenge to cultural definitions of male and female (Evans 1980; Harrison 1988).

The gender strategies and the conservative methods of Senator Smith were no longer salient. Gender discourse had shifted from liberal individualism to radical feminism. Where once the ERA had been considered the pinnacle of social change, to radical women seeking to alter social norms, it was inadequate and beside the point. As one activist put it, "the gut issues of women's liberation cannot be legislated away. We want revolution, not evolution" (Smith Papers). Those who still encouraged women to seek political office and use it to advance women's causes clustered in the liberal wing of the women's movement, including the National Organization for Women. Changing demographic patterns and the strategies of the President's Commission on the Status of Women, initially instituted by President Kennedy to sabotage the ERA, effectively narrowed the gap between ERA advocates and the liberal Women's Bureau coalition (which had earlier felt threatened with the loss of protective workplace legislation) in support of the ERA within a broader program for women's equality (Harrison 1988). As a result, assistance was extended primarily to political women who advocated a liberal agenda in addition to the ERA. Ironically, then, support for the ERA became equated with liberal politics where once it had been the hallmark of conservative women. In short, the ground had shifted while Smith had not. If anything, she had become increasingly conservative in an increasingly radical milieu.[8]

Wrong Kind of Woman

In 1972, during Senator Smith's final campaign, the president of the Maine chapter of the National Organization for Women called a press conference to denounce her as a "warmonger," an "elitist," and a "token woman" who cared nothing for women's concerns. Maine's by-now-senior Senator, she said, "represents everything women in the liberation movement want to eliminate" (*PPH*, 28 June 1972). Another group of Maine women, mothers and peace activists, holding militarism as repugnant as sexism, deemed Smith, as a member of the Senate Armed Services Committee, responsible for formulating and implementing military policies in the Vietnam War (*PPH*, 12 July 1972). Where once Maine women had been the mainstay of Margaret Chase Smith's campaign organization, the new more vocal women's groups were working actively to discredit her.

Changes in the perception of Margaret Chase Smith over more than two decades, from a trailblazer destined to lead women to political equality to the warmonger who deserted the women's movement, was as much a function of the changing composition of activist women as it was a critique of Smith's politics. Most of the women who greeted Smith in 1949 were women involved in business and the professions, as well as those who worked within the traditional political system or sought entry into it. Women activists in the late 1960s were young, radical and disdainful of traditional politics, and disdainful too of the few "token" women who had "made it."

For her part, Margaret Smith was angered and dismayed by their unladylike tactics and vulgar confrontations. Her political and personal philosophy favored moderation and negotiation aimed at practical if gradual change. She found radical feminism and the tactics of the women's movement inappropriate and counterproductive, and she was both angered and embarrassed by women whose "ambition and greed for power are out front. . . . Good people don't go out front and holler about it" (Interview, 8 December 1989). They insisted on being confrontational, adversarial, and extremist, when it was simply more sensible, she believed, to persuade than confront.

> I fear that the over-militancy and belligerency of some women's movements [sic] have been the real causes of the setback to the ERA. The effective method is respectful and courteous persuasion rather than militant and threatening pressure. (Smith Papers)

These women had ruined a worthwhile pursuit. "I still support the ERA," she wrote in 1981, "but I fear that the militant, belligerent, brassy bra burners by their repulsive tactics have killed it for several years" (Smith Papers).

Smith felt profoundly disheartened by what she took to be a show of disloyalty from women. Arguments for women's equality, she believed, could only be strengthened by her example. She had redefined the possibilities; she had blazed the trail for them; she had proved that women could handle the rigors of public office; she had infiltrated the system, and she had mastered it. Margaret Smith had achieved what her generation of women had sought. They should be, she said, "building on women of achievement" (*PEE,* 20 March 1972).

While Smith's rejection by radical feminists had little effect on the outcome of her last election, she remained wary of feminists ever after. Nearly twenty years later, she complained that they had not recognized her accomplishments nor realized the limits of her power.

> Here I was, a woman with this background and this record—I co-sponsored ERA throughout my Senate tenure, stopped Everett Dirksen from knocking the word "sex" out of the Civil Rights bill, got women full regular status in the Armed Services, and championed many women causes in Congress—and they said I didn't do anything. NOW was calling for a male candidate to re-

place me while at the same time calling for more women in political office. They didn't like me because I would not join them, fight with them. But I could not have gotten elected if I did those things. Women just don't understand the political reality. (Interview, 3 September 1989)

Impact

Margaret Chase Smith changed the face of politics. She was the first woman to breach several important barriers to become a visible and positive symbol of political attainment. She initiated, stimulated, and contributed to a complex public discourse that took the idea of women in high national political office seriously. She sustained a long, distinguished political career that, despite her status as a "token" woman, was defined by integrity and independence. Throughout, Smith's ambiguous relationship with other women and with her own gender identity highlighted both the intensity of ideological differences among women and the formal and informal obstacles that continue to check a political woman's potential for meaningful impact on American politics.

Notes

1. Representatives Mary T. Norton (D-N.J.), Edith Nourse Rogers (R-Mass.), Frances P. Bolton (R-Ohio), Helen Gahagan Douglas (D-Calif.), Chase Going Woodhouse (D-Conn.), Katherine St. George (R-N.Y.), Reve Beck Rosone (D-Utah), and Cecil M. Harden (R-Ind.).

2. Among them were the National Women's Party, the General Federation of Women's Clubs, the National Women's Democratic Club, the National Federation of Women's Republican Clubs, the American Association of University Women, the American Women's Association, the Committee of Women in World Affairs, Brooklyn Women's Bar Association, Advertising Women of New York, the National Education Association, the League of Women Voters, and the Woman Jurors Association.

3. Despite great expectations, the Multi-Party Committee ran into financial difficulties almost immediately and decided they could not go ahead with a national effort to raise a million dollars when they faced problems making up a $400 deficit from the "Special."

4. Scholars have noted the importance of women's club activities in politicizing women of the era. These single-sex organizations provided opportunities to learn leadership skills, organizational experience, and contacts with like-minded women within activities deemed acceptable forms of participation by women (Kirkpatrick 1974; Ware 1981; Carroll 1985).

5. Apparently a popular tactic with right-wingers, this technique was used unsuccessfully against Estes Kefauver in his bid for the Senate in Tennessee and led to Claude Pepper's defeat in Florida. This was the same guilt-by-association employed by Richard Nixon to defeat Helen Gahagan Douglas in the 1950 Senate race in California, in which his notorious "pink sheets" listed the parallels between her votes and Marcantonio's.

6. Women in the House in 1940: Mary T. Norton (D-N.J.), Jessie Sumner (R-Ill.), Clare Boothe Luce (R-Conn.), Edith Nourse Rogers (R-Mass.), Winifred Stanley (R-N.Y.), Frances P. Bolton (R-Ohio), and Margaret Chase Smith (R-Maine). Hattie W. Caraway (D-Ark.) was the only woman senator.

7. Although frequently quoted in this manner, the remark was a bit different in context. It came at the end of a long and acrimonious debate with Representative Blanton of Texas over the passage of a series of bills by the District of Columbia Committee, of which Norton was chair. "He kept referring to me patronizingly as 'the lady.' Finally I reminded him that I was not 'the lady,' but a member of Congress" (Norton Papers).

8. Smith's "liberal quotient," a rating of key votes by Americans for Democratic Action, reached its high point in the 1950s and early 1960s, where it topped out at 84 percent in 1964; by 1971 Smith's liberal quotient had slipped to 19 percent. Her rating by the conservative Americans for Constitutional Action rose during the same period, from a low in the mid-20 percent range in the 1960s to a high of 69 percent and 76 percent in 1969 and 1970 respectively (Sharp 1988).

References

Primary Sources

Congressional Record. 81st Congress, 2d Session, 23 January 1950: 770–771.
Lucy Somerville-Howorth Papers. The Arthur and Elizabeth Schlesinger Library on the History of Women in America, Cambridge, Mass. (Howorth Papers)
Mary T. Norton Papers. Alexander Library, New Brunswick, N.J. (Norton Papers)
Margaret Chase Smith Papers. The Margaret Chase Smith Library, Skowhegan, Maine. (Smith Papers)
Smith, Margaret Chase. 1946. *Statements and Speeches*, vol. III.
Smith, Margaret Chase. 1948. *Statements and Speeches*, vol. V.
Smith, Margaret Chase. 1949. *Statements and Speeches*, vol. VI.
Smith, Margaret Chase. 1972. *Declaration of Conscience.* William C. Lewis, Jr., ed. Garden City, N.Y.: Doubleday and Company.
Smith interviews with author: 8 January 1987, 16 March 1987, 18 January 1989, 26 July 1989, 30 August 1989, 3 September 1989, 8 December 1989.

Maine Newspapers

Bangor Commercial (*BC*), Bangor Daily News (*BDN*), Kennebec Journal (*KJ*), Lewiston Journal (*LJ*), Portland Sunday Telegram (*PST*), Portland Evening Express (*PEE*), Portland Press Herald (*PPH*).

National Newspapers

Christian Science Monitor (*CSM*), Chicago Tribune (*CT*), New York Times (*NYT*), New York World-Telegram (*NYWT*), New York Mirror (*NYM*), San Francisco Chronicle (*SFC*), Washington Star (*WS*), Washington Post (*WP*), Washington Times-Herald (*WTH*)

Secondary Sources

Anderson, Karen. 1981. *Wartime Women: Sex Roles, Family Relations, and the Status of Women during World War II*. Westport, Conn.: Greenwood Press.

Baker, Ross. 1980. *Friend and Foe in the U.S. Senate*. New York: The Free Press.

Bowman, Geline MacDonald, and Earline White. 1946. *A History of the National Federation of Business and Professional Women's Clubs, Inc. 1919–1944*. Washington D.C.: National Federation of Business and Professional Women's Clubs.

Brunelle, Jim. 1978. *The Maine Almanac*. Portland: Guy Gannett Publishing Company.

Campbell, D'Ann. 1984. *Women at War with America: Private Lives in a Patriotic Era*. Cambridge, Mass.: Harvard University Press.

Carroll, Susan J. 1985. *Women as Candidates in American Politics*. Bloomington: Indiana University Press.

Chafe, William H. 1972. *The American Woman: Her Changing Social, Economic, and Political Roles, 1920–1970*. New York: Oxford University Press.

Cott, Nancy. 1987. *The Grounding of Modern Feminism*. New Haven: Yale University Press.

Duverger, Maurice. 1955. *The Political Role of Women*. New York: United Nations.

Evans, Sara. 1980. *Personal Politics: The Origins of Women's Liberation in the Civil Rights Movement*. New York: Vintage Publishers.

Gallup, George H. 1972. *The Gallup Poll: Public Opinion, 1935–1971*. Wilmington, Del.: Scholarly Resources.

Gertzog, Irwin N. 1984. *Congressional Women: Their Recruitment, Treatment and Behavior*. Westport, Conn.: Praeger Publishers.

Harrison, Cynthia. 1988. *On Account of Sex: The Politics of Women's Issues 1945–1968*. Berkeley: University of California Press.

Kirkpatrick, Jeane J. 1974. *Political Woman*. New York: Basic Books.

Markel, Helen. 1964. "Twenty-Four Hours in the Life of Margaret Chase Smith." *McCall's* (May): 161.

Matthews, Donald R. 1960. *U.S. Senators and Their World*. Raleigh: University of North Carolina Press.

Oleszek, Walter J. 1984. *Congressional Procedures and the Policy Process.* 2nd ed. Washington D.C.: Congressional Quarterly Press.

Porter, Amy. 1943. "Ladies of Congress." *Colliers,* 28 August, 22.

Rawalt, Marguerite. 1979. *History of the National Federation of the Business and Professional Women's Clubs, Inc.* Vol. II. Washington, D.C.: The National Federation of Business and Professional Women's Clubs.

Sargent, Ruth. 1979. *Gail Laughlin: ERA's Advocate.* Portland: House of Falmouth Publishers.

Scobie, Ingrid Winther. 1992. *Center Stage: Helen Gahagan Douglas, A Life.* New York: Oxford University Press.

Sharp, J. Michael. 1988. *The Directory of Congressional Voting Scores and Interest Group Ratings.* New York: Facts on File Publications.

Sherman, Janann. 1990. "'They either need these women or they do not': Margaret Chase Smith and the Fight for Regular Status for Women in the Military." *The Journal of Military History* 54 (1): 47–78.

Smith, Beverly. 1948. "Senator from the Five-and-Ten." *Saturday Evening Post,* 9 November, 36.

Ware, Susan. 1981. *Beyond Suffrage: Women in the New Deal.* Cambridge, Mass.: Harvard University Press.

Whalen, Charles, and Barbara Whalen. 1985. *The Longest Debate: A Legislative History of the 1964 Civil Rights Act.* New York: New American Library.

White, William S. 1968. *Citadel: The Story of the U.S. Senate.* New York: Houghton Mifflin Company.

Foreign Policy Decision Makers
The Impact of Gender

Nancy E. McGlen and Meredith Reid Sarkees

Particularly in the United States foreign policy arena, women have seldom been interviewed on television, quoted in newspapers, or appointed to positions of authority (Hoynes and Croteau 1989). Affairs of the nation-state in dealing with other nation-states have been considered nearly off-limits to women. Men have been identified as the authorities in this area, and women, if they were seen as having any political expertise at all, were characterized as mostly concerned with social welfare or related domestic political issues. Thus the overall political context of foreign policy has not welcomed women. Ann Tickner has described this masculine domination of international relations in great detail in *Gender in International Relations* (1992).

The exclusion of women and women's interests from the U.S. foreign policy arena has been under serious challenge from feminist groups and women's peace groups for almost two decades, and yet with the possible exceptions of Jeane Kirkpatrick, Madeleine Albright, and Condoleezza Rice, it is almost impossible to identify visible women experts in this field. This state of affairs led us to pose the following questions: Are there less visible women in positions of authority in the foreign policy process? Are they having a distinctive impact on United States policies toward other nations? What problems do they confront in trying to influence the decision process?

Data Collection

With this focus on the role of women in foreign policy formulation, we centered our investigation on the two main foreign policy agencies: the

Department of State and the Department of Defense. The State Department has been the traditional center for American foreign policy, bearing the primary responsibility for the conduct of U.S. relations. However, developments in the 1970s and 1980s led to a decline in the Department's influence and a corresponding rise in power by the White House and the Pentagon. Much of this trend has been attributed to the personalities of recent presidents, such as Nixon, Carter, Reagan, and Bush (though perhaps less so with Clinton). However, it was also seen as a result of the function of the State Department itself, with its relatively passive role of observation, reporting, negotiation, and advisement, compared with the Defense Department's primary function of action (Bloomfield 1982, 42–43).

The military became the largest implementer of policy decisions. Additionally, reorganization measures, which consolidated five of the nine intelligence agencies within the Department of Defense, also made the Pentagon into the largest gatherer and supplier of information for the foreign policy formulation process (Rainey 1975, 179). As a result, the postwar record of U.S. foreign policy is replete with evidence of a military approach to foreign affairs, most recently seen in Eastern Europe. These trends reinforced our decision to examine the Departments of State and Defense.

Restricting ourselves to the two Departments in the Executive Branch most responsible for setting foreign policy, we next set out to identify the women in those Departments who were in positions of influence. We chose to include women (and a companion sample of men) political appointees plus career service employees in the upper echelons of both Departments (Senior Executive Service and Senior Foreign Service). Although, as most of our respondents noted, policy is influenced below the level of Senior Executive/Senior Foreign Service, most significant policy is made at those levels or higher.

Identifying the women in those positions we wanted to interview was not always easy. While the Department of Defense and its military branches were generally cooperative in sending along names, addresses, and sometimes phone numbers (only the Army's came too late to be included), the Department of State defied almost all our efforts to obtain the information. We suspect our difficulties and those of others who have sought this information stem from the numerous legal challenges the Department has faced for sex discrimination (see *Palmer v. Baker* 1987, 1989).

By the time we conducted our interviews, in the summer of 1988, we had names of 55 women in the Department of Defense and the Department of State who fulfilled our criteria. We were able to interview, in person or by mail, 41 (or 74.5%) of these women. In order to be able to compare the experiences of men and women, we also interviewed a group of 38 men, randomly selected from the same lists used to identify the women.

Our goal in conducting this research was to address three central questions: Do women have an impact on foreign policy formulation, and in what ways do women's impacts differ from those of their male colleagues? What are women's policy goals and accomplishments? And do women makers of foreign policy have different foreign policy priorities than male policy-makers? It is our general contention that the political context of foreign affairs has significantly shaped the answers to these questions.

Political Context

In a study of women federal executives, Danity Little noted that the culture of an executive department (similar to our concept of political context) played a critical role. This culture included "how a department felt about women in the workplace, determined how each woman was employed, what opportunities were available, and how much support she received" (1994, 124). In our conception, the political context of foreign policy (specifically in the State and Defense Departments) consists of a number of elements including departmental ethos, ecological context, and social demography. In an extended analysis of our data (McGlen and Sarkees 1993), we examined the means by which the interaction of the ethos, ecological context, and social demography of both Departments has limited and continues to limit the ability of women to influence foreign policy. For instance, in terms of departmental ethos, we found that the Departments of both State and Defense have historically explicitly excluded women from the decision-making process. Indeed, as late as 1989, the Appeals Court found in *Palmer v. Baker* that the State Department still systematically discriminated against female Foreign Service officers.

The ecological context, or organization, of both Departments also undermines women's positions. Since both are extremely hierarchical structures, women have found it difficult to break into the decision-making ranks at State and Defense. This finding dovetails with the perception of a "glass ceiling" which has made it difficult for women to reach senior policy-making positions throughout the federal government (Little 1994). Moreover, women who do find themselves in higher-ranking positions are often segregated by the internal topography of both Departments to areas with limited impact on foreign policy, such as personnel and legal services in Defense and consular and administrative affairs in State. As one women executive explained:

> The top positions are all filled by men. It is basically a power club, and you don't push your way into that world. They can pull a few of us up. But the major jobs, the more critical jobs, are basically held by men, military and civilian, in the Department of Defense.

Lastly, we found that the social demography, or the ability of women to fit into each Department, is severely hampered by traditional views of women's knowledge and training in foreign and military affairs. In the State Department, women reported that traditional stereotypes about women in other countries and our own served to hamper the effectiveness of women in positions of authority. As a high-ranking woman noted, when asked whether there were any views about women that limited her influence or the influence of other women in the Department:

> They tend to be mostly behavior views. The fear of the shrieker. The fear of a woman's uncontrolled anger. It's in that area of not being confident about how a woman would play the game. . . . I'm confident when I took this job three years ago there was great skepticism as to whether I would fit in. Could a woman fit in? Because you bring a new element to the physical appearance of a meeting, it changes, and it's upsetting. Are you going to make things difficult for them? Or are you going to be a great show? Are you going to be a bitch to deal with? And there is usually an effort to handle that problem by cutting you out.

In the Defense Department, women's ability to influence the decision-making process is further hampered because women generally lack the military training and background of many male decision makers in the Department. A woman in the naval weapons area outlines the problem:

> In the military, military themselves have a discrimination against civilians whether they're male or female, because most civilians have not been in operations. So there is that bias or perception that civilians don't know what they're talking about. Then when you put the women on top of that, it makes it even a little worse. So DOD is a very macho world. You just don't have that many military women at the top officer, at the admiral or general, level. And

the ones we have, we have laws that prevent females from serving in combat positions, and that, in essence, is the hard core of the military. If the military stays male, women will always be less effective because they have not had to demonstrate to peers, to male peers, that they know what they are talking about because they have not been "under fire." Put it in quotes because there's a lot of men who have not been "under fire" either.

Because neither Department has been very hospitable to women, the overall political context of foreign policy is even more difficult for women than other realms. The few women who have made it to positions of authority face a difficult task in attempting to influence foreign policy. Yet here our primary concern is more positive. We wish to examine what impact these women in foreign policy have had. How were they able to cope with a difficult political context? Were they able to influence policy in spite of the handicaps they faced?

Policy Impact

In trying to gauge impact on foreign policy, we asked a number of questions designed to tap a person's perception of his or her influence. Before examining their responses, it should be noted that the people in our sample were in positions that affect foreign policy in a variety of ways. Within the Defense Department, we interviewed people involved in weapons technology, force analysis, and bilateral or multilateral negotiations. In the State Department, our interviewees occupied positions such as area directors and ambassadors. In all, their job responsibilities ranged from providing legal advice, budgetary control, and personnel recruitment to specific formulation of U.S. foreign policy toward other countries. All those we talked to felt that they had an impact or influence on policy-making, in general, though the women were somewhat more likely than the men (82.9% versus 71.2%) to consider their jobs as directly involving foreign policy formulation. There were, however, departmental differences, with our respondents in Defense less likely than those in State (69.8% versus 86.1%) to characterize their jobs as involving the making or implementing of foreign policy. Interestingly, it was primarily the men in the Defense Department who were reluctant to see their positions as involving foreign policy. About 80 percent or more of the men in State and the women in both Departments saw their job involving foreign policy, while this was true for only 50 percent of the men we interviewed at the Defense Department.

Policy Goals

In attempting to gauge whether our respondents came to their positions with a pre-planned agenda, we asked them whether they had a specific policy goal or goals when they took their current job. Not surprisingly, a large majority (73.4%) could identify one or more policies they had hoped to implement, and in this there was no difference between men and women. In terms of those who had initial goals, the women were more likely than the men (45.7% versus 35.5%) to have had specific foreign policy goals. Some of the goals the women cited were far from minor, ranging from negotiations on INF and ICBM modernization to advancing human rights issues in the Middle East. We then tried to ascertain whether our respondents were able to achieve their goals. The overwhelming majority (94.5%) of those who had goals saw themselves as having at least partially achieved their goals, with no significant difference between men and women. In trying to gauge impact along another scale, we asked our respondents to list their major policy accomplishments. Men were more likely than women (58.8% versus 41.7%) to mention foreign policy as an area where they had some success, although the difference was not statistically significant.

However, it is when examining the other types of accomplishments (not in terms of policy formulation) that we really saw the first statistically significant differences between men and women. Women were twice as likely as men (63.2% versus 31.4%) to list management accomplishments, such as multiplying the programs in their area, introducing automation, increasing productivity of staff, and formalizing the strategic planning process. Women were also much more likely to list accomplishments that affect women (18.4% versus 5.7%) and accomplishments in improvement of human relations (24.3% versus 8.6%). These comments from one woman in the State Department give a flavor of the kinds of goals some of the women reported:

> My proudest accomplishment for this office is that if anybody walked in here now, they would say that my office would be a model of EEO goals. It is a personal thing of mine that I think about a great deal, because when I was first looking for a job in 1971 they didn't have any. A number of times I went to government agencies and they looked at me and said, "We have our woman lawyer, thank you very much." And that was in 1971. And it always stuck in my mind that I wouldn't do that. And I really work at, for myself, where I worked truly reflecting an integrated society. . . . That's a personal achievement I'm proud of.

Despite the fact that our women respondents saw themselves as having positive impacts on policy formulation, many also saw "being a woman" as a handicap. Thirty-six percent of women and 26 percent of men indicated that being a woman (for themselves or their female colleagues) limits women's ability to influence foreign policy. As one woman observed:

> That is the way society is. A man is assumed competent till he opens his mouth and proves he isn't, and a woman is assumed she isn't until she opens her mouth and proves she is. [It is] a very subtle kind of thing, but it requires energy and time to overcome, so it keeps us from being as effective as we might be.

One man expressed the same view in discussing his woman colleagues, "I think there is still a tendency to discount what they [women] say. I think it is unfortunate that women have to work 50 percent harder to get the same recognition as their male counterparts."

About a quarter of both the men and the women also agreed that public stereotypes about women's lack of knowledge concerning foreign affairs affect the ability of women in their department to have an influence on foreign policy. A man responded: "Yes, I think inevitably and unfortunately. Initial impact only [and] initial assumptions are easily overcome by demonstration. If a man or woman demonstrates competence, most people's attitudes will change quickly." Others were less certain that the effects of the stereotypes were so short-term. A woman described the limitation as follows:

> Sometimes you have to prove yourself first. I've had some advantages and disadvantages. When I came through with a very creative solution and a very useful solution to a problem when I was early into the position, I would get double credit for it because, "My God, she can think." . . . However, they might not have asked me because they might have assumed, "Well, she wouldn't know." But once you come through you'd get more credit than a man would have gotten. Now that I have been around for a long time, that has evened out. But it is harder for a woman to get to that position and be accepted and recognized. People assume [she] is a token.

Even larger numbers of women and men (71% and 49% respectively) cited other public views or characteristics of women that hindered their influence on policy decisions. Such views included "The usual cliches: emotional; detail-oriented; afraid to make unpopular decisions." Women also felt themselves limited by beliefs that it is somewhat unnatural for women to be working, that women are less serious about their careers, that they are less quantitative, that they are unable to understand military exigencies, and that they get bogged down on appearances and trivialities. Several women also reported that physical attractiveness was a negative attribute: "The public thinks that if she looks nice, it means you don't have any brains." "I have seen beautiful women not taken seriously because they were beautiful."

Interestingly, the recognition of stereotypes (publicly or personally held) about women's ability or knowledge did not seem to affect women's estimates of their own personal power in the foreign policy arena. Asked to rank their own influence on a seven-point scale from little to great influence, women's scores were not significantly different from the men's rankings. Having seen that women were as likely as men to come to their jobs with goals, achieve those goals and, at least in their own estimate, influence foreign policy, the next question we posed was: What kind of influence did they have in their jobs? Were their views on foreign policy questions the same as men's, or was there a "women's point of view" on issues of international affairs?

Foreign Policy Opinions and the "Gender Gap"

Our expectations regarding men and women's policy views are shaped by the theoretical and philosophic literature on women and peace, and by two conflicting bodies of data: that based on studies of citizens or public opinion, and that which relies on research conducted using responses from elites.

There is little consensus in the theoretical literature addressing the differences between women and men. While a few theorists focus on a biological explanation for differences between women and men (Burns 1992), others rely on differential socialization as the explanatory variable (Miller 1986). Variations on the latter include those who emphasize the influence of motherhood. Perhaps this view is best exemplified by the work of Sara Ruddick (1980, 1983a, 1983b, 1984). Borrowing heavily from the work of Chodorow (1978), Ruddick posits that women's training as mothers, or as daughters of mothers, gives rise to maternal thinking (1984) or preservative love (1983b). Maternal thinking, Ruddick posits, is not compatible with military practices. Mothers want to preserve life, not destroy it. Other feminists have criticized Ruddick, noting that there is little support for a special ethic of care among women (Conover and Sapiro 1993). Jean Bethke Elshstain (1987) in her work *Women and War* argues, for instance, that there are numerous examples from ancient and modern times demonstrating that women played important roles in war, as either supportive mothers and wives or actual combatants. The cultural conception of women's naturally peaceful nature, she posits, has only developed since the eighteenth century. Others, such as Cynthia Fuchs Epstein, conclude that there are no fundamental attitudinal differences between men and women (1988, 186), while still others posit that what may be critical is women's (or men's) levels of feminism (Conover 1988).

The data from citizen-level research tends to support the arguments of those who would expect women to hold different views from men. Indeed, we find a number of studies that report significant gender-based differences, labeled the "gender gap." Although it is the subject of much recent concern, polls dating from the 1930s also found women to be less hawkish than men on defense issues. For many years it was predicted that this gap would have a large impact on electoral behavior, yet no significant differences surfaced until 1980, when partisan behavior between the sexes benefited Democratic candidates (Carroll 1985; Frankovic 1982; Kenski 1988; Lake 1982; Miller 1983, 1986; Mueller 1988). The most widely accepted explanation for women's reluctance to vote for Ronald Reagan focused on women's more pacifist nature. This position, first offered by Frankovic (1982), holds that women rejected Reagan and the Republican Party because of the perception that Reagan would lead the nation into war (Lake 1982; Miller 1983, 1986).[1]

This emphasis on women as pacifists has been noted not only in electoral politics but in studies of foreign policy beliefs as well. An early analysis by Smith (1984) found significant differences between men and women on matters concerning the use of force in domestic and international relations, with the average difference between men and women around 9 percentage points. A follow-up study by Shapiro and Mahajan (1986), using thousands of survey questionnaires collected by the major polling organizations, also found significant differences between men and women on a whole range of issues. Looking specifically at questions dealing with force in foreign affairs (including issues of defense spending, missile systems, selling arms, and other related topics), Shapiro and Mahajan found that in the period from 1964 to 1983, women, on the average, were about 6.2 percentage points less likely than men to choose a "pro-force" response. Similarly, in their study of American voters and their attitudes concerning national security issues, the Daniel Yankelovich Group (1988) found that the "gender gap" existed on a number of issues. Women were more critical than men of the harmful effects of defense spending. They were also more concerned than men about a wider range of threats to our national security (Yankelovich 1988, 2).

Conover and Sapiro, using the responses in the 1991 National Election Study, found that even when controlling for background and attitudinal variables, women were more isolationist and more fearful of war than men. Interestingly, they found no significant differences in women's and men's willingness to consider the use of force in certain circumstances (1993, 1,089). Women were also significantly more upset than men by the conduct of the Persian Gulf War, although they were no less attentive to it (1993, 1,095). In searching for explanations of the gender gaps in foreign policy, Conover and Sapiro found no support for the mothering hypothesis and little for the feminism explanation. Income, education, and patriotism did help to explain some of the differences between women, yet they did not eliminate the gender gap. They conclude that

Gender differences, then, are greatest for emotional reactions to real conflicts, and they disappear for some cognitive assessments of hypothetical cases. Taken together, these patterns suggest that such differences are socially constructed and contextually driven. Moreover, the fact that they cannot be eliminated by controlling for the effects of a wide range of other explanatory elements points to a pervasive, gendered pattern of early learning of cognitive and especially affective orientation toward the use of violence, particularly in the form of conflict resolution. (1095–1096)

In contrast to the proliferation of studies examining the gender gap in mass politics, there has been relatively little written specifically addressing the question of foreign policy differences among elites. Probably most well known are the studies conducted by Ole R. Holsti and James N. Rosenau (1981, 1984, 1988, and 1995), examining foreign policy beliefs of people in leadership positions from 1976 to 1988. Their data were derived from mail surveys of America's leaders, within and outside government, including those in education, media, business, law, foreign service, public office, and the military. Originally, in analyzing the 1976 results (1981), they had found only limited support for a gender gap. "On many of the issues that have dominated foreign policy discourse during the post–World War II era, differences among men and women are substantially less impressive than are the similarities" (1981, 337, 338). There were some differences between women and men, however, with women opposing using the CIA to undermine hostile governments and being more inclined to favor a more restricted international role for the United States (1981, 339). Seeking to explain the origins of these differences, Holsti and Rosenau noted that there were significant differences between their male and female leaders in terms of their occupations, with women "clustered in two occupations (educators [26.8%] and media leaders [14.7%]), whose members are more likely to take a 'dovish' position on international issues, whereas a high proportion of male leaders are to be found in the more 'hawkish' occupations (military officers [24.3%] and business executives [13.4%])" (1981, 332). After controlling for occupation, few if any gender differences survived, leading Holsti and Rosenau to conclude that "the dominant lines of cleavage among this sample of respondents are those defined by occupation. Military officers and business executives, including both men and women, provide the strongest support" for Cold War issues (1981, 342). This lack of a gender gap among elites reappeared in a subsequent analysis, in which Holsti and Rosenau concluded:

These results do not necessarily relegate the "gender gap" to the status of myth, but they suggest that a distinction between leaders and others may be as important for women as it is for men. The evidence from three surveys during an eight-year span indicates that women in leadership positions hold political attitudes that are generally quite similar to those of men in comparable roles. Liberal women are likely to resemble liberal men; Republican women tend to resemble Republican men, and so on. (1988, 288)

In a later study Holsti (1990) did note that there might be some gender-based differences emerging because of shifting attitudes among women. Holsti and Rosenau's article (1995) specifically examined the impact of gender on foreign policy beliefs over the twelve-year period. They generalized that their studies showed a convergence between women and men in 1980 and 1984. Their results were more mixed in the 1988 data. Although, as in the earlier studies, occupation, ideology, and political party were the primary correlates of foreign policy beliefs, there remained a slight gender gap, with differences reflecting "a greater aversion among women to foreign entanglements that includes, but is not limited to, military interventions abroad." Yet their overall conclusion, that gender does not rival ideology, partisanship, or occupation as the predominant determinant of foreign policy beliefs among elites, provides a contrast to the general public opinion data indicating a gender gap. In investigating a similar topic, Caprioli and Boyer (1998) analyzed the international crisis behaviors of national leaders, focusing on women national leaders and other enlightened leaders. They similarly found that female leaders "were certainly aggressive in their actions and not observably more peaceful than men in their crisis interactions" (1998, 18). Correspondingly, in a review of several women national leaders, Michael Genovese concluded that "None of these women has been a 'revolutionary' leader, and overall they have tended to be spread across the ideological spectrum" (1993, 213). It is the divergence between the general public and elite data sets which creates the parameters for our study, providing differing expectations for behavior of those in the foreign policy formulation process.

The Gender Gap among Foreign Policy Decision Makers

In attempting to answer the question whether women in foreign policy decision-making positions hold different views from men in those positions, we first asked respondents whether they saw themselves as having different priorities in foreign policy than their counterparts of the opposite sex. Most of the respondents reported that they did not see any differences. Men were especially likely to think their views were similar, with only 5.6 percent seeing a difference. Among women, one out of five reported differences from their male colleagues, yet few of the answers given in the follow-up question focused on policy differences. Rather, those women and men seeing differences were more likely to focus on management style. Only a few gave any response which might be called policy differences, and even those were quite vague. For instance, a few of the respondents noted that women were more likely to be concerned about people.

It is possible, however, that the perception that women in the foreign policy arena hold the same foreign policy views as men may not reflect reality. To examine this possibility, we asked the respondents a long series of questions requiring them to indicate the importance of various foreign policy goals for the United States and their level of agreement with some general statements that have been made concerning U.S. foreign policy. Although the focus of our study is a narrower, more specialized, elite than those in the Holsti-Rosenau study, we saw their leaders as a valid comparison group. Therefore, we used a number of questions from the Holsti-Rosenau study in this part of our survey. In addition, we asked respondents to indicate their attitude toward current issues in American foreign policy, to classify their general views in political matters ranging from far right to far left, and to tell us their partisan affiliation.

Looking first at the general political orientation of the respondents, we found that the women in the sample were significantly more conservative than the men (See Table 6.1). Among the women, 44.8 percent

Table 6.1. Political Views of Men and Women in the Departments of
State and Defense[a]

	Overall	Overall		State		Defense	
Political Ideology		Men	Women	Men	Women	Men	Women
Far Left	0	0	0	0	0	0	0
Very Liberal	1.4	2.8	0	0	0	6.3	0
Somewhat Liberal	18.9	27.8	10.5	20.0	20.0	37.5	4.3
Middle of the Road	43.2	41.7	44.7	55.0	40.0	25.0	47.8
Somewhat Conservative	27.0	22.2	31.6	25.0	33.3	18.8	30.4
Very Conservative	9.5	5.6	13.2	0	6.7	12.5	17.4
		tau$_c$ = −.28*		tau$_c$ = −.13		tau$_c$ = −.35*	

[a]Figures represent the percentage of men and women in each of the categories. A negative correlation indicates women are more conservative. Correlations for the subgroups not reported in the table were as follows: Men and women appointees at State, tau$_c$ = −.14; men and women career at State, tau$_c$ =.18; men and women appointees at Defense, tau$_c$ = .04; and men and women career at Defense, tau$_c$ = −.38*. Respondents giving don't know, depends, or no response were excluded from the analysis.

*significant at the .05 level

**significant at the .01 level

indicated that they saw themselves as very or somewhat conservative, while only 27.8% of the men chose either of these two categories (tau$_c$ = −.28). These figures contrast sharply with those of the general public. A New York Times public opinion poll (Cowan 1989), taken at the same time as our survey, found that 32 percent of women and 37 percent of the men considered themselves conservative. This would seem to suggest that perhaps the types of policymaking positions of our interviewees appeal more to women with a conservative bent.

When we divided responses according to whether they were from the State Department or the Defense Department and whether they were political appointees or career civil servants, the picture became more complex. While there were no significant differences between men and women in the State Department generally or in the subcategories at State, there were significant differences between men and women in the Defense Department. Overall, women were significantly more conservative (tau$_c$ = −.35), and even among career civil servants, women

Table 6.2. Party Identification of Men and Women in the Departments of
State and Defense[a]

	Overall	Overall		State		Defense	
Party Identity		Men	Women	Men	Women	Men	Women
Strong Democrat	7.0	5.7	8.3	0	14.3	11.8	4.5
Weak Democrat	14.1	11.4	16.7	5.6	21.4	17.6	13.6
Independent— Leaning Democrat	14.1	22.9	5.6	27.8	14.3	17.6	0
Independent	15.5	20.0	11.1	22.2	7.1	17.6	13.6
Independent— Leaning Republican	11.3	17.1	5.6	16.7	0	17.6	9.1
Weak Republican	12.7	8.6	16.7	11.1	0	5.9	27.3
Strong Republican	25.4	14.3	36.1	16.7	42.9	11.8	31.8
		$tau_c = -.17$		$tau_c = .08$		$tau_c = -.41^*$	

[a]Figures represent the percentage of men and women in each of the categories. A negative correlation indicates women are more likely to identify with the Republican Party. Correlations for the subgroups not reported in the table were as follows: men and women appointees at State, $tau_c = -.42^*$; men and women career at State, $tau_c = .73^{**}$; men and women appointees at Defense, $tau_c = -.20$; men and women career at Defense $tau_c = -.40^*$
*significant at the .05 level
**significant at the .01 level

were also significantly more conservative ($tau_c = -.38$) than their male counterparts. Moreover, while the number of cases makes generalization difficult, women appointees in both Departments tended to be more conservative than men appointees, although the differences were not significant. Further examination revealed that the most conservative of the respondents were the women appointees, followed by the men appointees and the career women in the Defense Department. The most liberal members of the foreign policy establishment were the career women at State, although the career men in both Departments were also quite likely to adopt a moderate or liberal label for their political views (data not shown).

The results for party identification were similar (see Table 6.2). Overall, women were more likely to be Republican, although the difference is not statistically significant. Similarly, in three of the subgroups (career personnel in Defense, appointees in Defense, and appointees at State) women were more likely to be Republican. The one reversal is in the State Department, where women in career SES/SFS positions were more likely to be Democrats than men holding similar positions. The results for party identification are particularly striking given national figures that show women to be significantly more likely to identify with the Democratic Party (McGlen and O'Connor 1998, 72).

Overall differences in political views between men and women in the foreign policy establishment are, however, only half the picture. Of more importance than general political philosophy or partisan inclination are the specific foreign policy views of men and women. Table 6.3 reports those questions on which men and women in the sample held significantly different positions. Overall, only seven questions (out of eighty-seven) revealed significant gender variations. Moreover, no clear picture of a unique women's view was apparent. If there was a pattern, it was that women more often took the more conservative position. Given the findings on political views of men and women in leadership positions, these results were as expected. What is interesting from the perspective of the literature on the gender gap among the public is that no differences between men and women were found relative to questions dealing with the use of force in international affairs.

An examination of the foreign policy views of men and women in each of the two Departments found much the same picture. In the State Department only three policy questions found men and women taking divergent stands. Again no clear picture emerged. While the women at State were more likely to downgrade world peace as a foreign policy goal, they endorsed the idea that stationing American troops abroad encourages other nations to let us do their fighting and the view that if foreign interventions are undertaken, the necessary force should be applied in a short period of time rather than through a policy of gradual escalation.

In the Defense Department more questions separated men and women, and the pattern was clearer (see Table 6.4). Women, more so than men, were likely to take the hard line or the Reagan administration viewpoint. For instance, women were more likely to disagree on the need to enlist the support of the United Nations in settling international disputes and to reject the desirability of giving foreign aid to poor foreign nations. Similarly, the women in Defense accepted the Cold War view that revolutionary forces are not nationalistic but rather controlled by the Soviet Union or China. These findings are particularly interesting in comparison with the Holsti-Rosenau study. They

Table 6.3. Overall Policy Differences between Men and Women in the Department of State and Defense Combined

	Correlation
Policy Goal:	
Strengthening the U.N.[a]	$tau_c = -.20*$
Policy Issue:	
Revolutionary forces in the "Third World" countries are usually nationalistic rather than controlled by China or the USSR[b]	$tau_c = -.37**$
Détente permits the USSR to pursue policies that promote rather than restrain conflict	$tau_c = .25*$
It is vital to enlist the cooperation of the U.N. in settling international disputes	$tau_c = -.26**$
The press is more likely than the government to report the truth about the conduct of foreign policy	$tau_c = -.32**$
Third World conflicts cannot jeopardize vital American interests	$tau_c = -.21*$
The U.S. has a moral obligation to prevent the destruction of Israel	$tau_c = -.25*$

[a]Figure represents the tau_c correlation between ranking this goal as very important and sex. A negative correlation indicates women were less likely to rank it as important.

[b]Figures represent the tau_c correlation between agreement with the statement and sex. A negative correlation indicates women were more likely to disagree.

*significant at the .05 level
**significant at the .01 level

found that women leaders overall were more likely to favor enlisting the support of the United Nations and were less inclined to see revolutionary forces as being controlled by the Soviet Union or China (1995, 124). Their gender gap was also based on women's disinclination to give foreign economic aid to poorer countries if it meant higher prices at home (1995, 124).

In dividing our sample still further between appointees and career civil servants, we have to be tentative in our generalizations because of

Table 6.4. Policy Differences between Men and Women in the
Department of State and the Department of Defense

STATE DEPARTMENT	
Policy Goal:	Correlation
Keeping Peace in the World[a]	$tau_c = -.13^*$
Policy Issue:	
Stationing American troops in other countries encourages them to let us to do their fighting for those countries[b]	$tau_c = .31^*$
If foreign interventions are undertaken, the necessary force should be applied in a short period of time rather than through a policy of graduated escalation	$tau_c = .37^*$
DEFENSE DEPARTMENT	
Policy Issue:	Correlation
Revolutionary forces in "Third World" countries are usually nationalistic rather than controlled by China or the USSR	$tau_c = -.45^*$
It is vital to enlist the cooperation of the U.N. in settling international disputes	$tau_c = -.34^*$
The press is more likely than the government to report the truth about the conduct of foreign policy	$tau_c = -.43^*$
The U.S. has a moral obligation to prevent the destruction of the State of Israel	$tau_c = -.33^*$
The U.S. should give economic aid to poorer countries even if it means higher prices at home	$tau_c = -.33^*$

[a]Figures represent the tau_c correlation between ranking this goal as very important and gender. A negative correlation indicates women were less likely to rank it as important.
[b]Figures represent the tau_c correlation between agreement with the statement and gender. A negative correlation indicates women were more likely to disagree.
*significant at the .05 level
**significant at the .01 level

the problem of diminishing cases. With this caveat in mind, we examined the distribution of this further breakdown in Tables 6.5 and 6.6, and the results are quite revealing. Looking first at the State Department, we found the first evidence of a consistent gender gap between the men and women career civil servants (see Table 6.5). On eighteen separate issues women's views diverged from those of men, and generally in unique ways. We can divide these eighteen policy questions into four areas: overall view of the world of foreign affairs; use of force in foreign affairs; policy goals; and methods of implementing goals. With respect to the first, we found women more likely to reject the hard-line or Cold War view of the world, as they were more likely to disagree with propositions that the domino theory is valid and any Communist victory is a defeat for America's national interests. Similarly, the career women were more likely than men to oppose the statement that the United States should take all steps, including the use of force, to prevent the spread of Communism.

Along the same line, in choosing policy goals for the United States, the career women at State were more likely than the men to reject promoting capitalism, containing Communism, and bringing democracy to other nations and to favor combating world hunger and giving foreign aid to poor countries. In selecting strategies for foreign policy implementation, the career women at State favored cutting the Defense budget and fostering international cooperation. They also soundly disagreed with the use of the CIA to undermine hostile governments. These findings are particularly interesting in comparison with both the Holsti-Rosenau leadership data and the general public opinion data. The differences between men and women career government people at State correspond fairly closely to those of Holsti and Rosenau, but the magnitude of difference in this sector of our sample is greater. Where they found only modest sustenance for female "dovishness," in terms of opposition to use of the CIA and Soviet expansionism, the picture here is more pronounced. In general, the view of career civil servants in the State Department looked like what we might expect on the basis of studies of citizen-level opinion.

The picture for political appointees at State, however, is nearly the opposite. Women appointees diverged significantly from male appointees on eight of the policy questions, and on all eight their views are more hard-line or conservative (see Table 6.5). They strongly endorsed the Cold War view of an expansionist Soviet Union and the need to contain Communism. More modern goals such as combating world hunger were rejected, as was the tactic of fostering international cooperation. Instead we see the policy of using the CIA to undermine hos-

Table 6.5. Policy Differences between Men and Women Career and
Political Appointees in the Department of State

	Career	Political Appointees
Policy Goal:		
Containing Communism[a]	−.41*	.57**
Promoting capitalism	−.35*	
Helping to bring a democratic form of government to other nations	−.33*	
Combating world hunger	.34*	−.57*
Strengthening the U.N.	−.41*	
Fostering international cooperation to solve common problems such as food, inflation, and energy	.45*	−.59*
Policy Issue:		
Détente permits the USSR to pursue policies that promote rather than restrain conflict[b]		.54*
If foreign interventions are undertaken, the necessary forces should be applied in a short period of time rather than through a policy of graduated escalation	.40*	
There is considerable validity in the "domino theory" that when one nation falls to Communism, others nearby will soon follow a similar path	−.36*	
An effective foreign policy is impossible when the executive and Congress are unable to cooperate	−.36*	
Any Communist victory is a defeat for America's national interest	−.37*	.69*
The Soviet Union is generally expansionist rather than defensive in its foreign policy goals		.57*

Continued on next page

Table 6.5 *Continued*

	Career	Political Appointees
The U.S. has a moral obligation to prevent the destruction of Israel	−.48*	
Third World conflicts cannot jeopardize vital American interests	−.40*	
There is nothing wrong with using the CIA to try to undermine hostile governments	−.53*	.86**
The U.S. should give economic aid to poorer countries even if it means higher prices at home	.46*	
The U.S. should take all steps including the use of force to prevent the spread of Communism	−.36*	
The U.S. defense budget should be: (a) increased, and taxes should be increased to pay for it; (b) increased, and domestic programs should be cut to pay for it; (c) maintained at about the present level; (d) reduced, and spending on domestic programs should be increased; (e) reduced, and taxes should also be reduced	.33*	−.68*

[a]Figures represent the tau_c correlation between ranking the goal as very important and gender. A negative correlation indicates women were less likely to rank it important.

[b]Figures represent the tau_c correlation between agreement with the statement and gender. A negative correlation indicates women are more likely to disagree.

*significant at the .05 level

**significant at the .01 level

tile governments being strongly supported. Several possible explanations arise as to why women appointees at State in the late 1980s would have been so hard-line, especially compared with the women in career positions. One possibility is that there was a greater preponderance of outsiders or political ideologues among the women appointees in the State Department. This was particularly true of the Reagan administration, in which appointees were selected on the basis of an ideological litmus test. However, the status of the political appointees at the State

Table 6.6. Policy Differences between Men and Women Career and
Political Appointees in the Department of Defense

	Career	Political Appointees
Policy Goal:		
Helping to bring a democratic form of government to other nations[a]	−.30*	
Protecting the jobs of American workers	−.33*	
Protecting the global environment	−.37*	
Policy Issue:		
Revolutionary forces in "Third World" countries are usually nationalistic rather than controlled by the USSR and China[b]	−.48*	
It is vital to enlist the cooperation of the U.N. in settling international disputes	−.37*	
The press is more likely than the government to report the truth about the conduct of foreign policy	−.51*	
Efforts to protect weaker domestic industries from foreign competition are not a viable policy		.46*
Third World conflicts cannot jeopardize vital American interests		−.43*
The U.S. has a moral obligation to prevent the destruction of the state of Israel		−.46*
The U.S. should give economic aid to poorer countries even if it means higher prices at home	−.33*	

[a]Figures represent the tau_c correlation between ranking the goal as very important and gender. A negative correlation indicates women were less likely to rank it important.

[b]Figures represent the tau_c correlation between agreement with the statement and gender. A negative correlation indicates women are more likely to disagree.

*significant at the .05 level

**significant at the .01 level

Department is clouded by the fact that a number of women appointees were former career Foreign Service officers. Perhaps the orientation sessions for appointees conducted by the Heritage Foundation made the Reagan policies clear to both newcomers and insiders who were appointed to influential positions in both departments (Maranto 1993, 683). Maybe the difficult struggle to make it as women in that hostile environment allowed only the solidly doctrinaire to survive, at least to survive in the fine fashion of political appointees. Our data do not allow us to differentiate between these and other possible explanations. One thing is clear: The gender gap at State was complex, and the absence of an overall gap was largely a function of the sharply divergent views *among women* in the Department.

Turning to the Defense Department, we find a neater set of results (see Table 6.6). Among career SES members of the Defense Department, the women differed significantly from the men on only seven policy questions. As we might expect, given our earlier discussion of the political views of the career women at Defense, on almost all these differences the women took the more hard-line position. For instance, they were more likely than their male counterparts to disagree with the idea that revolutionary forces are nationalistic and not under the control of the USSR or China. They also were more likely to discredit the goals of protecting the global environment or giving aid to poor countries. Similarly, in terms of strategies, they rejected enlisting the United Nations in settling international disputes. They also were more likely to reject the ability of the press to report fairly on foreign policy. Interestingly, they were less likely than men to adopt the foreign policy goal of protecting the jobs of American workers. The women appointees at Defense also showed few differences from their male colleagues, but where there were significant differences it was mostly a result of the more conservative stance of the women.

To summarize our results, only among career officials in the State Department did the gender gap look similar to that found in general public opinion polls. Among career men and women at State we found a strong tendency for women to adopt a more moderate stance on world issues, rejecting many of the hard-line policy views and the use of force or subterfuge in favor of more global concerns and international cooperation. In contrast, women political appointees at State and Defense and women career SES officers at Defense (in the few instances in which they differ from their male counterparts) seemed to be more hard-line and conservative. Just why we should get such divergent results is a most interesting question.

The Impact of Political Context

Several possible explanations for our divergent findings center on the different political contexts, or cultures, of the two Departments: the direct effects of the contexts, and the ways in which people respond to their constraints. Most observers of foreign policy formulation would characterize the Defense Department and its positions on most foreign policy positions as more hard-line than that of the State Department. Indeed, the battles between State and Defense on foreign policy questions are legendary. For instance, while controlling for occupation, Holsti and Rosenau (1981, 346) found the military officers taking strong "Cold War" positions sixteen times while Foreign Service officers took such stances only twice. In a 1987 survey of high-ranking career and noncareer government officials, Robert Maranto found that both appointees and careerists in Defense agencies were consistently more conservative and pro-administration than were government officials in other agencies (although State was not included) (1993, 688). Given these two political environments, the socialization experience for women careerists may be quite different in State and Defense. Women coming into Defense may, in their attempt to fit in to an overwhelmingly male-dominated and conservative organization, overcompensate and become too conservative, while women in State might overcompensate and become more liberal.

A similar process (of adapting to the political context) has also been noted by Susan J. Carroll in her study of state legislators (this volume), in which she argues that women officeholders may find themselves pressured to conform to male norms and standards for behavior. Carroll expected that this pressure would be particularly strong in situations in which the proportion of women is small, which is certainly the situation in the Departments of Defense and State. Georgia Duerst-Lahti (1985, 20) and Cathy Johnson (Duerst-Lahti and Johnson 1989, 20) have referred to this phenomenon as the need to "go native to succeed." Furthermore they noted that "Probably from trying to fit preconceptions of nature, culture, or maybe because they 'read' the prerequisites for top jobs better, women seem to erase much of the feminine and adhere more closely to the masculine than men do" (Duerst-Lahti and Johnson 1989, 20). Indeed, in our study women at Defense were more than twice as likely (45.8% versus 20%) as women at State to say that their gender limits their ability to influence foreign policy. Interestingly, they correctly perceived that there were few policy differences between women and men in Defense and they were less likely than women at State to see any difference between their policy priorities and those of their male colleagues (16.7% versus 26.7%). There was some additional evidence in the survey that this organizational ethos has had a large impact upon women, particularly in the Defense Department, where some women claimed to have a difficult time establishing credibility due to their lack of military experience. As one of our women respondents in Defense noted in response to a question asking her to estimate her influence in policy decisions of her Department:

> To be *allowed* to make policy decisions. I am willing to make a lot of decisions. DOD tends to be a male-chauvinistic master. It is very difficult. I was on an assignment and I went into this office and they said to me, "This is the most critical project for the Department of Defense. It is much too important for a woman to work here." I was detailed there for eight months, and they let me know it every day that I was just a woman and couldn't make these decisions. In the Department of Defense, it is much more difficult to be a woman and to be accepted and have people listen to what you have to say. There is a military macho image, so you have to prove yourself. Before they listen to you, you have to prove yourself, over and over and over again.

Another woman reiterated this need to deny her femininity in order to fit in: "There isn't any room for women who dress cute or act sexy, or accentuate the fact that they are very different. But if you effectively blend in, then you are taken as seriously as anybody else." The same process, though in the opposite direction, may be happening at State, where the more moderate policy position of the Department produces more moderate women.

The political contexts also affect political appointees, though in a magnified fashion combining the contexts of the political party (and the appointment process itself) with that of the department itself. This may have been particularly true in the Reagan administration. These factors may be reflected in the more conservative stance of the Reagan women appointees. Women wishing to fit into the Republican Party, especially into the very conservative Reagan administration, may have overcompensated in adopting the hard line of the political right. Perhaps, as Duerst-Lahti and Johnson noted, women have to try harder because they feel less secure or more privileged in executive positions (1989, 20). We also have some evidence from our respondents that a selection process was at work that put special emphasis on checking for the correct conservative views of women. A career woman at Defense explained: "In order to get cleared for the White House to get nominated as a political appointee, during the first Reagan administration, you had to have worked for Reagan in 1966 when he was campaigning. You had to be that ideologically pure." As both Maranto and Steven Stehr explained, this attempt to politicize the agencies of the executive branch was an element of the Reagan administration's program to seize control of policy-making. As Stehr noted:

> Key administrative positions in the departments and agencies were staffed with loyal appointees who were philosophically unsympathetic to most forms of government activism; and, political executives were encouraged to exclude career professionals from important policy-making duties and responsibilities. (1989, 1)

Maranto also reported that appointees were encouraged to "punish" careerists who did not follow the administration's policies (by denying merit pay and transferring them out of the agency) (Maranto, 683).

In addition to having an impact on people within the organization, the political context may also influence the choices of those who come into the organization in the first place. It is likely that a self-selection process is at work, with women who espouse more moderate views being drawn to the State Department or more conservative women being drawn to Defense. Indeed, Maranto's 1987 research concerning high-ranking careerists and appointees in a variety of federal agencies found that both groups were consistently more conservative and pro-administration in the Defense Department. Correspondingly, the views of careerists and appointees were much more similar in Defense-related agencies than in non-Defense agencies (he did not interview officials at State). Maranto argued that the difference between Defense and other sectors of the government could be traced to the more conservative mission of Defense. He reasoned this mission would attract more conservative individuals as careerists who, in turn, would be promoted based on their support of this mission (1993, 684, 688–692). While we have no way of testing the latter proposition directly, as Table 6.1 makes clear, women in the Defense Department were more conservative than the women at the State Department. Nearly one-fifth (17.4%) of the women we interviewed at Defense stated that they were very conservative, but only 6.7 percent of the women at State said so. At the other end of the continuum, 20 percent of the women at State claimed the liberal label compared with only 4.3 percent of the women at Defense.

Additional evidence for the self-selection hypothesis can be found in responses to a question we asked concerning why our respondents chose their career. Interestingly, women at the Defense Department were more likely than the women at State to indicate military experience (12% versus 0%), private industry experience (28% versus 6.3%), and experience in an internship or other government agency (48% versus 31%). Reasons for joining government also were somewhat different for the two groups, with women at Defense (compared with State women) more frequently mentioning serving the government or the nation (36% versus 6.3%) and opportunities for advancement (48% versus 12.5%) and less likely to mention interest (68% versus 87.5%) and family or family connection reasons (24% versus 43.8%). The education backgrounds of the two groups of women also varied, with women in the Defense Department more likely than those at State to have degrees in science, math, engineering, or computers (24% versus 0%). Most of these differences between the two groups of women were sharper for career women in the two Departments than they were for political appointees.

One thing is clear: The women in the foreign policy process, at least during the Reagan administration, were not a homogeneous group. There was no women's view adopted, even in part, by all women. Indeed, the closest we come to a unified position would be the more conservative stance of the appointees and the career women at Defense. A review of the historical role of women in the foreign policy process especially as it relates to war would find our results not all that surprising. As Jean Bethke Elshtain (1987) details in *Women and War,* women have been found on both sides of the war issue, as peace activists and as war supporters. Thus we should not be surprised to find different stands on policy issues among women in the foreign policy establishment.

Implications

The question that provides the focus for our research is whether adding women to the foreign policy process will change the output of that process. When we did our research, in 1988, women were a distinct minority in the senior ranks of both Departments. They constituted only 4.8 percent of the Senior Foreign Service and 3.9% of the Senior Executive Service at Defense (Office of Equal Employment and Civil Rights 1988; U.S. Office of Personnel Management 1986; DOD 1987). One might speculate that adding more women to these Departments would alter how foreign policy is made or the policy outcome. However, our interviewees generally did not think this would be so. In response to the question whether having more women in the Departments of State and Defense would have an impact on foreign policy, 74.7 percent of our respondents replied in the negative. Even in instances in which a change was anticipated, it was not of great proportions. "Policy wouldn't be different, but a better cross section would give a wider range of opinions, lead to more diversity." Women were not seen as having a united or "women's" position on foreign policy. Moreover, at the time we did our analysis, as the results indicate, women could be found at both ends of the foreign policy issue continuum. Which of the various "women's views" might be influential in the process in the future will depend on the relative power of the two Departments, the locus and influence of women within the Departments, and the means by which appointees are selected. As we noted, women in Defense appear to have been socialized into the values of the conservative and patriarchal system of their department. Under such circumstances, as Dodson also noted (1989a, 1), there is less chance that the presence of women will make a difference. In fact, if the Defense Department dominates the foreign policy process, or becomes more influential in that process, then the addition of more career and appointed women in the Department might actually shift U.S. foreign policy more in the direction of a hard-line, Cold War stance. If the State Department controls the process, then the more moderate view of the career women at State might hold sway, but this would only be true if careerists are allowed to influence the policies of the Department. The appointment of Madeleine Albright as Secretary of State has not apparently moved the United States toward a more pacific foreign policy. She is credited with embodying the foreign policy vision which pushed the United States into war in Kosovo (Isaacson 1999, 27). Indeed, her tenure has been characterized as creating the "Albright Doctrine," a "tough-talking, semi-muscular interventionism that believes in using force" (Isaacson 1999, 28). Also critical, of course, is the policy position of the administration. Not only can the President appoint individuals of like-minded views, he or she and his or her appointees can shape the policy that the career officials are legally bound to follow.

Another important variable in predicting women's influence may be the status of women in the two Departments. We have argued elsewhere (McGlen and Sarkees 1993) that after years of discriminatory behavior, the State Department in particular is under court pressure to allow women a wider role in the Department. Thus, women might be more able to press their point of view at State. Indeed, there are more women moving up through the ranks at State than at Defense, although Sheila Widnall's appointment as Secretary of the Air Force signifies change there as well. Other aspects of the cultures in both Departments appear to make State more permeable to women's views (although by no means are women treated equally or equitably at State or are their views given equal hearing). Thus, we might expect women to have a greater opportunity to have a say at State. In a positive vein, 60.3 percent of our respondents felt that the influence of women in both Departments would increase in the future (38.1 percent thought it would remain the same, and 1.6 percent felt it depended on future changes in administrations). Unfortunately, there is always the possibility that administration officials who might not favor the view of women or the role of women might shift decision making in foreign policy even more to political appointees, or to other executive agencies, in which women may be having an even more difficult time exercising influence. Indeed, the trend has recently intensified by which foreign policy and defense issues have become increasingly privatized (or turned over to nongovernment agencies entirely). Women's representation in upper-echelon posts in private enterprise is exceedingly low. On the other hand, women's representation in the workforce overall is growing, and one might anticipate that the addition of women to the Departments, whether their policy priorities are different from men's or not, might shape how policy is made. We have some evidence that women add a "people dimension" to their management style (McGlen and Sarkees 1993). Thus even if women's policy priorities are not distinct from men's, the influence of women on the process may still be significant.

Notes

We would like to thank the following people for the considerable help they provided us in gathering the information for this chapter: Georgiana M. Prince; Alison Palmer; Monica Wagner, esq. (Terris, Edgecombe, Hecker, & Wayne); Hon. John La Falce; Maryann Jacob, Air Force; Sharon Bobb, OSD; Carmen Arrowood, Navy; Ken Dalrymple, OPM; Maria Melchiorre, State; Bob Zenda, Army. We would particularly like to thank the women and men in the State and Defense Departments who gave so graciously of their time to be interviewed.

This project was supported in part by a grant from the Center for American Women and Politics (CAWP), a unit of the Eagleton Institute of Politics at Rutgers University. This chapter reflects the views of its authors and not necessarily those of CAWP.

1. Recent research on the 1992 and 1996 elections by Kaufmann and Petrocik (1999) found that foreign policy differences between men and women were not a significant factor in either election. Domestic issues, namely social welfare, were the keys in those years. Kaufmann and Petrocik argue that the saliency of this issue combined with differences in views between men and women produced the Clinton victories and their large "gender gaps."

References

American Forces Information Service. 1987. *Defense '87 Almanac.* Washington, D.C.: Department of Defense.

American Forces Press Services. 1976. *Women in the Armed Forces.* Washington, D.C.: Department of Defense.

Bardes, Barbara. 1986. "Gender and Foreign Policy: A Comparative Perspective." Presented at the annual meeting of the American Political Science Association, Washington, D.C.

Bloomfield, Lincoln. 1982. *The Foreign Policy Process: A Modern Primer.* Englewood Cliffs, N.J.: Prentice-Hall, Inc.

Calkin, Homer. 1978. *Women in the Department of State: Their Role in American Foreign Affairs.* Washington, D.C.: Department of State.

Caloss, Dario Jr. 1989. "The Foreign Policy Belief Systems of Americans: National Idealism and National Self-Interest as Central Value Systems among the American Public." Presented at the annual meeting of the International Studies Association, London.

Caprioli, Mary, and Mark Boyer. 1998. "Women in Crises: Gender and the Character of International Crises." Presented at the annual meeting of the International Studies Association Northeast, Boston, November.

Carroll, Susan J. 1985. "Gender Schema and Mass Politics." Presented at the annual meeting of the Midwest Political Science Association, Chicago, April.

Carroll, Susan J. 1988. "New Strategies to Increase the Number of Women Appointed to Recent Presidential Administrations in the United States." Presented at the Vater Staat und Seine Frauen Conference, West Berlin.

Chodorow, Nancy. 1978. *The Reproduction of Mothering.* Berkeley: University of California Press.

CBS. 1989. "60 Minutes," July.

Conover, Pamela Johnston. 1988. "Feminists and the Gender Gap." *Journal of Politics* 50 (4): 985–1010.

Conover, Pamela Johnston, and Virginia Sapiro. 1993. "Gender, Feminist Consciousness, and War." *American Journal of Political Science* 37 (4): 1079–1099.

Cowan, Alison Leight. 1989. "Women's Gains on the Job: Not Without a Heavy Toll." *New York Times,* August 21.

Daniel Yankelovich Group. 1988. "Americans Talk Security: A Series of Surveys of American Voters: Attitudes Concerning National Security Issues." No. 3.

Department of Defense. 1980. *Selected Manpower Statistics.* Washington, D.C.: DOD. September.

Department of Defense. 1987. *Selected Manpower Statistics.* Washington, D.C.: DOD. September.

Dodson, Debra. 1989a. "Are Parties Gender-Neutral?" Presented at the annual meeting of the Midwest Political Science Association, Chicago.

Dodson, Debra. 1989b. "A Comparison of Women and Men's Attitudes on Their Legislative Behavior: Is What They Say What They Do?" Presented at the annual meeting of the American Political Science Association, Atlanta.

Duerst-Lahti, Georgia. 1985. "Gender, Position and Perception: Communicating Power in State Organizations." Presented at the annual meeting of the Midwest Political Science Association, Chicago.

Duerst-Lahti, Georgia. 1986. "Organizational Ethos and Women's Power Capacity: Perceived and Formal Structure in State Administrative Organizations." Presented at the annual meeting of the American Political Science Association, Washington, D.C.

Duerst-Lahti, Georgia. 1987. "But Women Play the Game Too: Gender Dynamics in Administrative Decision Making." Presented at the annual meeting of the American Political Science Association, Chicago.

Duerst-Lahti, Georgia, and Cathy M. Johnson. 1989. "Gender, Style, and Bureaucracy: Must Women Go Native to Succeed?" Presented at the annual meeting of the American Political Science Association, Atlanta.

Elshtain, Jean Bethke. 1987. *Women and War.* New York: Basic Books.

Epstein, Cynthia Fuchs. 1988. *Deceptive Distinctions: Sex, Gender, and the Social Order.* New Haven: Yale University Press.

Frankovic, Kathleen. 1982. "Sex and Politics—New Alignments, Old Issues." *P.S.* 15 (Summer): 439–448.

Genovese, Michael, ed. 1993. *Women as National Leaders.* Newbury Park, Calif.: Sage.

Goodman, Ellen 1989. "Women's Meeting Poses Question: Is It Worth Getting into Public Service?" *Niagara Gazette,* October 20, 4A.

Holsti, Ole R. 1990 "Gender and Political Beliefs of American Leaders, 1976–1988." Presented at the annual meeting of the International Studies Association.

Holsti, Ole R., and James N. Rosenau. 1981. "The Foreign Policy Beliefs of Women in Leadership Positions." *Journal of Politics* 43: 326–347.

Holsti, Ole R., and James N. Rosenau. 1984. *American Leadership in World Affairs.* Boston: Allen & Unwin.

Holsti, Ole R., and James N. Rosenau. 1988. "The Domestic and Foreign Policy Beliefs of American Leaders." *Journal of Conflict Resolution* 32 (2): 248–294.

Holsti, Ole R., and James N. Rosenau. 1995. "Gender and the Political Beliefs of American Opinion Leaders." In Francine D'Amico and Peter R. Beckman, eds., *Women in World Politics.* Connecticut: Bergin & Garvey.

Hoynes, William, and David Croteau. 1989. "Are You on the Nightline Guest List?" *Extra,* January/February.

Isaacson, Walter. 1999. "Madeleine's War." *Time,* May 17: 27–35.

Kaufmann, Karen M., and John R. Petrocik. 1999. "The Changing Politics of American Men: Understanding the Sources of the Gender Gap." *American Journal of Political Science* 43 (3): 864–887.

Kegley, Charles, and Eugene R. Wittkopf. 1982. *American Foreign Policy: Pattern and Process.* 2nd ed. New York: St. Martin's Press.

Kenski, Henry C. 1988. "The Gender Factor in a Changing Electorate." In *The Politics of the Gender Gap,* ed. Carol M. Mueller. Beverly Hills: Sage.

Lake, Celinda. 1982. "Guns, Butter, and Equality: The Women's Vote in 1980." Presented at the annual meeting of the Midwest Political Science Association, Milwaukee.

Little, Danity. 1994. *How Women Executives Succeed: Lessons from the Federal Government.* Westport, Conn.: Quorum Books.

Maranto, Robert. 1993. "Still Clashing after All These Years: Ideological Conflict in the Reagan Executive." *American Journal of Political Science* 37 (3): 681–698.

McGlen, Nancy E., and Karen O'Connor. 1998. *Women, Politics, and American Society.* 2nd ed. Upper Saddle River, N.J.: Prentice Hall.

McGlen, Nancy E., and Meredith Reid Sarkees. 1993. *Women in Foreign Policy: The Insiders.* New York: Routledge.

Miller, Arthur H. 1983. "The Emerging Gender Gap in American Politics" *Election Politics* 1 (Winter): 7–12.

Miller, Arthur H. 1986. "Gender Politics in the United States." Presented at the 1986 ECPR Joint Workshops, Gothenburg, Sweden.

Mueller, Carol M. 1988. ed. *The Politics of the Gender Gap.* Beverly Hills: Sage.

Mueller, John. 1994. *Policy and Opinion in the Gulf War.* Chicago: University of Chicago Press.

Mueller, John E. 1973. *War, Presidents, and Public Opinion.* New York: Wiley.

Office of Equal Employment and Civil Rights. 1987. *Secretary's Annual Report to Congress on Equal Employment Opportunity Efforts Fiscal Year 1987.* Washington, D.C.: Department of State.

Office of Equal Employment and Civil Rights. 1988. *Update of the Affirmative Action Plan and Annual Accomplishment Report of Equal Employment Activities for Fiscal Year 1987.* Washington, D.C.: Department of State.

Olmsted, Mary S., Bernice Baer, Jean Joyce, and Georgina M. Prince. 1984. *Women at State: An Inquiry into the Status of Women in the United States Department of State.* Washington, D.C.: Women's Research and Education Institute of the Congressional Caucus for Women's Issues.

Palmer v. Baker. 1987. 662 Federal Supplement. 1551–1575.

Palmer, et al. v. Baker. 1987. Defendant's Brief on Remand from the Court of Appeals.

Palmer, et al. v. Baker. 1987. Plaintiffs' Brief on Remand to the District Court.

Palmer v. Baker. 1989. Remedial Order. U.S. District Court for the District of Columbia.

Rainey, Gene. 1975. *Patterns of American Foreign Policy.* Boston: Allyn and Bacon.

Ruddick, Sara. 1980. "Maternal Thinking." *Feminist Studies* 6 (Summer): 342–367.

Ruddick, Sara. 1983a. "Pacifying the Forces: Drafting Women in the Interest of Peace." *Signs* 8: 471–489.

Ruddick, Sara. 1983b. "Preservative Love and Military Destruction: Reflections on Mothering and Peace." In *Mothering: Essays in Feminist Theory*, ed. Joyce Trebilcot. Totowa, N.J.: Littlefield Adams.

Ruddick, Sara. 1984. "Feminist Questions on Peace and War: An Agenda for Research, Discussion, Analysis, Action." *Women's Studies Quarterly* 12 (Summer): 8–11.

Schreiger, E. M. 1978. "Education and Change in American Opinions on a Woman For President." *Public Opinion Quarterly* 42 (Summer): 171–182.

Shapiro, Robert Y., and Harpreet Mahajan. 1986. "Gender Differences in Policy Preferences: A Summary of Trends from the 1960s to the 1980s." *Public Opinion Quarterly* 50: 42–61.

Smith, Tom W. 1984. "The Polls: Gender and Attitudes toward Violence." *Public Opinion Quarterly* 48: 384–96.

Stehr, Steven D. 1989 "Top Bureaucrats and the Distribution of Influence in Reagan's Executive Branch." Presented at the annual meeting of the American Political Science Association.

Stiehm, Judith Hicks. 1989. *Arms and the Enlisted Woman*. Philadelphia: Temple University Press.

Tankard, James W. 1984. "Nuclear Weapons Literacy and Its Correlates." *Peace Research* 16: 30–34.

Task Force on Women in the Military. 1988. *Report Task Force on Women in the Military*. Washington, D.C.: Department of Defense.

Tickner, J. Ann. 1992. *Gender in International Relations*. New York: Columbia University Press.

Tronto, Joan C. 1987. "Beyond Gender Differences to a Theory of Care." *Signs* 12 (Summer): 644–663.

U.S. Office of Personnel Management. 1979. *Federal Civilian Force Statistics: Equal Employment Opportunity Statistics*. Washington, D.C.: USOPM. November.

U.S. Office of Personnel Management. 1980. *Federal Civilian Force Statistics, Equal Employment Opportunity Statistics*. Washington, D.C.: USOPM. November.

U.S. Office of Personnel Management. 1986. *Federal Civilian Workforce Statistics: Affirmative Employment Statistics*. Washington, D.C.: USOPM. September.

Seven

Do Women Leaders Make a Difference?

Substance, Style, and Perceptions

Sue Tolleson-Rinehart

Through thinking, training, experience, the woman in politics has a most definite original contribution to make in such fields as child welfare, education, the removal of inequities of women before the law, and international relations. More women assisting in the delicate contact between country and country would mean, I firmly believe, more surety of world peace.
—Representative Ruth Bryan Owen (D-Fla., 1929–33)

In 1988, twelve of America's one hundred largest cities had women mayors, and women were mayors of 11.4 percent of cities with populations of 30,000 or more. Three times as many women held local office at the end of the 1980s as had done so in the mid-1970s (Center for the American Woman and Politics 1989). This dramatic rate of increase did not continue. The rate of growth of women big-city mayors is roughly on a par with the corresponding rate of increase of women state legislators. The rate of increase in the share of mayoral offices held by women is dwarfed by the growth rate of successful female contestants for United States House seats. Table 7.1 presents a simple illustration of the change.

We must also, however, consider the absolute numbers underlying these rates of change. There are now sixty-five women in Congress and almost 1,700 women in statehouses across the country. Even as late as 1999, only sixteen women were mayors of the nation's largest cities, and only forty-five were mayors even of moderately sized cities, those with populations of 30,000 or more (Center for American Women and Politics 2000). Looked at in this light, the occurrence of a woman urban chief executive appears to be a much rarer phenomenon. As I write, fewer women are mayors of the largest cities than are sitting as lieutenant governors, and the nation's two largest cities, New York and Los Angeles, have never had a woman mayor. The women who have been

149

Sue Tolleson-Rinehart

Table 7.1. Changes in Percentage of Women in Different
Types of Office

% Women in office	1989	1999	% Change
State Legislatures	17%	23%	35.3%
U.S. Congress	5%	12%	140.0%
Mayors, 100 largest cities	12%	16%	33.3%
Mayors, > 30,000 pop.	11.4%	19.6%	71.9%

Source: CAWP 1989; CAWP 2000. % change calculated by the author.

mayors of large cities are not only few in number; they are also highly likely to be the first woman to hold the office in their cities. Singularity focuses the gender role expectations like a prism, putting these women under a strong observational light.

These women are also chief executives, although some have more direct governing power than others. They, like the even smaller number of women governors in our history, act within and are constrained by a variety of political contexts, as is true of all public officials. But they are also surrounded by two unique, interacting contexts—that of the singularity of their sex and their "first woman to . . ." status, and that of the executive nature of the office—that attach strongly gendered expectations to leadership (Cann and Siegfried 1990). For these reasons, models of women's political leadership that are derived from study of women in legislatures may leave us insufficiently informed.

Given the dramatic increases in the numbers of women who hold elective office, it is not surprising that our assumptions about women's leadership behavior, and policy-making, would emerge from studies of legislators. The culture as a whole now seems to expect women to speak in Gilligan's (1982) "different voice," although at least one study that tested the two putatively different moral voices—abstract justice and caring—found that women use both (Plutzer 2000). This cultural expectation has filtered into our assumptions about women in politics. A large literature has documented that women legislators appear to favor policy agendas that differ from those of men (Thomas 1994; Gertzog 1995). Voters seem to use those gendered expectations as cues about what candidates stand for, especially in the absence of other information (McDermott 1997; Dolan 1998).

Because political leadership is greatly affected by context, however, our understanding of women political leaders, women's policy-making, or the nature of leader-follower relations when the leader in question is a woman will be limited if we assume that the legislative contexts shaping these behaviors can be generalized to other domains. We know that people make a distinction between legislative and executive leadership, and that those distinctions parallel gender role beliefs; the feminine stereotype is associated with legislative leadership, while the masculine stereotype and expectations of executive leadership are in close accord (Huddy and Terkildsen 1993). Studies of women governors (Tolleson-Rinehart and Stanley 1994), women in the judiciary (Mezey 2000), women Cabinet secretaries (Borelli 2000), women in the military (Baldwin 1996), and women in the defense and foreign policy establishments (McGlen and Sarkees 1995, this volume) have all found that the context in which a woman finds herself may sharply constrain her behavior.

I chose to study women and men who were, or recently had been, mayors of some of the nation's largest cities in order to determine what difference the intersection of gender role context and political context makes. While what follows might be seen as a qualitative study, it is structured no differently than if it were quantitative. The point of the study is to measure the influence of gender roles on political chief executive leadership. The implications from the study are significant for our understanding of the movement of women not just into legislative roles but also into those executive roles, including that of the presidency, that continue to be seen in more masculine ways. These implications also enable us to challenge whether such leadership is, in fact, "masculine," even when it is practiced by men.

Design of the Study

Because both gender role contexts and political contexts are complex, detecting their intersection is challenging. Choosing female-male pairs of mayors from the same cities enabled me to impose a kind of control on political context while exploring for gender role effects; to the extent that gender differences would (or wouldn't) emerge under these circumstances of "controlling for" the local political environment, they might be said to be significant. At the same time, choosing as diverse a collection of cities as possible would give us at least a preliminary look at the range of gender-political context intersections. Although these interviews were conducted a decade ago, relatively little has changed, in the numbers and kinds of women who have been big-city mayors, in the demands of the mayoralty, or in the sense on the part of both mayors and citizens that a woman mayor must somehow be different.

The five pairs of men and women introduced in these pages are a sample of sorts. Not all cities among the twelve of the nation's largest that had recently had women mayors offered the possibility that interviews could be conducted during the life of the study. In one city, the woman mayor had quite recently died. In another, the woman mayor was running for higher office and unavailable for an interview. Some cities were too much alike on key variables to provide the diversity I sought.

From the remaining cities, I chose a combination of the five largest cities that would give me the most diversity in geography, city government type (strong versus weak mayor) and interaction of race and sex among the five pairs.

I began by contacting the woman mayor or recent mayor first, and upon scheduling an interview with her, I tried to schedule an interview with her male counterpart as close to the same day as possible. All interviews were conducted by me and in person during 1989 and 1990. With the respondents' permission, I tape-recorded the interviews and took notes. The analysis presented here is based on transcripts of the tape recordings. The interviews ranged in length from about twenty-five minutes to about two hours, depending on individual conversational and stylistic variations and scheduling constraints. The conclusions presented below are based on interviews with the resulting five pairs of men and women in cities in the Northeastern, Southeastern, Midwestern, and Southwestern United States. Other characteristics of the men and women can be seen in Table 7.2. Among the pairs of mayors are one in which both the woman and man are black, one in which the man is black and the woman is white, and one pairing of a black woman and a white man. In the remaining two pairs, both the man and the woman are white.

Each person was asked the same questions and invited to respond as completely and individually as possible, with one exception. At the end of the interview, women were asked whether "being a woman made any difference to you as a candidate . . . to people's perceptions of you . . . to being the kind of mayor you are." The men were asked whether they thought that sex made a difference in the kind of mayors each were or had been, and were also asked whether they thought their female counterpart's sex had made a difference to people in general. Mayors are usually expert judges of people and of public opinion. I wanted the male mayors' assessment of their *city's* views of their female counterparts, rather than simply their own opinions about these women. While they did give me their own opinions, all but one of them clearly seemed to understand the kind of assessment I was seeking and provided it.

Table 7.2. Some Descriptive Characteristics of Mayors Interviewed

Characteristics of context	Women	Men
Strong-mayor government type	3	3
Weak-mayor government type	2	2
White	3	3
Black	2	2
Democrat	4	5
Republican	1	0

Women and Men Leading Their Cities

In many ways, men and women do not differ. Among the mayors, for example, the female-male pairs were in extraordinary agreement on the characterizations of their communities and their constituencies, although in one case the woman was pessimistic about her city's future, while her male counterpart was more optimistic. One city was characterized by both its mayors as a challenging combination of wealth and poverty, with each spontaneously pointing out that the middle class needed and demanded less from government than either the rich or the poor. Two other cities, both having experienced crises of racial integration and unpredictable growth, were noted by both mayors for their large groups of unselfish, activist, and committed citizens, despite the strains both cities had experienced.

It is not surprising that men and women who have been active for, campaigned in, and led a city would be in close agreement on its essence. Almost all of the mayors are noteworthy, in my view, for intelligence, acumen, and shrewdness of observation. And their success must be kept in mind: These are people who knew their cities well enough to win the confidence of the electorate. Nor is it surprising that men and women would be in the same strong agreement when it comes to identifying the city's most important problems; the mayoralty offers a distinctive viewpoint to whoever is in office. Both men and women stressed the problems of growth and economic development, and similar community issues such as education and housing. Only men mentioned drugs, and women mentioned a broader range of issues, but gender does not, in this instance, lead to many real differences. The political context of the mayoralty was more determinative of their responses.

A similar pattern emerged when I asked the mayors about the three most important problems facing the nation. Women provided a broader range of answers, and men mentioned national economic policy while women did not, but both men and women frequently mentioned issues of social welfare or social justice, peace, education, and the environment. In four of the five cities, both the men and the women were unusually internationalist in their perspectives. When I asked about the three most serious problems facing the world, any gender differences vanished. Both men and women mentioned the same small but profound list of issues: peace, world hunger and population growth, the environment, international economic development and trade, and drugs, something that mayors saw as problems susceptible only to multinational cooperative efforts. Most of the mayors, at some point, talked in terms of "my city and the world"; none was even faintly parochial.

I began to wonder whether, in many cases, the immediacy and intimacy of their relations with their constituencies—several mayors pointed out to me that they were physically the closest representatives of the people of any level of government—had not had a subtle influence on their approach to global politics. Perhaps few gender differences emerged in these areas not because the women were more like men but because the men were more like "women." The issues that men as well as women mayors raised were, after all, also issues long thought to be the special purview of women's "nurturance": education, social welfare, peace, world hunger, and the environment. Here, men mayors fit the gendered expectations as well as do the women mayors, an example of the importance of considering the influence of political context.

Orientations to Leadership

More obvious gender differences emerged when I began to ask the mayors about their leadership style and requested their views on the nature of leadership and followership. Four of the five women, for example, said that they had an involved, "hands-on" style and emphasized collegiality and teamwork. Four of the five men, in contrast, said that their staffs were their implementors and sounding boards. The men were more likely to mention delegating responsibilities and seemed to be speaking more frequently in the "command" idiom that we have come to associate with "male" or executive leadership.

I asked which political leaders, no matter when or in what circumstances, the mayors admired most. John F. Kennedy, Franklin Delano Roosevelt, Truman and Lincoln appeared on both lists, but men also mentioned Jefferson, Washington, Adam Clayton Powell and Adlai Stevenson. Women, and women alone, admired women leaders Margaret Thatcher and Shirley Chisholm, and one woman but no men mentioned Jesse Jackson and Mario Cuomo. This variation in the choice of role model is a significant indicator that men are still unlikely to adopt female leaders as personal models.

The men and women were very similar in their views of the essence of leadership, and individual pairs were in especially close agreement, no doubt as a result of the kind of political environment—the nature of the city—in which each pair cut its political teeth. But once again, the lack of gender differences here comes less because the women are like men than because the men are "like women." The qualities of leadership all seemed to admire most are motivation, concern for people, vision, commitment, listening, and communication. These seem closer to the stereotypical qualities valued in femininity than the sterner, more aggressive qualities our culture has attached to male leaders. Surely part of this arises from the context: I have talked to mayors and not international leaders or generals. But even this recognition of contextual differences underscores the limits of a stereotypically "masculine" definition of leadership, a definition that would certainly fail to capture much of what the male mayors themselves value. Similarly, both men and women told me forcefully that the best follower is a leader-in-the-making, a participator in the vision, and not an unthinking, loyal soldier.

Another instance of the effects of the local context softening rigidly masculine stereotypes of leadership appeared when I asked the mayors whether the essence of politics is conflict or cooperation. Stereotypes and extant research might have led me to expect that more of the men would embrace politics as conflict and more of the women would emphasize cooperation. Four of the five men adamantly chose politics as cooperation, while three of the five women chose conflict. One male mayor said that "The essence of politics is cooperation, as is all of life . . . people working together and figuring out how to work with each other . . . coalition building." His female counterpart said "Conflict . . . philosophical differences, personal prejudices and financial interests . . . when this city is in trouble, people will rally to the cause, then when things are going great everybody is fighting for their own."

Another male mayor said, "Well, I'm a positive person and I guess I've come to it by way of cooperation. I tend to be the kind of person who's absolutely certain that I can take five or six divisions . . . and by trying to hear them out, you get all five or six [ready to] cooperate . . .

but that requires a high degree of energy on the part of that person trying to get them there." While his orientations were those we have come to expect of women leaders, his female counterpart said, "I think that the only way anything gets done is conflict: [You put conflict] out in the open, then it takes cooperation to carry it through."

Another woman mayor saw politics in pessimistic terms, emphasizing the deepness of divisions between people, while her male counterpart firmly stuck to the belief that politics is *both* conflict and cooperation. The two remaining female mayors chose cooperation, both using the phrase "the art of compromise," and both stressing the power of persuasion. But so did their two male counterparts: one, defining cooperation, said, "I think that conflict comes about when you *don't* do things that you should be doing," and the other said that politicians who emphasize conflict "don't last very long."

These somewhat surprising findings are not evidence of a massive gender role reversal in the American mayoralty. It is possible that some of the women mayors had simply seen more conflict, at least partly in response to their cities' difficulties in adjusting to a woman mayor. In two of the cases, indeed, the cities these women have led are subject to deep enough divisions that their male counterparts might almost be seen as unduly optimistic, and both women first became mayors earlier than anyone else I interviewed, at a time when the acceptance of women in office may have been somewhat less than it is today. The interaction of gendered expectations about the women with unusually challenging political environments may have produced a more conflictual context than others saw.

While that may be so, it is also true that the two black women and two black men, who might have expected at least as much difficulty as the white women in gaining acceptance, all espoused cooperation as the essence of politics. The most important conclusion to be drawn from the mayors' views of conflict and cooperation is that simpleminded stereotypes about the orientations of female and male leaders contribute little to our understanding of their outlooks or behavior.

Gender and Perceptions of Gender

For all their apparent similarities, do the mayors see gender in the same ways? They do not. Three of the male mayors were thoughtful about gender differences and usually made good guesses about what the women mayors experienced, but, for obvious reasons, they did not see the differences to be as serious as did their female counterparts. And all of the men spoke in somewhat abstract terms, while the women were nothing if not immediate, and personal, in their responses. All of the men spoke in terms of equality of abilities; for them, that was what mattered most. The women all seemed to see things in more complex terms. Below, the mayors speak for themselves. In each case, the remarks of pairs of men and women mayors will be presented, with the man's comments coming first. But from pair to pair, we will see that one's sex seems more determinative of reactions to questions about gender than one's leadership of any particular city.

Is there a difference? "Not by their sex," says one man. " . . . [O]nly a woman, by her sex, often has to confront issues, reactions, different from what males do. Otherwise, it's personalities. . . . " He continued:

We're still dealing, living in a male world, and there are times when one has to confront that bias. But that's folly. Not only just as a general attitude, but because there are more capable women who're assuming all these responsibilities, and demonstrating that they're getting results, a capacity to lead which has always been there, it's just never been recognized.

His female predecessor was not so sanguine:

I think, you know, most of the time, a woman tends to feel that our sex has no bearing, but in reality it does, and while we work very hard to, umm, minimize whatever impact that may have, I think that still is an issue. I think we have reached a point, though, whereby communities now are more silent on their apprehensions and more willing to take the "wait and see" posture. And so that may provide the better opportunity, better in the sense that you don't initially start getting all these negatives about what will or will not happen. . . . I still feel that every move I make is, for some reason, still a test. . . . [I still don't think that] if I make a mistake it would be considered just, you know, "that was a bad day," it would still be a measure of competence, capability, whether or not women are sending forth this kind of activity. . . . The bottom line: I think women, especially in politics, are still measuring their moves, much more than men measure theirs.

Both of these mayors clearly saw that the expectations of a woman were different from what was expected of a man.

Those words were spoken by a white man and a black woman. The next remarks were made by a black man and a white woman. I did not ask about race differences, but the similarity of the men's and the women's remarks seem to transcend race. The male mayor made a simple egalitarian argument about the lack of meaningful differences:

> It's hard for me to talk about [whether gender makes a difference] in the abstract, without getting into the personalities, and I don't know that you could, that there are any differences. . . . I've seen Kathy Whitmire, and Donna Owens, and a host of other mayors, male and female, who, I couldn't tell much difference on the basis of their sex, as to whether they had a different outlook toward their leadership roles, or a different style. . . . I don't believe all that stuff I've heard about kinder, gentler, softer, more compassionate.

The woman, the lone Republican in this group of mayors, also started with an egalitarian perspective. Quickly, though, the tenor of her comments changed. She suggested that women were, in fact, "kinder, gentler, softer," even though she was one of the women who saw politics as conflict rather than cooperation. She also tentatively articulated the difficulty of being accepted by her constituency:

> No, it never has [made a difference to be a woman candidate]. The only difference it makes is that you have to work twice as hard and prove yourself much more, to prove your capabilities. A male comes into it totally accepted because he's a male. A female, people look at questionably and say, "Well, is she really qualified?" so you've got to go that extra mile to convince people that yes you are qualified and that you're starting out on equal footing with [whoever] the male opponent might be. . . .

She seems to be saying that the differences are no more than differences of perception. But she suddenly veers toward a view of differences as innate:

> I very much do [believe that being a woman makes her a different mayor] because of two things. One, the female is not as confrontational as a male because of the way we're raised, what's expected of a male, what's expected of a female. And the motherly instinct you have, being a female, those characters [sic] are very, very good attributes, because you aren't as quick to anger, you don't go into a meeting confrontationally, you go in looking for cooperation. . . . Now the downside of that is sometimes you don't, when you first start out, it takes you a little longer to get to the point where you really have to put your foot down and say, "Okay, this is the way it's going to be."

Of the remaining three pairs, in one case both the man and woman are black, and in the others both are white. Once again, though, race seems less significant than gender in differentiating the mayors' responses. The third male mayor, one of the two black men in the group, began with a liberal feminist perspective for himself while simultaneously emphasizing the strength of common perceptions:

I think [gender makes a difference] to people's perceptions. I don't think it makes any difference at all. I [was involved in the National Council of Black Mayors and the United States Conference of Mayors], and you had fifty females in that group and the rest were all male. And I had a chance to dialogue with many of them. . . . And actually, it makes no difference at all in the way they govern, or in their responsibilities, but I think the attitudes of people have to change. . . . They say, well, a woman can't do this, a woman can't do that, a woman can't be effective. I think it's an old-boys'-school kind of thing that has to be changed not just in government but in the workplace as well.

But he used a common stereotype about women's maternal orientations to explain women mayors' effectiveness:

I've watched her and other female mayors, and they're just as effective and better than a lot of male mayors, and I think one reason for that is because of their basic commitment and concern as parents, as mothers . . . no, I don't think that they're any less effective, I think they're just as effective or more so.

He is not alone. Four of the five male mayors, and four of the five female mayors, made references to women's feelings and experiences as mothers to explain women mayors' behavior. No mayor, man or woman, linked effective political leadership to the lessons of fatherhood, even though "the father" has been a powerful trope of political leadership in much of human history. To some extent, women chief executives, at least as mayors, are acceptable today because maternal orientations are now valued in politics, just as Victorian suffragettes hoped that they would be. But this kind of positive stereotyping is still significantly constraining, especially as we try to envision these maternal women in higher executive offices such as governor or president. The black woman who followed this man as mayor was forthright about the power of descriptive representation while clearly recognizing the paradoxes created by the intersection of gendered contexts and political contexts. She said:

It made a big difference. It made a difference in my running. I ran because, you know, I thought there was a need for a black woman to try for the office so that people could see that diversity in representative government is such a thing. There was some resistance in both sexes for women in leadership roles. In both sexes there are those who are more comfortable with male leadership, and I have a double whammy in being black and a woman. . . . So people's perceptions of me—on one hand, expectations are more, because women have a reputation for being exhaustive workers, and constantly reaching out and giving of themselves. And on the other hand, there's some misunderstanding about your intellectual capacity and ability to be tough. . . . Can you be tough, can you make the tough decisions?

She was frustrated by what she saw as the endless need to negotiate gender role expectations:

So after becoming mayor, you always strive to become non-invisible. . . . In many instances you aren't seen, you know, because they aren't accustomed to women being around the table. . . . Now they can't tell women jokes, they can't tell black jokes . . . in the past it would lead to tension. . . . some of the difficulties would come as much from black men as white men. I call it condescension. . . . in order to persuade you, rather than presenting a convincing argument to you, and let's have some dialogue, they want to touch you, or hug you, or like "Oh, you see it my way" and that's the whole content of the discussion! "Oh, you see it my way. Come here and give me a kiss on the cheek."

Her understanding of the power of descriptive representation and her exasperation with stereotypical behavior, however, do not mean that she does not expect women in politics to be different on some essential level:

I think those of us who are out there, we preach it constantly, that we're not about being clones of men. We want to bring that extra dimension to affairs of state. . . . So we have to understand the rules, but we have to bring, like I said, another dimension. Because then why not elect all men? Why have a woman?

Why elect women to office if we don't expect them to do and be something different? And yet, as her comments make clear, the political context may be demanding the same things from women and men.

The fourth man mayor, who is white, made a simple liberal feminist argument and said that voters were rewarding women candidates in order to right past wrongs:

I think that, if I heard your question right, the answer is no. I do feel, however, that we're in a period of American political history that, where to be female is to have an advantage, because there is a voter attitude of affirmative action for past injustices, past injustices done to females. . . . I think male and female are equally able to lead, and I think that the success of female politicians in the last few years has proved that conclusively. And they are good leaders or bad leaders depending on their ability not their gender. . . . [But women now have an advantage]: You take for example [the woman mayor's recent high-level appointment of a woman to a city post]. And just everybody, everybody I know wants her to succeed, because the idea that women have broken into this previously all-male-dominated institution . . . is an exciting idea.

His female counterpart was crisp and unsentimental about gender. She was very astute about the perceptual role it played in her first election, but she refused to accept a gendered explanation of herself or her behavior. She was the only woman not to invoke a maternal stereotype:

It allowed me to have some advantages, in that [my first campaign] attracted considerably more volunteers than I would have had, had there not been the cause of electing the first woman. . . . So that was an advantage. Another advantage was more press attention. The press was much more interested in me as a candidate than they would have been if I had not been female. The negatives were: much harder to raise money, and much more questioning of [whether I could] really do the job. . . . If your question was [whether it mattered to me], no, it didn't matter to me, but it changed the elements of the campaign. It was more difficult to convince [the city's political elite] that I was going to be able to win, and as a result that made it more difficult to raise money. And it was more difficult to convince the press, who translate everything to everybody else, that I was a serious candidate. So those were the impediments that I had to deal with. Now, it never has mattered to me. . . . I don't subscribe to the belief that women are somehow automatically different from men. I believe all people are individuals. They are influenced by their own environment, their own culture, their own background. To the extent that women as a group are subjected to a different environmental or cultural background, then you can generate some assumptions about what women are going to be like, you know, but I think that's all background-generated. It's not genetic! [Laughs.]

But as her male predecessor noted, she worked hard and successfully to advance other women, using her position to bring other women forward. She did it out of a straightforward notion of egalitarian justice:

I will say, I have adopted as one of the causes that I work hard for, the cause of opportunities for women, because of my experiences of being discriminated against as a woman. That has become a very, very important cause of mine.

But she once again rejects any notion of essential difference, and in particular dismisses the picture of women as morally pure. Differences, she claims, are just the result of women entering a context with which they have little familiarity.

In the short run there's a lot of belief that women will subscribe to higher standards of integrity, and will be less likely to be involved in corruption, etc. I hate to be cynical, but my view of that is that's just because women have traditionally been outsiders. You know, fifty years from now, [when men and women will be completely equal,] you will no longer be able to make those distinctions.

The final pair of mayors functioned in an exceptionally hard-edged political environment. Both are white, but both governed one of the nation's most racially and ethnically diverse cities. Questions about gender appeared to have caught the man by surprise, and he is the only one of the men who did not invoke motherhood stereotypes. The woman, not surprised, was more than generous with her thoughts. But she also seemed unaccustomed to speaking of gender—indeed, she never used the terms "gender" or "feminism"—in the language that has become second-nature to many women in politics.

Well [the man responds], of course the perception of others, it makes a difference if it's a Hispanic mayor, if it's a woman mayor, if it's a black mayor, if it's a—I guess today, sure, I mean it does. The reality is, it does. But they're perceptions. No, I don't think it makes any difference.

His female counterpart, on the other hand, reacted enthusiastically.

Yes. I mean it's yes to every one of those questions. Except a "no" to the first. It did not bother the people [of her city] at all that I was a woman. Nor did I campaign, or use the woman's issue to run. At all. Yes, it did affect the term, and the way you are governing, the way you are perceived to govern, because your immediate critics, at least at City Hall, were all male. Your entire press corps is male. They have clichés, they had stereotypes, they will reinforce that in the things that you are doing even though it has nothing to do with being a woman.

But she too, like all but two of her counterparts of either sex, quickly turned to the "added dimension":

> I think [more women in politics is] one of the most needed aspects of society, too. I really and truly believe it . . . women have the brainpower, they have the physical strength, they certainly have as sound a nervous system, as the man. And a woman has an added dimension, I think, I don't want to use the word mothering nature, or whatever, but femininity in whatever you want to define it. I never even read the book [*The*] *Feminine Mystique,* but whatever it is, there is a sensitivity. . . . A man would not have that sensitivity.

She concluded, though, with a wry recognition of the importance of learning the rules of the game, and women's comparative inexperience in it:

> I'm not the Madison Avenue type, this networking business, and stuff like that, that's just a word to me . . . [but after dealing with a businessman who had agreed to raise a large sum of money for the city that very day, at lunch], he left, and I thought to myself, "Now how many women could I toss this off on, and she could, absolutely sure of herself, say, oh, I'll see all those guys at lunch? Those women at lunch? And know that they could commit to a minimum of $75,000 without asking?" Not very many.

Conclusion

What can we conclude about gender and leadership from these reflections of ten people who have governed large cities? First, if we were guided by the results of legislative and congressional research, we would say that the men mayors looked more like "women." The issues they thought most important, and their views of the nature of politics, all correlate with what the culture has come to expect of women in (legislative) office. These men have been political chief executives, and yet their political context—the city—may call for "feminine" orientations.

But second, four of five men said that only personalities, not gender, created differences, and the fifth did not even make that distinction. The same four who emphasized individual differences, though, acknowledged past or present discrimination, and some were insightful in their attempts to gauge what their female counterparts might have endured. They nonetheless had gendered expectations of women in politics that centered on motherhood, as did four of the five women. The mayors may have thought it socially desirable to make such references, but even the fact that such references would seem socially desirable em-phasizes the strength of gender role contexts.

Third, when I asked merely whether they thought men and women mayors were different, all five men interpreted "difference" to be a measurement of women's performance against that of men. Men's "ef-fectiveness" was their standard for evaluating women, even when they evaluated women quite highly, and even when their own behavior might be seen as closer to what we have come to expect of women in office than to what we have expected of men.

Fourth, the women did not see "difference" as a measurement against a male standard of performance, although all five admitted, with vary-ing degrees of humor, weariness, or frustration, that the public was in fact measuring them that way. Although they did not think they should be measured against a male standard, they did not treat the political context itself as part of that male standard. The political context, in-stead, is a terrain with which women must become familiar. Perhaps the terrain is shaped by masculine stereotypes, but the women mayors did not discuss it in those terms.

Fifth, only one of the five women did not believe that women were and should be substantively different from men—but she has nonethe-less achieved a great deal for her "cause" of creating opportunities for other women. She does not believe that women truly will differ from men, but that has not deterred her from working hard and effectively on behalf of other women. The remaining four women all did believe that women bring an "added" or "extra dimension" to politics. In one case, the dimension was phrased largely in terms of style, whereas with the other women, it seemed to color policy orientations as well, even if im-plicitly.

Sixth, and finally, these women, most of whom are exceptionally vi-brant and gregarious, can be seen as somewhat lonely figures. All of them understood how singularity made them unique, and all of them pointed to the fishbowl-like aspects of their lives. All of them were eager to end that condition and were quick to point to more women in office as the solution.

Gender differences among political leaders are subtle, and they can-not be elucidated in crude assumptions about issue orientations. These men and women used their cities' needs as the criterion for assessing political problems. Gendered *expectations* are more influential than any measurable gender *differences*.

Gender does not act as a filter, allowing some needs to pass only into female fields of vision while others fall only within a male field. It is not that differences are not there. It is, instead, that the presence of women in leadership itself can free us from stereotypical thinking. Three of the men mayors I talked to could easily be called "nurturant." Certainly all of the women are decisive and strong. It is only the presence of women in leadership positions, however, that liberates us to ask these kinds of questions and to be prepared for surprising answers.

References

Baldwin, J. Norman. 1996. "Female Promotions in Male-Dominant Organizations: the Case of the United States Military." *Journal of Politics* 58 (November): 1184–1197.

Borelli, MaryAnne. 2000. "Gender, Politics, and Change in the United States Cabinet: The Madeleine Korbel Albright and Janet Reno Appointments." In *Gender and American Politics*, ed. Sue Tolleson-Rinehart and Jyl Josephson. Armonk, N.Y.: M. E. Sharpe.

Cann, Arnie, and William D. Siegfried. 1990. "Gender Stereotypes and Dimensions of Effective Leader Behavior." *Sex Roles* 23 (Nos. 7/8): 413–419.

Center for American Women and Politics. 2000. "Women in Elective Office 2000." Fact Sheet.

Center for the American Woman and Politics. 1989. "Women in Elective Office 1989." Fact Sheet.

Dolan, Kathleen. 1998. "Voting for Women in the 'Year of the Woman.'" *American Journal of Political Science* 41 (January): 270–283.

Gertzog, Irwin N. 1995. *Congressional Women: Their Recruitment, Integration, and Behavior.* 2nd ed., rev. and updated. Westport, Conn.: Praeger.

Gilligan, Carol. 1982. *In a Different Voice.* Cambridge, Mass.: Harvard University Press.

Huddy, Leonie, and Nayda Terkildsen. 1993. "Gender Stereotypes and the Perception of Male and Female Candidates." *American Journal of Political Science* 37 (1): 119–147.

McDermott, Monika L. 1997. "Voting Cues in Low-Information Elections: Candidate Gender as a Social Information Variable in Contemporary United States Elections." *American Journal of Political Science* 41 (1): 270–283.

McGlen, Nancy, and Meredith Reid Sarkees. 1995. *The Status of Women in Foreign Policy.* New York: Foreign Policy Association.

Mezey, Susan Gluck. 2000. "Gender and the Federal Judiciary." In *Gender and American Politics*, ed. Sue Tolleson-Rinehart and Jyl Josephson. Armonk, N.Y.: M. E. Sharpe.

Plutzer, Eric. 2000. "Are Moral Voices Gendered? Care, Rights and Autonomy in Reproductive Decision Making." In *Gender and American Politics*, ed. Sue Tolleson-Rinehart and Jyl Josephson. Armonk, N.Y.: M. E. Sharpe.

Thomas, Sue. 1994. *How Women Legislate.* New York: Oxford University Press.

Tolleson-Rinehart, Sue, and Jeanie R. Stanley. 1994. *Claytie and the Lady: Ann Richards, Gender, and Politics in Texas.* Austin: University of Texas Press.

Eight

The Impact of Women in State Legislatures
Numerical and Organizational Strength

Sue Thomas and Susan Welch

Over the past thirty years, the number of women state legislators in the United States has increased dramatically. From a mere 5 percent in the early 1970s, women now make up more than one-fifth of the membership of state legislatures. An important question arising from this growth is how women's presence has affected governmental agendas and products. This chapter explores women's political priorities in relation to two features of the wider political context: the proportion of women in legislative bodies and the presence or absence of a women's legislative caucus. We do so using data from a twelve-state survey of legislators.

Literature Review

This study is designed to uncover any evidence that women legislators' priorities have changed over time, and that the women are more active than men in areas concerning women, children, and families. Why do we expect an increase in the willingness of women to raise women's issues? One reason is that now most women work outside the home and the problems of women's dual role affect most families. It would be natural for women legislators to try to ease that burden by supportive legislation. Women legislators are further encouraged to make public women's issues by their increased numbers. This increase means a larger potential supportive network for women who push issues of importance to them. Small numbers of women officeholders mean women are likely to feel outnumbered and less willing to pursue their concerns.

Rosabeth Moss Kanter's (1977) pioneering study of women in corporate sales forces illustrates the connection between minority status and behavior on the job. She concluded that "relative numbers of socially and culturally different people in a group are seen as critical in shaping interaction dynamics" (965). She suggested that when a minority of 15 percent or less exists within an organization, members of that minority are seen as tokens, and that this status constrains their behavior. Rather than blending into the mainstream, tokens continuously respond to their differential status. On the other hand, as a minority becomes larger, it becomes more active.

These ideas suggest that token status, along with relatively less political experience individually and collectively, may have affected the behavior of women officeholders of the 1970s and earlier. Evidence that this was so is abundant. For example, women tended to participate less than men legislators in a range of legislative activity, such as speaking in committees and on the floor, bargaining with their colleagues, and meeting with lobbyists (Diamond 1977; Kirkpatrick 1974).

Women were also less aggressive in pursuing issues of concern to them, especially if they were not generally in the legislative mainstream. Gehlen quotes a female member of Congress stating: "I can't imagine a woman being successful in Congress if she narrows her interests to these fields [social welfare]" (1977, 316). Carroll (1984) terms one form of this restraint the "closet feminist syndrome." She suggests that despite expressing feminist points of view, some women officeholders did not push their views because it might be detrimental to their careers in environments dominated by men. They feared being labeled as too narrow or only interested in women's issues.

That women did have differing views from men but didn't fight as strongly for those positions as they might is well cataloged. Research on issue attitudes, roll-call voting, and policy priorities indicates that women and men had different viewpoints on issues but a tendency to rank issues similarly. Generally, women officeholders had been more supportive of women's issues than men (Diamond 1977; Johnson and Carroll 1978) and more liberal on many other issues (Frankovic 1977; Gehlen 1977; Leader 1977; Hill 1983; Lilie, Handberg, and Lowery 1982; Welch 1985).[1] However, these concerns had not impelled female officeholders to give women's issues or liberal issues a higher priority than did men (Gehlen 1977; Mezey 1978; Johnson and Carroll 1978).

Thus, women legislators' token status may depress or alter behavior. In a more encouraging environment, they might be more active and assertive. As Mueller commented about women state legislators and members of Congress, "Increasingly, they recognized that the experience of officeholding is different for women and men. [There is a] widespread sense of membership in a minority accompanied by varying perceptions of exclusion of 'not being taken seriously.' Where this collective sense of group membership has emerged, women no longer shun the idea of joining together as women legislators" (1982, 57–58).

As evidence of Mueller's claims, one study of the Santa Clara, Calif., County Board of Supervisors showed that, as the numbers of women on the Board increased, the women felt freer to speak out and participate fully in the legislative process. Further, the presence of women in office and the perceived clout of women voters raised the overall amount of legislation pertaining to women that was introduced and passed (Flammang 1985).

More recent empirical research suggests that women's increased representation in elected office has resulted in a significant impact on both attitudes and behaviors of officeholders. For example, female officeholders of both parties continue to be more supportive than men of issues relevant to women, including funding for domestic violence shelters, funding for medical research on women's health care issues, and child support enforcement (Thomas 1990, 1994; Saint-Germain 1989; Dodson and Carroll 1991; Welch 1985). Women, regardless of party, also tend to be more liberal than their male counterparts (Thomas 1994; Carey, Niemi, and Powell 1998; Thomas and Wilcox 1998). Representing the interests of women in the electorate is more often seen as very important by female officeholders than male officeholders. Women are also more likely than men to take pride in accomplishments that further the status of women (Thomas 1994; Thomas and Welch 1991).

Most tellingly, attitudes translate into direct legislative support. Women legislators tend, more often than men, to make priorities of issues important to women and to introduce and successfully usher those priorities through the legislative process. It is important to note that women in politics do not limit themselves only to certain kinds of issues; they are involved in and are successful in the full range of items in the political arena. What is clear, however, is that women are now more active and involved than men on issues that flow from their different life experience (Thomas 1994; Dodson and Carroll 1991; Tamerius 1995).

This chapter examines three hypotheses derived from these ideas. They focus on the likelihood of women organizing their priorities and their successes in getting legislation passed. The greater the proportion of legislators who are women,

the more women legislators will display distinctive priorities, especially in giving priority to women's, children's and family issues;

the more women legislators will be successful in getting legislation relevant to women and families passed; and

the more likely women are to organize into women's legislative caucuses.

Data and Methods

The Survey

The data for this study come from a 1988 survey of members of the lower houses of state legislatures in twelve states: Arizona, California, Georgia, Illinois, Iowa, Mississippi, Nebraska, North Carolina, Pennsylvania, South Dakota, Vermont, and Washington.[2] State legislatures were chosen for our study because women's membership in them far exceeded, on average, that of Congress (as is still the case). Moreover, states vary widely in their proportion of women members, thus allowing useful cross-sectional comparisons.

These particular states were chosen primarily because they represented the full range of proportions of women in state legislatures at the time of data collection, from barely 3 percent in Mississippi to 30 percent in Washington. Diversity in geographical region and political culture were additional criteria for selection, with chosen states representing three major political cultures (Elazar 1984). All women legislators (n = 226), ranging from four in Mississippi to forty-one in Vermont, were surveyed along with thirty male legislators in each state (except in Vermont, where we sampled forty-one men to match the forty-one women legislators).[3]

A four-wave mailing procedure was undertaken (surveys were sent four times to each legislator to encourage a response). The first two waves were sent to state Capitol office addresses and the last two were sent to home addresses in each state, except California. California's third wave was sent to the state Capitol since the legislature was still in session. The fourth wave, which occurred after adjournment, was sent to district offices since those were the only ones publicly available. The waves were mailed approximately four weeks apart during summer 1988. The response rate was 54 percent, ranging from 78 percent in Washington to 22 percent in Mississippi.[4] Nine states had good response rates of 40 to 60 percent. Two states, Nebraska and Washington, were above that level. Mississippi was the only state below 40 percent.[5] Finally, the total number of responses was 322.

We also interviewed women legislators in six of the twelve states:

California, Georgia, Mississippi, Nebraska, Pennsylvania, and Washington. Each legislator was asked a set of questions relating to the role of women in the legislature. A total of sixty-six women were interviewed between August 1988 and May 1989, including fifty-seven legislators and nine staff members. (Those interested in reviewing the survey instruments may find them in Thomas 1994).

The Variables

The unit of analysis is the state (n = 12). The independent variable of interest is the proportion of women in each state's lower house (plus Nebraska's unicameral legislative body). For ease of presentation and interpretation, we group the twelve state legislatures into three categories (Table 8.1): those with fewer than 10 percent women (Mississippi and Pennsylvania), those with 10 to 20 percent women (California, Georgia, Illinois, Iowa, Nebraska, North Carolina, and South Dakota), and those with more than 20 percent women (Arizona, Vermont, and Washington).

Three sets of dependent variables are of interest. The first, derived from the mail questionnaire, measures legislative priorities. Legislators were asked to list their five top-priority bills from the last complete legislative session. Coding categories differentiate bills dealing with women, children and families, budget and taxes, education and health care, business and the economy, energy, environment and public land use, and welfare. An average score was derived for each gender group in each state. For example, in calculating a score for the women's issues priority variable for women legislators in Washington, the scores could range from 0 if none of the women had women's issues as a priority to 1 if all did.

A second set of dependent variables assesses whether women are more successful than men in the passage of bills dealing with women, children, and the family. A measure of success was constructed for each legislator by dividing the number of the legislator's priority bills dealing with women, children, and the family (if any) that were passed by the total number of their priority bills focusing on women, children, and the family. This proportion was averaged for all women in each state and all men in each state and could range from 0 to 1 for each group.

The third category of dependent variable is whether the legislature had a formal women's legislative caucus.

With only twelve states under consideration, it is impossible to control for many variables that could affect the dependent variables. However, each of the three groups of states is a mixture of political cultures,

Table 8.1. Women in State Legislatures

State	% of Women	Legislators in Lower House	Caucus
Higher proportions of women			
Washington	31	98	0
Vermont	27	150	+
Arizona	25	60	0
Medium proportions of women			
South Dakota	19	70	0
Nebraska	18	49	0
Iowa	18	100	**
Illinois	17	118	*
North Carolina	17	120	*
California	15	80	**
Georgia	13	180	0
Lower proportions of women			
Pennsylvania	7	203	0
Mississippi	3	122	++

Nebraska's is a unicameral legislature. The information is from 1987, the year the survey was designed. Data were provided by the Center for the American Woman and Politics, Eagleton Institute of Politics, Rutgers University.

* = presence of a formal caucus; ** = formal caucus with an agenda; + = informal caucus; ++ = informal caucus with an agenda; o = no caucus.

allowing us to assess whether political culture is an alternative explanation for whatever variation we find in the dependent variables.[6] For example, in the first category, all have traditional political cultures.

Findings

Our hypotheses included the expectation that women place a higher priority than men on issues related to women, children, and families and that these gender differences are strongest in legislatures with the highest proportions of women. Table 8.2 illustrates that this was largely the case. These gender differences were consistent in the three states with the highest proportions of women. The gender differences were much smaller in the two states at the other end of the spectrum. Indeed, in

Table 8.2. Gender Differences in Types of Priority Bills

	Women	Children & Family	Business	Welfare	Educ Health	Budget Taxes	Environ.
Washington	W	W		W		W	W
Vermont	W	W		W		W	W
Arizona	W	W					W
South Dakota		W				W	
Nebraska	W				W	W	W
Iowa	W					W	W
Illinois	W	W			W	W	
N.C.	W	W					
California	W						
Georgia	W	W				W	W
Pennsylvania		W				W	
Mississippi						W	W

Note: W denotes that women have more bills in this area as one of their top five priorities. All differences are statistically significant.

Mississippi, women and men appeared equally uninterested in this sort of legislation. In Pennsylvania, neither women nor men made women's bills a priority, although women legislators gave higher priority than men to bills dealing with children and families. States in the middle category displayed no clear trend, as might be expected from the truncated range of percentages.

On the other hand, supporting our theory, political culture does not explain gender differences in women and family issue priorities. Within the traditional political culture states, no difference between women and men was found in Mississippi, but in the other states (Arizona, Georgia, and North Carolina), women gave higher priority than men to women and family bills. Within the moralistic political culture (California, Iowa, South Dakota, Vermont, and Washington), one presumably more open to remedying the unequal status of women (Diamond 1977), results were mixed.

Given the relative paucity of information about how women and men compare in their legislative priorities, it is also of interest to note gender differences and similarities on other issues. As expected, in most states, women were more likely than men to make environmental issues a priority. In every state, men gave higher priority to business bills. Contrary to traditional patterns and to our expectations, however, women were also considerably more likely than men to give priority to tax and budget bills and considerably less likely to give priority to welfare, education, and health bills. Thus, at the same time that women have focused more than men on bills specifically relating to women and the family, they gave less priority than men to traditional women's concerns such as education, health, and welfare, and more to traditional men's concerns, such as taxes and budgets. It is possible that, in part, increased attention by women to issues of women, children, and the family displaced attention from what have been considered more traditional women's issues. It is also possible that women legislators have tried to communicate balance to constituents and colleagues—by devoting attention to women's issues, they may have felt the need to be active on issues that are considered harder or more important. In this way, they might hope to reverse some of the vulnerabilities resulting from a focus that can be portrayed as feminist or liberal (Thomas 1997). A final possible explanation for these issue category findings is simply that women legislators are more diverse and knowledgeable about the range of issues than their foremothers.

Success in Passing Priority Bills

In Table 8.3, we compare the success rates of women and men in getting their priority bills relating to women, children, and the family passed. There is substantial gender-based difference in the mean level of success, with only 13 percent of men's priority bills dealing with women, children, and families passing, compared with almost 29 percent of women's priority bills on these topics. The differences were fairly consistent across the states. In all but three of the states, women's priority bills on these issues were more likely to be passed than men's. While not a direct indicator that women work harder for these priorities, these differences support the interpretation that women spend more energy and effort in passage of these bills than do men. Another interpretation is that women have more credibility on these issues and that their bills are taken more seriously.

Our personal interviews with women legislators in California, Georgia, Mississippi, Nebraska, Pennsylvania, and Washington support these findings. Women legislators believed that they were more concerned than men with issues relevant to women, children, and families. As one legislator explained: "Most of the women are or have been married and have kids. Since they had that experience, those issues are very

Table 8.3. Proportion of Bills on Priority Women, Children, and
Family Passed by Women and Men

State	% of Men's Priority Bills Passed	% of Women's Priority Bills Passed	Ratio of Women's/Men's Bills Passed
Washington	11.1	30.4	2.74
Vermont	0.0	11.3	—
Arizona	17.6	12.5	0.71
South Dakota	11.8	22.2	1.88
Nebraska	7.1	50.0	7.04
Iowa	15.0	61.7	4.11
Illinois	23.1	36.9	1.60
North Carolina	16.7	23.8	1.43
California	51.5	37.5	0.73
Georgia	7.7	25.0	3.25
Pennsylvania	0.0	20.0	—
Mississippi	0.0	0.0	—
Overall mean	12.9	28.5	2.17

Note: — means a ratio has a o divisor and hence cannot be calculated.

important to them. They see it as their responsibility." Moreover, these
women legislators believed that women are freer than men to voice concerns about family issues and that women are seen as having expertise
in these issue areas. This finding supports the theory that women have
greater credibility in these issue areas.

We next compare these relative successes of women and men legislators to the proportion of women in the legislature (Table 8.3). The results do not conform to our expectations. That is, the three states where
men do as well or better than women in getting their priority legislation
on women, children, and the family passed (lowest ratios in Table 8.3)
include one state with a large proportion of women (Arizona), one with
a medium percentage (California), and one state with a low percentage
(Mississippi), where no priority bills passed at all. The highest ratios of
women's to men's success (i.e., highest ratios in Table 8.3) were in three
states in the middle bracket of women's membership (Nebraska, Iowa,
and Georgia).

Another measure of the impact of women legislators is whether legislatures with more women pass more legislation relating to women and families. In other words, the overall output of the legislature, not just how women and men compare within it, is an important indicator of policy impact. Thus, we examined the relationship between the proportion of women in these legislatures and the success of legislators in getting bills relating to women, children, and families passed. For each legislature, the overall success score was calculated by averaging the proportion of each legislator's priority bills on women, children, and families that passed.[7]

There was a slight relationship between the proportion of women in the legislatures and the passage of policies in these areas (Table 8.4). In particular, states with the lowest proportions of women also had the lowest proportion of these bills that passed. Having less than 10 percent women's membership does seem to be a deterrent to successful passage of these bills. However, states with the highest percentages of women legislative members were not the states with the most legislation. In fact, those states ranked fourth, seventh, and tenth respectively.

What other factors might affect legislative output on women's and family issues? One we have discussed is political culture. However, the top five states in legislative output are a mix of cultural types, as are those at the bottom end of the output.

Women's Caucuses

Another explanation for greater legislative attention to women's issues is the presence of organized political caucuses. Of the top five states in the production of women's and family legislation, four had formally organized women's caucuses (Table 8.4). Indeed, they were the only states with such caucuses. The other state among the top five, Washington, was the state with the largest proportion of women members.

These numerical relationships are supported by other evidence. As one western state caucus member noted, "The caucus can be a power bloc; it can make an impact." "Women can work together," another reported. One California assemblywoman reported that "the caucus was an important help in her [finally successful] nine-year push to crack down on private clubs that refuse to allow women members" (Zeiger and Jeffe 1988). A staff member for one state women's caucus remarked that "The issues the caucus works on include domestic violence, family law, homelessness, child care, pay equity, child abuse, and pre-natal care. . . . The caucus is very effective in the legislature; when the bills go before committee, the legislators are afraid to vote against a power bloc."

Table 8.4. Ranking of the States on Legislative Output Relating to Women and Families

State	% Women in Legislature	Caucus
California	15	Yes
Iowa	18	Yes
Illinois	17	Yes
Washington	31	No
North Carolina	17	Yes
Georgia	13	No
Arizona	25	No
Nebraska	18	No
South Dakota	19	No
Vermont	27	Informal
Pennsylvania	7	No
Mississippi	3	Informal

Note: California has the most legislative output relating to women and families, Mississippi the least.

Thus, it appears that, to promote more legislation of special relevance to women and families, the existence of a formal women's caucus might be at least as important as the sheer proportions of women legislators.

We hypothesized that the higher the percentage of women in the legislature, the more likely a state would be to have a women's caucus. Table 8.4 indicates that our hypothesis was not supported. Of the states with the highest percentage of women members, only Vermont had a women's legislative caucus, in this case an informal one. Moreover, while we would expect states with few women members not to have women's caucuses, Mississippi also had an informal one (although it was new). In fact, no pattern in the presence of women's caucuses existed that can be explained by either proportion of women in the legislature or political culture. The absolute size of the legislature did appear to be related to the formation of women's caucuses, although our explanation of this is rather post hoc. Only one of five lower houses with fewer than one hundred members had a caucus (California). In larger legislatures, five of seven had caucuses. Perhaps the small legislatures were more collegial or there were norms against special-interest caucuses. Or perhaps the absolute number of women in these legislatures was fairly small even when the proportion was high (although there were thirty women in the Washington lower house). In any event, legislatures of 100 to 150 seemed to be the most conducive to the formation of women's caucuses.

Mueller (1982) has suggested that the formation of a women's caucus depends on the partisan environment of the legislature, how threatened male colleagues feel, and whether women are wary of collective organizations because of past legislative history. These factors seem relevant here. In Washington, a woman's caucus was created early in the 1980s, but the leadership forced it to disband. Because of the strong partisanship within the legislature, the speaker felt sure of the necessary votes to move his legislative agenda without losing the women of his party. The rewards and sanctions of partisan loyalties were stronger than identification with the caucus, which, on its own, could deliver neither. However, our personal interviews indicated that, in Washington, the women legislators supported one another informally and many were also quite powerful individually. That, combined with their numbers, may be why women in this state were so successful in getting their priorities passed.

One-party dominance in combination with strong leaders can also inhibit caucus formation. Interviews in Mississippi and Georgia revealed that although Mississippi had many fewer women legislators than Georgia, Mississippi women legislators were much more optimistic that adding to their number would stimulate the formation of a formal caucus and lead to policies reflecting more concern for women and the family. The Georgia women legislators repeatedly complained about the effect the powerful speaker had on the one-party-dominated state. They believed that even if women banded together, it would not be enough to challenge the speaker's power unless there was a tremendous increase in the number of women members. Women in Mississippi, on the other hand, where the speaker was much less powerful, believed that, with increased numbers, their informal caucus would have more clout and more impact on policies. Thus, the strength of the leadership, the degree of partisanship in the legislature, and party competitiveness can all affect the development of a formal women's caucus.

Conclusions: When Do Women Make a Difference and Why Does It Matter?

For a number of reasons, women legislators can make a difference. Women legislators, like women in the mass public, have slightly more liberal issue attitudes, and women legislators, compared with their male counterparts, give a higher priority to women's issues. These are preconditions for women to have a distinctive influence, but some of the preconditions were in place twenty to twenty-five years ago. What has changed that has enhanced women's influence?

Two contextual factors seem to increase this influence. A big change is simply the larger numbers of women. Women are no longer a small minority in most legislatures. (This is even more true today than when this survey was conducted.) Our study reveals that where women were a noticeable group, they were better able to focus their own attention, as well as that of their male colleagues, on issues of importance to them and to other women (see also Berkman and O'Connor 1993 for evidence that proportionality of women in state legislatures is linked to abortion policy). Women were more willing to give higher priority to women's issues than they had in earlier eras. With more women in legislatures, men legislators were more likely to perceive the legitimacy of women's legislative priorities.

A second, even more powerful contextual factor enabling women to make a difference was banding together for collective action. The existence of a women's caucus appears to be related to the successful passage of women's legislation. In our study, women's caucuses were not limited to states with the largest proportions of women members. However, they did not occur in any state with fewer than 15 percent women's members. Thus, having a noticeable number of women may be a necessary, although not sufficient, condition for the formation of such a caucus. Among the top states in production of legislation on women, children, and families, all but Washington had a women's caucus. And in Washington, women made up more than 30 percent of the legislative membership, the highest proportion in our sample of legislatures; moreover, they appeared to work together to pass legislation of interest to women.

In sum, women are most likely to make a distinct contribution to U.S. state legislatures when they are not tokens and when they organize to work together on mutual goals. Women legislators adapt their behavior as they move from the status of tokens to that of mainstream members. This finding may have implications for our understanding of the behavior of other groups too, particularly minorities.

Our results also have implications for our understanding of public agendas. As women move into the mainstream of legislative membership, they change legislative agendas to include topics that heretofore have been slighted. Issues such as latchkey children, domestic violence, comparable worth, and family leave, previously thought mostly to belong to the private sphere, have been moved onto the public agenda.

It is not surprising that emergent political minorities bring their social concerns to the governmental agenda. Future research needs to focus on the ways in which this is most effectively achieved and the factors that promote success of that agenda. Another scholarly goal might include the point or points at which the perspectives and goals of political minorities take on a mainstream focus. As Susan Carroll notes in the introduction to this volume, there is much work left to do.

Notes

The authors are grateful for the financial support for this project given by the Center for American Women and Politics and the National Science Foundation. They also express thanks to Rebekah Herrick and Kidae Kim for data collection and processing assistance.

1. The exception is the Thomas (1990) study of the California Assembly showing that women legislators were more supportive of women's issues than were men legislators but not more liberal overall. Consistent with these findings, the present study shows women in California and Arizona to be less liberal than their male counterparts.

2. Since Nebraska has a unicameral legislature, its one house is the focus of our survey there. Lower houses were chosen because more women held office there than in upper houses.

3. Thirty was chosen somewhat arbitrarily. We planned to match the number of women in each house with an equal number of men but decided to sample at least thirty men in each state. Only Vermont had more than thirty women in its lower house, which is why Vermont is the only state where more than thirty men are sampled. The total number of women is 226, reflecting the number of women in the legislature at the time we designed our survey.

4. The response rate for each state was as follows: Arizona 59 percent, California 43 percent, Georgia 53 percent, Illinois 48 percent, Iowa 57 percent, Mississippi 22 percent, Nebraska 64 percent, North Carolina 53 percent, Pennsylvania 40 percent, South Dakota 52 percent, Vermont 49 percent, Washington 78 percent. Gender-based differences in response rates were as follows: Arizona, 62 percent male, 53 percent female; California, 37 percent male, 58 percent female; Georgia, 43 percent male, 65 percent female; Illinois, 37 percent male, 65 percent female; Iowa, 38 percent male, 89 percent female; Mississippi, 18 percent male, 50 percent female; Nebraska, 70 percent male, 44 percent female; North Carolina, 41 percent male, 70 percent female; Pennsylvania, 43 percent male, 36 percent female; South Dakota, 60 percent male, 38 percent female; Vermont, 43 percent male, 56 percent female; Washington, 63 percent male, 93 percent female; total for all states combined, 46 percent male, 63 percent female.

5. The overall response rate compares well with other studies of state legislators, including those of Ambrosius and Welch (1988) and Welch and Pe-

ters (1977). In the subsequent analysis, individual respondents were weighted so that the proportions of each sex by state in the sample equaled that in the universe of bodies that we sampled. In fact, weighting makes no significant differences in findings reported here; unweighted and weighted coefficients are similar.

6. States can be classified into three major political cultural types specified by Elazar (1984). Arizona, Georgia, Mississippi, and North Carolina are best classified as traditional; Nebraska, Illinois, and Pennsylvania as individualistic; and California, Iowa, South Dakota, Vermont, and Washington as moralistic.

7. This measure was imperfect, relying as it did on survey responses.

References

Ambrosius, Margery M., and Susan Welch. 1988. "State Legislators' Perceptions of Business and Labor Interests." *Legislative Studies Quarterly* 13: 199–209.

Berkman, Michael B., and Robert E. O'Connor. 1993. "Do Women Legislators Matter? Female Legislators and State Abortion Policy." *American Politics Quarterly* 21: 102–124.

Carey, John M., Richard G. Niemi, and Lynda Powell. 1998. "Are Women State Legislators Different?" In *Women and Elective Office: Past, Present, and Future*, ed. Sue Thomas and Clyde Wilcox. New York: Oxford University Press.

Carroll, Susan. 1984. "Women Candidates and Support for Feminist Concerns: The Closet Feminist Syndrome." *Western Political Quarterly* 37: 307–323.

Dodson, Debra L., and Susan J. Carroll. 1991. *Reshaping the Agenda: Women in State Legislatures.* New Brunswick, N.J.: Center for the American Woman and Politics.

Diamond, Irene. 1977. *Sex Roles in the State House.* New Haven, Conn.: Yale University Press.

Elazar, Daniel J. 1984. *American Federalism: A View from the States.* 3rd ed. New York: Harper and Row.

Flammang, Janet A. 1985. "Female Officials in the Feminist Capital: The Case of Santa Clara County." *Western Political Quarterly* 38: 94–118.

Frankovic, Kathleen A. 1977. "Sex and Voting in the U.S. House of Representatives 1961–1975." *American Politics Quarterly* 5: 315–331.

Gehlen, Freida. 1977. "Women Members of Congress: A Distinctive Role." In *A Portrait of Marginality*, ed. Marianne Githens and Jewel L. Prestage. New York: McKay.

Hill, David B. 1983. "Women State Legislators and Party Voting on the ERA." *Social Science Quarterly* 64: 318–326.

Johnson, Marilyn, and Susan Carroll with Kathy Stanwick and Lynn Korenblit. 1978. *Profile of Women Holding Office II.* New Brunswick, N.J.: Center for the American Woman and Politics.

Kanter, Rosabeth M. 1977. "Some Effects of Proportions on Group Life: Skewed Sex Ratios and Response to Token Women." *American Journal of Sociology* 82: 965–990.

Kirkpatrick, Jeane. 1974. *Political Woman*. New York: Basic Books.

Leader, Shelah G. 1977. "The Policy Impact of Elected Women Officials." In *The Impact of the Electoral Process*, ed. Louis Maisel and Joseph Cooper. Beverly Hills: Sage.

Lilie, Joyce R., Roger Handberg, Jr., and Wanda Lowrey. 1982. "Women State Legislators and the ERA: Dimensions of Support and Opposition." *Women & Politics* 2: 23–38.

Mezey, Susan Gluck. 1978. "Support for Women's Rights Policy: An Analysis of Local Politicians." *American Politics Quarterly* 6: 485–497.

Mueller, Carol. 1982. "A Scholar's Perspective." In *Women State Legislators: Report from a Conference*. New Brunswick, N.J.: Eagleton Institute of Politics.

Saint-Germain, Michelle. 1989. "Does Their Difference Make a Difference? The Impact of Women on Public Policy in the Arizona Legislature." *Social Science Quarterly* 70: 956–968.

Tamerius, Karen L. 1995. "Sex, Gender, and Leadership in the Representation of Women." In *Gender Power, Leadership, and Governance*, ed. Georgia Duerst-Lahti and Rita Mae Kelly. Ann Arbor: University of Michigan Press.

Thomas, Sue. 1990. "Voting Patterns in the California Assembly: The Role of Gender." *Women & Politics* 9: 43–56.

Thomas, Sue. 1994. *How Women Legislate*. New York: Oxford University Press.

Thomas, Sue. 1997. "Why Gender Matters: The Perceptions of Women Officeholders." *Women & Politics* 17: 27–53.

Thomas, Sue, and Susan Welch. 1991. "The Impact of Gender on Activities and Priorities of State Legislators." *Western Political Quarterly* 44: 445–456.

Thomas, Sue, and Clyde Wilcox, eds. 1998. *Women and Elective Office: Past, Present, and Future*. New York: Oxford University Press.

Welch, Susan. 1985. "Are Women More Liberal Than Men in the U.S. Congress?" *Legislative Studies Quarterly* 10: 125–134.

Welch, Susan, and John G. Peters. 1977. "Some Problems of Stimulating Responses to Mail Questionnaires." *Political Methodology* 71: 139–151.

Zeiger, Richard, and Sherry Bebitch Jeffe. 1988. "Women in Politics." *California Journal* 19: 7–11.

PART III

THE EFFECTS OF IDENTITY POLITICS

Nine

Black Women in State Legislatures

The Relationship of Race and Gender to the Legislative Experience

Edith J. Barrett

The number of women and minorities entering public office has increased with every election in recent years. In 2000, 22.5 percent of state legislators were women, and although the percentage of women now in office is far from proportional to the population, it represents a large advancement for women. Likewise, blacks make up 7.9 percent of state legislators (as of 1999), a proportion that is closer than ever to parity with the 12.3 percent of the U.S. population that blacks embody. Intersecting both of these groups and often overlooked by scholars writing on either group are black women (who made up 2.5 percent of all state legislators in 1999). While still a disproportionate minority among both women and blacks, black women have nonetheless achieved greater parity with respect to black men (about 30 percent of black legislators are women) than white women have achieved with respect to white men.[1] Of course all legislators have many affiliations, from political party membership to interest group affiliations, but black women are distinctive in being members of two traditionally excluded groups: women and blacks.

Experiences as both women and members of a historically oppressed racial minority group have provided African American women a unique standpoint on feminism (Collins 1991). Black feminist women share with white feminist women the burden of living and working within a male-dominated society, and this has, to some extent, shaped their identity as feminists. However, black women face the additional hardship brought on by not being a member of the dominant racial group. Their membership in an underrepresented racial group plays as much, if not

185

more, of a role in defining their singular black feminist identity (Gay and Tate 1998; Collins 1991; hooks 1984). Furthermore, and perhaps because of their racial experiences, black women have been stauncher supporters than white women of gender equality (Baxter and Lansing 1983), and they remain more likely than white women to identify as feminists (Mansbridge and Tate 1992).

The attitudes black women hold about politics and policy are no doubt informed by their experiences as women and as African Americans (Gay and Tate 1998; King 1988). There is clear evidence that black and white politicians differ in their political outlook, with blacks much more likely than whites to associate with the Democratic Party and liberal policies (Dawson 1994; Tate 1993). Women politicians, likewise, lean more than men toward liberal policies and the Democratic Party (Witt, Paget, and Matthews 1994; Carroll 1991; Mezey 1978; Leader 1977). Past research demonstrates the hurdles both women and blacks have had to overcome, and the literature points out the policy differences among female, black, and white male legislators. Scholars have paid little attention, however, to the situations faced by black women politicians and even less to the policy priorities of these demographically unique legislators. The purpose of this chapter is to broaden the discussion of black women as state legislators by examining their attitudes and policy preferences and by comparing the views of black women with those of other women and with those of black men.

Data Collection

In the spring of 1992, questionnaires were sent to all black women serving in state legislatures, as well as to a geographically matched sample of African American male, nonminority female, and nonminority male legislators. Whenever possible, each black woman respondent was matched with a black man, a white woman, and a white man from the same state and the same region within the state. When this was not possible, matches were made with legislators from neighboring regions or states. Only Democrats were included in the survey, because all members of the primary population of interest—black women legislators— were Democrats. The items on the questionnaire asked specifically about gender and race issues, and, since it was anticipated that men would respond to the survey at lower rates than women, a larger sample was taken from the two male populations.

A personalized letter, the questionnaire, and a postage-paid return envelope were mailed to 518 potential respondents in January 1992, just after the legislative session resumed after the winter break. Six weeks later, at the end of February, those who had not yet responded were sent a second survey and return envelope. In order to increase the minority participation and yet stay within a limited postage budget, a third mailing was sent at the end of March to black legislators only. A total of 230 legislators returned completed questionnaires, yielding an overall response rate of 44.5 percent for the survey. White women returned questionnaires at the highest rate (n = 71, 58.2%), followed by black women (n = 53, 50.0%), white men (n = 54, 37.2%), and finally, black men (n = 52, 35.9%). While the response rates for men are lower than for women, they are not unexpectedly low. Response rates in the 30 to 40 percent range are quite common for surveys of elites (Miller 1991). Despite the difference between male and female response rates, the samples remain similar with regard to region of the country, the matching variable. The majority of respondents lived in either the South (ranging from 36 percent of white women to 46 percent of black men) or the East (ranging from 28 percent of black women to 33 percent of black men), and there was no statistically significant regional variation across groups.

With a few exceptions, the respondents did not differ in their personal characteristics. The female respondents were less likely to be married than their male colleagues, and this was especially the case among black women. The women were also much less likely to have children—especially school-age children—than the black men but did not differ from the white men. And although at the time of the survey there were no age differences across the gender and race groups (the mean age was 52.4 years), the women tended to have been older than the white men, but not the black men, when first elected into office. Given this, it was inevitable that the women also had a shorter tenure in office than the men.[2] There were, however, no racial differences in either the proportion who had held previous office (mean 37.8%) or the number of years they spent in that previous position (an average of 6.7 years). These observed demographic characteristics were similar to those found in other studies (see Thomas 1994).

On average, as reported by the legislators, 36 percent of the constituents within each of the districts were African American (ranging from 0% to 98%), and 32 percent of the constituents were "poor" (ranging from 0% to 99%). Not surprisingly, districts represented by blacks tended to have higher proportions of African Americans (mean 57%) than districts represented by whites (mean 17%), and African American legislators tended to have higher proportions of low-income residents in their district (mean 40% for black legislators and 25% for white). Controlling for race, the demographic composition of districts represented by women was similar to that of the men's districts.

The Legislative Environment for
Women and Minorities

Although rarely easy for any candidate, for women and minorities the path into elected office can be particularly onerous. Women and minorities may face obstacles not placed before their white male opponents. Most obvious among these is public prejudice against nontraditional candidates, such as women and minorities. Women have had to overcome public sentiment that "women should stay at home and leave politics to men." Blacks have confronted racism at every point of their public lives. As recently as 1992, a poll found that 8.4 percent of North Carolina residents would refuse in general to vote for a woman even if she were a party-endorsed candidate, and 7.6 percent would hold out against an endorsed black candidate (Carolina Poll 1992). Nontraditional candidates often find themselves having to spend campaign time and money trying to persuade voters that they can do the job as well as white men rather than focusing on more politically pertinent issues.

Once in office, women and minorities also may find themselves facing difficulties integrating fully into the legislative environment. For example, Blair and Stanley (1991) discovered that women legislators regularly avoid close collegial relationships with men legislators for fear that such relationships would be misconstrued as romantic. Yet in forgoing close contact with male peers, women legislators lose an important potential avenue of opportunity for political support and career advancement (Blair and Stanley 1991). Likewise, minority legislators may have a difficult time achieving equal professional respect from their white colleagues (Simon 1987). Consequently, women and minorities may find themselves feeling denied leadership positions or prestigious committee assignments. Women and minority legislators may feel that any one of a number of barriers blocks them from becoming completely integrated into the legislative environment. One might expect minority women to feel especially impeded.

In the survey, legislators were asked a series of questions concerning the potential barriers faced by women and by minorities. Respondents were asked the degree to which they agree that: (1) once elected, women/minorities "have to work harder to prove themselves" than do men/whites; (2) in general, women/minorities "are not as aggressive" as men/whites in getting legislation passed; (3) most men/whites "are better suited emotionally for politics" than most women/whites; (4) women/minorities "are less likely than men/whites to interact with legislative leaders"; (5) "in general, the public is less willing to elect women/minorities to state legislatures"; and (6) women/minorities "bring unique assets into the policymaking arena." All respondents answered the six questions with respect to women as well as with respect to minorities. There were no questions directly asking about the experiences of minority women.

In their perceptions of the barriers faced by women, black women sometimes agreed and sometimes disagreed with white women (Table 9.1). Both black and white women agreed that women must work harder than men to prove themselves, that women bring unique assets to the legislature, and that, emotionally, women are as well-suited for politics as men. In these beliefs they were dissimilar from their male colleagues, who were less likely to see differences between men and women legislators. On the other hand, while white women were more likely than both black and white men to perceive women as having fewer opportunities to interact with legislative leaders, black women failed to see any gender-based disparity and agreed with men that the two genders have relatively equal access. White women and white men were in agreement that the public did not make gender distinctions, but black women—and, to a slightly lesser extent, black men—saw the situation differently. Both black women and black men felt more strongly than whites that the public was less willing to support female candidates. All legislators tended to generally agree that women are no less aggressive then men in their role as legislators.

Turning to their beliefs about the experiences of blacks in state legislatures, black and white women were more consistently in agreement. However, their views tended also to be similar to those of black men. White men alone seemed to differ from their colleagues in perceptions of the black legislative experience. Black men and women as well as white women tended to agree with the statement that blacks must work harder than whites to prove themselves, and they believed this to be the case more than did white men legislators (Table 9.1). Black men and all women tended to agree that blacks bring unique assets to the legislature, and they felt more strongly about this than white men. Although all legislators tended to maintain that blacks and whites are equally suited emotionally for legislative office, blacks and white women held this belief more strongly than white men. Black men were most likely to perceive that the public is less willing to elect black candidates; their

190

Table 9.1. Mean Scores on Beliefs about the Legislative Environment
for Women and Blacks Controlling for Years in Office and
District Composition[a] (by Race and Gender)

	Black Women (A) n = 53	Black Men (B) n = 52	White Women (C) n = 71	White Men (D) n = 54
Must Work Harder to Prove Self				
Women	1.77 (B,D)	2.48	1.62 (B,D)	2.69
Blacks	1.79 (C,D)	1.92 (D)	2.10 (D)	2.85
		*	+	
Bring Unique Assets				
Women	1.24 (B,D)	1.65	1.26 (D)	1.92
Blacks	1.44 (D)	1.33 (C,D)	1.58 (D)	1.96
	+	*	+	
Men/Whites Better Suited Emotionally				
Women	3.81 (B,D)	3.38	3.72 (B,D)	3.18
Blacks	3.81 (D)	3.81 (D)	3.68 (D)	3.40
		+		+
Less Likely to Interact with Leaders				
Women	3.08 (C)	2.92	2.49 (B,D)	2.92
Blacks	3.02	2.94	2.78	3.03
			+	
Public Less Willing to Elect Women/Blacks				
Women	2.74 (C,D)	2.76	3.16	3.20
Blacks	2.25	1.91 (C,D)	2.42	2.66
	*	*	*	*
Not as Aggressive as Men/Whites				
Women	3.11	3.16	2.94	3.17
Blacks	3.18	3.25	3.27	3.16
			+	

[a]Defined as the proportion of white residents within the district. Scores range from 1 (strongly agree) to 4 (strongly disagree). Letters denote other groups from which the given group differs significantly ($p < .05$).

*Denotes cases in which the mean with respect to blacks is significantly lower than mean with respect to women.

+Denotes cases in which the mean with respect to women is significantly lower than mean with respect to blacks.

beliefs differed significantly only from those of whites (both men and women). Black women did not differ from whites in their attitudes about public support. Finally, there were no racial or gender differences in legislators' beliefs about the aggressiveness of black politicians or in their beliefs about the access black legislators have to political leaders.

Although white women tended to agree with black men and women that blacks face barriers in the legislative environment, white women nonetheless tended to feel that women are at a greater disadvantage than blacks. White women believed that women must prove themselves against men more often than blacks must prove themselves against whites; that women interact less with leaders compared with men than blacks compared with whites; that the difference between women and men in their aggressiveness in pursuing policy is greater than the corresponding difference between blacks and whites; that women have an added responsibility of proving a broad agenda; and finally, that women are more different from men than blacks are from whites.

Black men tended to be of the opposite viewpoint. They were more likely to believe that blacks have a harder time proving themselves than women; that the public is more anti-black than it is anti-women; that women are less emotionally suited for politics compared with men than blacks are compared with whites; that blacks are more important for the advancement of minority policy than women are for women's policy; that blacks must show a broader agenda than women; and that, compared to women, blacks bring more unique attributes into office.

Unlike white women or black men, though, black women appeared to make few distinctions between the barriers faced by women and those faced by blacks. They agreed only that women bring more unique attributes and that the public is less accepting of blacks—a perception shared by all legislators regardless of race or gender. Thus, the data suggested that black women were similar neither to white women in their belief that women's fate is worse nor to black men in believing that blacks face higher hurdles. Black women sensed that both groups confront equally difficult obstacles.

Policy Priorities of Women and Minorities

In 1916, Jeannette Rankin (R-Mont.) became the first women elected to the United States Congress. Rankin fulfilled her congressional duties as any other member, but perhaps her most memorable vote was the first she cast. In a House that voted 373 to 50 in favor of U.S. involvement in World War I, Rankin stood firm against sending American troops. Although some congressmen also voted against involvement, her vote mirrored an expectation of women's general antiwar, pro-family stand. Shirley Chisholm, the first African American woman elected to Congress, showed her strong interest in bettering the situation for minority and poor Americans when, in her campaign, she placed attention on seven specific policy issues: jobs, job training, equality education, adequate housing, enforcement of anti-discrimination laws, support for day care, and an end to the Vietnam War. The belief that women and ethnic minorities fulfill a particular niche within the legislature remains. Although they may not always have the opportunity to pursue their own policy agenda, most legislators no doubt enter office with a sense of what they would like to accomplish legislatively, if given the chance.

Women and minority legislators may at times feel such strong pressure to meet others' expectations that they act as group representatives. Women and minority members of the public pay close attention to the actions of women and minority legislators, believing that these politicians may be their closest allies (Mezey 1978; Kilson 1989; Meier 1979; Rohr 1986). It is not surprising, therefore, that black legislators tend to pay especially close attention to issues affecting their black constituencies (Smith 1990; Sokolow 1971), nor that women tend to focus a disproportionately greater amount of time on the concerns of women (Carroll 1991; Leader 1977; Merritt 1982). Although this may be an advantage in terms of voter support, it can also place an added obligation on women and minority legislators. Few black politicians can afford to alienate whites (Hochschild 1993; Kilson 1989), and women politicians must work within the male-dominated establishment. Thus, women and minority legislators may find themselves pulled in two directions: Their female or minority constituents may demand special attention while their white male constituents and colleagues may push them to show breadth.

On the whole, women legislators have shown themselves to be different from men in their policy priorities. Studies have found women state legislators to be more liberal than men, even when controlling for party membership (Leader 1977), and women state legislators tend to be more concerned with feminist issues than their male colleagues (Mezey 1978). When asked about their most important policy concerns, women are more likely than men to offer at least one women-oriented issue (Carroll 1991, this volume; Thomas and Welch, this volume). Women are more likely than men to work on legislation addressing traditional women's issues (Carroll 1991, this volume; Merritt 1982), especially when the number of women within a legislature increases. Saint-Germain (1989) notes that as the number of women in the Arizona state legislature has increased, women have begun introducing legislation addressing traditional women's concerns (e.g., abortion, children, education, family, public health, sex, and welfare) more often than their male colleagues. (See also Thomas and Welch, this volume.)

There is less evidence that African American legislators are distinctive in pursuing policy aimed at the minority population, in part because black issues are perhaps less clearly defined than women's issues (Kilson 1989; Tate 1993). During the racially volatile 1960s and 1970s, many black politicians focused their policy initiatives on the needs of blacks and were able to win the white liberal vote as well because of their attention to the poor and blighted urban areas (Smith 1990). Research from that period shows black state legislators paying especially close attention to issues such as health, education, and crime (Sokolow 1971). Today as well, state-level black legislative caucuses appear to successfully introduce policy aiding blacks (Miller 1990). No study to date has examined the potentially unique policy position of African American women.

Beliefs about Legislative Obligations

Included in the survey of state legislators described earlier were three items asking respondents whether they believed that women and minority legislators have a special responsibility to address the policy needs of women and minorities. Respondents were asked the degree to which they agree that: (1) "it is necessary to have women/minorities in state legislatures to ensure that women's/minority concerns get addressed," (2) "women/minority legislators should pay attention foremost to women's/minority issues," and (3) "to rise within the ranks, women/minority legislators must show concern for a broader range of policy issues than must men/whites." All respondents answered the questions with regard to both women and minorities.

Black women held beliefs similar to white women's concerning the policy role of female legislators (Table 9.2). Both black women and white women believed quite strongly that women's policy needs are best served when women legislators are present. In this belief, though, they differed only from white men; black men were just as likely as women to agree that women legislators are needed to advance women's policy issues. Black and white women also tended to agree with each other and disagree with black and white men that women legislators must prove to their male colleagues that they are pursuing a broad policy agenda. Finally, none of the four groups of legislators tended to believe that

Table 9.2. Mean Scores on Beliefs about the Legislative Obligations for
Women and Blacks Controlling for Years in Office and District
Composition[a] (by Race and Gender)

	Black Women (A) n = 53	Black Men (B) n = 52	White Women (C) n = 71	White Men (D) n = 54
Necessary for Women/Minority Issues				
Women	1.54 (D)	1.77 (D)	1.61 (D)	2.27
Blacks	1.41 (D)	1.36 (C,D)	1.74 (D)	2.23
		*		
Must Show Broader Agenda				
Women	2.06 (B,D)	2.51 (D)	2.20 (B,D)	2.98
Blacks	2.02 (C,D)	2.03 (C,D)	2.52 (D)	2.95
		*	+	
Must Pay Attention to Wom/Min Issues				
Women	2.88 (D)	3.16	2.92 (D)	3.34
Blacks	2.66	2.50 (C,D)	2.94	3.09
		*		*

[a]Defined as the proportion of white residents within the district. Scores range from 1 (strongly agree) to 4 (strongly disagree). Letters denote other groups from which the given group differs significantly (p < .05).

*Denotes cases in which the mean with respect to blacks is significantly lower than mean with respect to women.

+Denotes cases in which the mean with respect to women is significantly lower than mean with respect to blacks.

women are particularly obligated to pay foremost attention to women's issues, but to the degree that such a pressure was felt, it was women—both black and white—who sensed it the most.

Both black men and black women expressed a strong belief that minorities are a necessary ingredient in the success of minority policy, and in this belief they differed greatly from white men and not as much from white women. The same pattern showed for attitudes about the breadth of the black policy agenda. Black men and women felt much more strongly than white men that blacks must maintain a broad agenda, and although significantly different from their black colleagues, white women also tended to believe more so than white men that blacks must demonstrate wide policy interests. Finally, black men were most likely to maintain that blacks must pay special attention to minority issues, and in this they differed significantly from white men and women.

Black women tended to see women and minorities sharing an equally strong burden of representing the policy interests of minorities and women. On the other hand, white women sensed that women have a greater burden than minorities to prove policy breadth. And black men believed that blacks are more necessary for minority policy than women are for women's policy; that blacks have a greater responsibility to pay foremost attention to minority issues compared to women's responsibility; and finally, that more pressure is put on blacks to show breadth than is put on women. As with the barriers faced by legislators, the data once again suggested that black men and white women make distinctions between blacks and women that black women do not make.

Support for Targeted Policy

The questionnaire asked respondents how they felt about a number of current policy issues, some of which focus especially on the needs of women, some on the needs of minorities, and some on neither group specifically. Five items were included in a scale as measures of support for women's policy: publicly funded parental leave, affirmative-action and equal-opportunity programs, state-mandated comparable worth, government-subsidized child care, and legislation preventing housing discrimination against families with children.[3] Affirmative-action and equal-opportunity programs also target the needs of minorities, and this item tended to fit better in the minority-policy factor. It has been included, therefore, in the minority-policy factor, along with items questioning the validity of mandated government contracts with minority-owned businesses, state divestment from South Africa, and minority hiring quotas.[4]

The remaining miscellaneous policy items correlate neither with the women's scale, the minority scale, nor one another and therefore cannot be considered a single factor. These issues include financial incentives for banks to invest in the local community, flag burning, tax credits to businesses, and creating jobs to reduce inflation. Table 9.3 provides the exact wording of the policy issue questions and the mean responses shown by gender and race.

In general, women tended to be more favorable than men toward policy that targets the specific needs of women. However, black women legislators felt more strongly about such policies than did white women legislators. Black women were more supportive than white women of

Table 9.3. Mean Scores on Beliefs about the Policy Role of Women and
Black Legislators Controlling for Years in Office and District
Composition[a] (by Race and Gender)

	Black Women (A) n = 53	Black Men (B) n = 52	White Women (C) n = 71	White Men (D) n = 54
Support for Women's Issues				
Government should mandate publicly funded parental leave policy.	1.68 (B,C,D)	2.22	2.06 (D)	2.51
State law should mandate the payment of comparable wages for comparable jobs.	1.37 (C,D)	1.60 (D)	1.78 (D)	2.30
Government-funded child care is essential to addressing the problems of poor women.	1.58	1.57	1.49 (D)	1.92
Except in the case of apartments for the elderly, landlords should be forbidden from discriminating against families with children in renting property.	1.49 (B,C,D)	1.73 (D)	1.98	2.24
Support for Minority Issues				
Affirmative action/equal opportunity programs are essential if inequalities are to be reduced.	1.51 (C,D)	1.50 (C,D)	1.81 (D)	2.24
Government agencies should be required to award a portion of public contracts to minority-owned business.	1.39 (C,D)	1.37 (C,D)	2.02 (D)	2.43
States should have been forbidden from investing state pension funds in South Africa.	1.50 (D)	1.54 (D)	1.81	2.06
Quotas do not force employers to lower their hiring standards.	1.50 (C,D)	1.62 (C,D)	2.17 (D)	2.70

Table 9.3 *Continued*

	Black Women (A)	Black Men (B)	White Women (C)	White Men (D)
Support for Other Issues				
State government should give financial incentives to banks to invest in the local community.	1.92 (D)	2.12 (D)	2.30	2.49
State legislatures should pass a law forbidding the burning of the American flag.	2.71 (C)	2.97 (C)	3.42 (D)	2.84
States should entice new business with tax credits.	2.08 (C)	2.23	2.52 (D)	2.17
Creating jobs for the unemployed is more important than holding down inflation.	1.76 (D)	1.83 (D)	1.86	2.18
Special schools for inner-city minority males is a viable way of addressing the problems of ethnic youth.	2.36	2.23 (C)	2.71	2.41

[a]Defined as the proportion of white residents within the district. Scores range from 1 (strongly agree) to 4 (strongly disagree). Letters denote other groups from which the given group differs significantly ($p < .05$).

state-mandated comparable-worth policy, of laws forbidding landlords from discriminating against families with children, and of publicly funded parental leave. White and black women agreed only in the level of strong support they held for state-sponsored child care for poor women. The support black men held for the women-oriented policies tended to be similar to that of white women.

Blacks tended to be more supportive than whites of policy targeting minorities, and black women and black men tended to think alike (Table 9.3). Further, although white women were more likely than white men to believe that affirmative action is an important step toward reducing inequalities, that public contracts should give priority to minority-owned businesses, and that hiring quotas do not diminish the quality of the workforce, they were nonetheless not as positive in their support as black women. Black women also tended to believe more strongly than white men and somewhat more strongly than white women that states should not be allowed to invest state pensions in South Africa.[5] Thus, in their support for minority-targeted policy, black women were more similar to black men than they were to white women.

Finally, it is important to note that, although black women were most supportive overall of women- and minority-targeted policies, they did not necessarily differ from their colleagues on other policy topics (Table 9.3). Blacks (both men and women) were more supportive than white men of the state government's providing incentives to banks to invest in the local community and of creating jobs for the unemployed. Black men and black women were the most supportive and white women the least supportive of laws forbidding flag burning. Black and white women disagreed strongly on the use of tax credits to entice new business: Black women supported such policies, and white women opposed them.

In sum, then, regardless of whether the policy targets minorities or women, black women legislators tended to be more supportive than their colleagues. Furthermore, black women did not appear to distinguish between the targeted recipients when determining their level of support. They were as likely to support minority-targeted policies as women-targeted policies, and they tended to favor both types of policies over the general legislation questions also included in the survey. Black women did not appear to be predisposed to support the needs of one group above another, while both white women and black men seemed to hold clearer preferences.

The Policy Agenda

Every legislator in the survey was asked to list the three issues that he or she believed were of greatest concern to him or her as a legislator. To avoid prompting certain answers, the item was placed early in the questionnaire before the specific policy issues discussed above. The responses generally fell into 20 separate agenda items. Some of the issues were listed by many legislators (for example, 64 percent mentioned education or education reform), while others were mentioned infrequently (for example, only 1 percent expressed concern with redistricting and 2 percent with transportation policy). More than half the legislators included education, health care, or both on their top priority list (Table 9.4). About one-fourth of the respondents wrote down economic development, employment, tax reform, and state budget issues. The remaining top issues were given by fewer than 15 percent of the legislators.

Education was the most frequently mentioned policy concern among all legislators responding to the survey. Black women were generally

Table 9.4. Percent of Legislators Citing the Ten Most Frequent
Listed Issues, Shown by Race and Gender

	Blacks		Whites		Number of
	Women	Men	Women	Men	Respondents
1. Education	73.6	59.6	62.0	63.0	148
2. Health care	73.6	40.4	46.5	55.6	123
3. Economic Dev.	41.5	28.9	25.3	18.5	65
4. Employment	47.2	17.3	8.4	13.0	47
5. Taxes	11.3	19.2	22.5	27.8	47
6. Budget	5.7	17.3	23.9	20.3	40
7. Environment	7.5	5.8	19.7	20.3	32
8. Crime	13.2	11.5	12.7	11.1	27
9. Social Services	1.9	7.7	16.9	13.0	24
10. Children's Issues	11.3	1.9	14.1	5.6	20
Other Issues	24.5	38.5	31.0	24.1	68
Number of Respondents	53	52	71	54	

more likely than any other group to bring up the topic—three-quarters
of the black women responding to the survey mentioned education,
compared with two-thirds of the other respondents—although the proportions were not statistically different. Black women were equally
likely to mention health care reform and education, yet in this they were
unlike their colleagues. Attention to health care reform was the second
most commonly mentioned agenda issue among all respondent groups,
but black women were far more likely to be concerned with it than were
others (chi square $[3] = 12.6$, $p < .01$).

Black women legislators were more likely than black men, white men,
and white women legislators to mention economic development and employment, and indeed these were two key concerns of minority women.
More than 40 percent of black women legislators described their desire
for greater economic development compared with just one-fourth of
other legislators, and nearly 50 percent of black women mentioned employment concerns compared with fewer than 20 percent of their colleagues. Even when controlling for the fact that black women legislators
gave more responses overall, the proportion of black women's responses
going to economic development and employment concerns was still

greater than for any other group of legislators (chi square $[3] = 10.5$, $p < .05$).

Traditional women's issues were less likely than other issues to be named. Overall, 8.7 percent of the legislators mentioned child care as one of their top three concerns, and 5.2 percent mentioned abortion—the only traditional "women's" issues the legislators gave. Twelve legislators said that they believed abortion rights was a key issue facing their state legislature, and nine of those legislators were white women. Additionally, two white men and one black woman brought up the concern; no black men mentioned abortion. Stated in terms of the sample size, 12.8 percent of white women, 3.7 percent of white men, and 1.8 percent of black women declared abortion rights central to their agenda. As a top concern, abortion was clearly a white issue and, more specifically, a white women's issue. Child care, on the other hand, crossed both races but was more likely to be mentioned by women than men: 14.3 percent of white women, 11.1 percent of black women, 5.6 percent of white men, and 1.9 percent of black men brought up child care when asked to list primary policy areas to be addressed.

Among the important policy areas, three traditionally "black" issues were mentioned: seven legislators suggested that their legislature should look into civil rights policies, six offered economic justice as a key issue, and three would have liked to see greater attention placed on the way congressional redistricting is taking form. In total, sixteen legislators mentioned at least one of these issues, and all but three of those legislators were black. On the other hand, white women (4.3%) were nearly as likely as black women (5.6%) to mention any of the issues. Black men were more likely than anyone else to bring up one of these policy themes (18.5% of black men mentioned at least one). Thus, what are generally considered "black" issues were more likely to represent the principal policy concerns of black men than of black women.

The main policy concerns that black women would like to see addressed were not necessarily representative either of the policy interests of black men nor of white women. Instead, black women seemed to share with each other a uniquely fine-tuned agenda. While gender and race did not necessarily explain well the interests of white women and black men, there was a striking level of agreement among black women as to the key issues facing state legislatures. The four issues cited most frequently by black women represent 75.7 percent of all their citations. The four areas mentioned most frequently by black men account for just 59.2 percent of all their responses, for white women 63.8 percent, and for white men 61.6 percent (note that the four issues may be different for each group).

A Singular Group: Black Women Legislators

The purpose of this chapter has been to describe the beliefs of black women legislators and to show how those beliefs compare with those of other legislators. The data illustrate several important findings. First, they suggest that black women were less likely than either black men or white women to distinguish between the experiences of blacks and those of women. While black men were likely to see themselves facing greater obstacles than were faced by women, and white women tended to see their barriers as worse than those confronted by blacks, black women rarely noted a difference. Second, the data reveal that, although black women were quite supportive of policies targeting minorities and women, they made little separation between the deservingness of the target groups. Black men, on the other hand, tended to be more supportive of minority-targeted policies, and white women were more likely to support women-targeted policies. Third, reports of key policy issues demonstrated that traditional women's issues (in this case, abortion and child care) were given somewhat more often by white women than by black women, and traditional minority issues (e.g., civil rights, economic justice, redistricting) tended to be listed by black men and not black women. Finally, black women exhibited a cohesive and almost universal concern for similar policy issues. Unlike their colleagues, the 53 black women surveyed tended to express a singular legislative agenda.

Black women have not been in public office long. Although African American men gained suffrage in 1870 with the Fifteenth Amendment and women in 1920 with the Nineteenth Amendment, in practice, poll taxes and other hurdles prevented many blacks from voting. Not until the Voting Rights Act of 1965 were all African Americans free to practice their constitutional right to participate through voting. This is not to say, of course, that no woman was elected before 1920 and no black before 1965; after all, Jeannette Rankin won her United States House seat four years before universal suffrage (although women did have the vote in her home state of Montana), and the post–Civil War Congress included seven African American men. Nonetheless, black women were late entering electoral politics, and although their numbers have been increasing rapidly over the past decade, they remain an extreme minority. No doubt this experience has an impact on the views of black women. In a separate article (Barrett 1995), I discuss plausible explanations for the remarkableness of black women's unity, including their personal and professional background and the characteristics of their constituency. Perhaps the fact that there are so few black women in office offers the best explanation for their uniqueness. The majority of the black women serve in legislatures with very few other black women, and these are the women who tend to be in greatest agreement about the importance of education, health care, economic development, and employment. It is altogether likely that as more black women enter public office, their diversity will become greater as well. With more black women entering office, future studies may discover less unanimity among the group. For the present, however, black women remain a minority dedicated to addressing the interests of both women and minorities equally.

Similar to findings from studies of the general public (Gay and Tate 1998), the data presented in this chapter demonstrate the relevance of both race and gender in forming the identity of black women politicians. Black women use their experience both as women and as blacks to shape their role as legislators. When asked about the legislative experiences of blacks, they share beliefs similar to those of black male colleagues. When asked about the legislative experiences of women, their views appear similar to those of their white female colleagues. Yet, unlike their black male and white female colleagues, black women see the relevance both of racial identity and of gender identity. Race and gender combine to form a unique black female legislative identity.

Notes

1. Numbers are from the Joint Center for Political and Economic Studies (www.jointcenter.org) and from the Center for American Women and Politics (www.cawp.rutgers.edu).

2. Seventy-eight percent of black men were married, compared with 77.8 percent of white men, 69.6 percent of white women, and 56.6 percent of black women. Ninety-two percent of black men had children, compared with 79.6 percent of black women, 75.9 percent of white men, and 75.7 percent of white women. Thirty-six percent of black men had children under 18, compared with 33.3 percent of white men, 18.5 percent of black women, and 17.1 percent of white women. At the time elected, the average white man was 39.8 years old, the average black man 44.0, white woman 46.1, and black woman 47.2. Black men had an average of 10.2 years experience in the current office, compared with 9.2 years among white men, 6.7 years among white women, and 6.0 years among black women.

3. Cronbach's alpha—a measure of internal consistency that ranges from 0 (no consistency) to 1 (perfect consistency)—for the women's issue factor is .81.

4. These four items form an internally consistent single factor of support for

minority-targeted policy (Cronbach's alpha = .83). One additional item intended to measure beliefs about a minority-policy issue—the highly controversial suggestion of special inner-city schools for minority males—does not correlate highly with the other four items and is therefore not included as a minority-policy issue.

5. The survey was conducted before South Africa held its national election and apartheid was finally ended.

References

Barrett, Edith J. 1995. "The Policy Priorities of African American Women in State Legislatures." *Legislative Studies Quarterly* 20: 223–247.

Baxter, Sandra, and Marjorie Lansing. 1983. *Women and Politics: The Visible Majority.* Ann Arbor: University of Michigan Press.

Blair, Diane D., and Jeanie R. Stanley. 1991. "Personal Relationships and Legislative Power: Male and Female Perceptions." *Legislative Studies Quarterly* 16: 495–507.

Carolina Poll. 1992. Institute for Research and Social Sciences, University of North Carolina, Chapel Hill.

Carroll, Susan J. 1991. "Taking the Lead." *The Journal of State Government* 64: 43–45.

Collins, Patricia Hill. 1991. *Black Feminist Thought: Knowledge, Consciousness, and the Politics of Empowerment.* New York: Routledge.

Dawson, Michael C. 1994. "A Black Counterpublic? Economic Earthquakes, Racial Agenda(s), and Black Politics." *Public Culture* 7: 195–223.

Gay, Claudine, and Katherine Tate. 1998. "Doubly Bound: The Impact of Gender and Race on the Politics of Black Women." *Political Psychology* 19: 169–184.

Hochschild, Jennifer. 1993. "Middle-class Blacks and the Ambiguities of Success." In *Prejudice, Politics, and the American Dilemma,* ed. Paul M. Sniderman, Philip E. Tetlock, and Edward G. Carmines. Stanford, Calif.: Stanford University Press.

hooks, bell. 1984. *Feminist Theory: From Margin to Center.* Boston: South End Press.

Joint Center for Political and Economic Studies. 1997. *Black Elected Officials: A National Roster.* Washington, D.C.: Joint Center for Political and Economic Studies Press.

Kilson, Martin. 1989. "Problems of Black Politics: Some Progress, Many Difficulties." *Dissent* 36: 526–534.

King, Deborah. 1988. "Multiple Jeopardy, Multiple Consciousness: The Context of a Black Feminist Ideology." *Signs: Journal of Women in Culture and Society* 14: 42–72.

Leader, Shelah G. 1977. "The Policy Impact of Elected Women Officials." In

The Impact of the Electoral Process, ed. Louis Maisel and Joseph Cooper. Beverly Hills: Sage.

Mansbridge, Jane, and Katherine Tate. 1992. "Race Trumps Gender: Black Opinion on the Thomas Nomination. *P.S.: Political Science and Politics* 25: 488-492.

Meier, Kenneth J. 1979. *Politics and the Bureaucracy: Policymaking in the Fourth Branch of Government*. North Scituate, Mass.: Duxbury Press.

Merritt, Sharyne. 1982. "Sex Roles and Political Ambition." *Sex Roles* 8: 1035.

Mezey, Susan Gluck. 1978. "Does Sex Make a Difference? A Case Study of Women in Politics." *Western Political Quarterly* 31: 492-501.

Miller, Cheryl M. 1990. "Agenda-setting by State Legislative Black Caucuses: Policy Priorities and Factors of Success." *Policy Studies Review* 9: 339-354.

Miller, Delbert C. 1991. *Handbook of Research Design and Social Measurement*, 5th ed. Newbury Park, Calif.: Sage.

Rohr, John A. 1986. *To Run a Constitution: The Legitimacy of the Administrative State*. Lawrence: University of Kansas Press.

Saint-Germain, Michelle A. 1989. "Does Their Difference Make a Difference? The Impact of Women on Public Policy in the Arizona Legislature." *Social Science Quarterly* 70: 956-968.

Simon, Lucinda. 1987. "Who are the Leaders. . . . " *Journal of State Government* 60: 246-247.

Smith, Robert C. 1990. "Recent Elections and Black Politics: The Maturation or Death of Black Politics." *P.S.: Political Science and Politics* 23: 160-162.

Sokolow, Alvin D. 1971. "Black Members—White Legislators." *Black Politician* 2: 23-30.

Tate, Katherine. 1993. *From Protest to Politics: The New Black Voters in American Elections*. Cambridge, Mass.: Harvard University Press.

Thomas, Sue. 1994. *How Women Legislate*. New York: Oxford University Press.

Witt, Linda, Karen M. Paget, and Glenna Matthews. 1994. *Running as a Woman*. New York: Free Press.

Ten

Feminist Judges
Challenging the Status Quo

Elaine Martin

A non-feminist might say: why is feminism different from
any other "ism" which ought to be left out of judging?
—Kay 1989

The judiciary has certain unique features which set it off from other,
more political, institutions. The judicial role is circumscribed in ways
that the legislative role is not. Popular images of appropriate judicial
behavior and formal socialization of future judges into role patterns by
our legal education system operate to create a widely accepted set of
criteria for judging judges. The official, approved image of a judge is
that of a person who is "impartial, disengaged, and independent" and
who does not "pre-judge" the merits of a case before hearing the evidence presented by advocates for each side (Resnik 1988). What this
means in a nutshell is that a good judge is supposed to put aside his or
her personal feelings and values when donning the robe. The robe and
all its trappings are designed to hide individual physical characteristics
and, in so doing, also symbolically represent the impersonal nature of
the act of judging.

The formal rules of the judicial game reinforce these basic role expectations. For example, canons of judicial ethics prohibit a judge from
engaging in acts which have an appearance of impropriety on or off the
bench; most judges are selected by means other than "dirty" partisan
politics; and cries of outrage were heard when it was rumored that Reagan administration officials had asked potential federal judicial nomi-
nees how they might decide future cases (Totenberg 1986).

Institutional forces add yet another dimension to the elements con-
spiring to pressure judges to leave out "isms" such as feminism from
the process of judging. The law itself, statutes and precedents, the facts
of the case, the requirements of evidence, the possibility of being over-

turned on appeal, even the nature of the adversarial system all restrict the freedom of judicial discretion. Indeed, the authors of a leading text on the federal trial courts, while maintaining that who the judge is makes a difference in certain types of cases, acknowledge that "the best way to predict the given outcome of any case is to determine which litigant has the weightiest evidence and the best controlling precedents" (Carp and Rowland 1983, 165).

This maxim is lent validity in its application to women as well as to men by a story about Judge Susan Weber Wright (United States District Court, Arkansas). Judge Wright dismissed Paula Jones' sexual assault case against President Clinton, despite her clear distaste for the allegations: "[Although] the governor's alleged conduct, if true, may certainly be characterized as boorish and offensive, even a most charitable reading of the record in this case fails to reveal a basis for a claim of criminal sexual assault." Judge Wright was widely praised for "exceptional courage" for underscoring that "judges must be above politics."

Nevertheless, judges do differ from one another in ways that judicial scholars have long investigated. In fact, the extent to which judicial decisions are based on the facts of a case (the legal model) or on the judge's own policy preferences (the attitudinal model) is a question that continues to dominate judicial research (Flemming, Holian, and Mezey 1998). A key feature of judicial role studies is the attempt to measure judges' notions about what legal and attitudinal factors they think are legitimate to consider in reaching their decisions (Becker 1966; Flango, Wenner, and Wenner 1975; Gibson 1978, 1981; Howard 1977; Scheb, Ungs, and Hayes 1988). The basic conclusion is that a judge who prefers a particular outcome, say a liberal one, may nevertheless produce the opposite, say a conservative one. This happens because the judge feels that adherence to the legal rules of the game *requires* such an outcome. We would say that such a judge shows a restraintist role orientation—restraining his or her personal preferences during the process of reaching a decision. Activist judges, on the other hand, are more likely to produce outcomes in line with their personal political or social preferences, feeling this to be legitimate. However, even activism is tempered by respect for the mythic impartiality of the "good" judge. Thus, theoretically, activists act on their personal preferences *only* in cases in which law or precedent are unclear or conflicting.

In deference to this notion, most role theory studies of appellate judicial behavior focus exclusively on non-unanimous cases. The outcomes of unanimous cases are presumably governed by "the law" while non-unanimous cases represent situations in which the law is unclear. In these latter cases, judges' attitudes and role orientations come into play as they exercise the required discretion, with role orientations act-ing as an intervening variable between attitudes and decisions. As direct information about judges' attitudes is rarely available, researchers typi-cally use political party affiliation as a substitute measure of political ideology.

What happens when a judge's role orientation is focused not only on the process of doing justice but also on the justice of the outcome? What happens to a judge's conception of her job when she considers herself a feminist? Does she view feminism as just another "ism" best left out of the process of judging? Or does her feminism itself call her to action of a particular sort?

In this chapter I will argue that for a woman judge, feminism is not analogous to political ideology, at least as ideology functions in the judi-cial role model. That is, I claim that feminism is more than a set of attitudes that may or may not be acted upon, depending on whether the judge is an activist or not. I will argue that for feminist judges, women's-rights cases may trigger a response that overrides the usual variables of political ideology and judicial role. I will argue that the de-cision to call oneself a feminist includes a commitment to action on behalf of other women irrespective of judicial role or political party af-filiation.

Literature Review

Three groups of studies are relevant to the discussion of gender differ-ences between men and women in their judicial behavior: studies con-ducted when the number of women judges was still tokenistic; feminist jurisprudence literature; and "different voice" judicial studies.

The earliest studies of gender and judicial behavior by and large sup-ported the conventional wisdom prevalent at that time that women judges would behave no differently than men judges when confronted with similar cases. The handful of studies conducted in the 1970s and early 1980s concluded that although there were small differences be-tween men and women judges in their courtroom behavior, those differ-ences were not significant (Kritzer and Uhlman 1977; Gruhl, Spohn, and Welch 1981; Walker and Barrow 1985; Gottschall 1983). These re-searchers explained their findings by suggesting that the common so-cialization that men and women received through law school training and legal experience before their judgeships made them more alike than different.

This failure to find gender difference could also be explained by to-kenism theory. Tokenism theory says that token women conform, either because selection methods in male-dominated institutions, such as the judiciary, favor women who follow the male model (Cook 1980) or because tokens recognize the futility of non-conforming action against the odds of male-entrenched norms. Women judges in the 1970s and early 1980s certainly fit the classical criterion for tokenism (Kanter 1977; Epstein 1970). Women were widely dispersed throughout the fifty states and often sat as the only representatives of their gender in their judicial districts. In 1976, when President Carter was elected, there were only five women judges out of more than five hundred federal district and appellate court judges. In the same year, although there were more than sixteen thousand state and local judges in the United States, twenty states had no women on major trial courts whatsoever. At the founding meeting of the National Association of Women Judges in 1979, many women reported that they had never before met another woman judge (Cook 1979).

However, as Ruth Bader Ginsburg remarked after her inauguration as an Associate Justice of the U.S. Supreme Court, "Times are changing" (1993). In 1992 when President Clinton was elected, only 11 percent of federal judges were women. By the end of 1996, more than 17 percent of federal judges in active service were women. Overall, fewer than half of Clinton's judges were white men, an amazing break with historical precedent (Goldman and Slotnick 1997). From 1992 to 1997, the number of women who held seats on their state's supreme courts increased from 39 to 71, or 80 percent, and only seven states had no women justices. Two states, Minnesota and Michigan, for a time had a female majority on their state supreme courts (Martin 1997).

More recent studies indicate that, as women's numbers move beyond the token stage and as younger women educated after the women's movement become judges, differences based on gender emerge more clearly. It seems likely that some of the differences in findings can be attributed to differences in the types of women who were drawn to judicial office during the two periods (Martin 1997) and the impact of women's increased representation. Sue Thomas in her studies of women legislators asserts that higher proportions of women encourage women to adopt more nonconformist policy priorities, including so-called women's issues (Thomas 1994, 104).

In any case, studies conducted in the 1990s clearly contradict early findings. For example, Allen and Wall (1993) found that women on state supreme courts are more likely than men to be the most pro-female members of their court on women's issues, and more likely to engage in nonconformist or "outsider" voting behavior. A Florida study found that in contested custody appeals, all-male appellate panels were more likely to rule in favor of fathers than mothers, but mixed-gender panels showed no favoritism for either parent (Jackson 1997). A study of President Clinton's first-term appointees found that both women and black judges were more supportive of minority claims than were men or white judges (Segal 1997).

Since the 1970s a new, controversial, feminist stream of scholarship labeled "feminist jurisprudence" has developed in the nation's law schools (Binion 1993; Rhode 1990). These scholars exhibit a fascination with psychologist Carol Gilligan's claims that women speak about moral issues in a "different voice," a voice of care and connectedness, compared with the male "voice" of universal values and hierarchically ordered values (Goldstein 1992, 27). In this literature men are characterized as more "instrumental" and women as more "contextual" in their modes of thinking and feeling (Gilligan 1982). It is suggested that women lawyers and judges, because of either biological or culturally induced differences in moral thinking, will bring a different perspective to the law (MacKinnon 1983; Menkel-Meadows 1985; Minow 1987; Resnik 1988). What this new jurisprudence might eventually look like is not yet clear. However, significant changes in both procedural and substantive law to better fit with women's presumably unique ways of thinking and relating are predicted, if women achieve proportionate representation in the legal field.

Scholars of judicial politics have seized upon this "difference" theory, and studies in recent years have tested for the presence of a "different voice" among women judges (Allen and Wall 1993; Davis 1993; Davis, Haire, and Songer 1993; Martin 1993a; Maule and Hague 1997). It is important to understand that this different voice is defined as a *feminine* voice, not a feminist voice. Thus it ought to be discernible in cases as seemingly far removed from feminist concerns as search and seizure (Songer, Davis, and Haire 1994) and environmental policy (Songer and Crews-Meyer 1996). Most of these studies have failed in their attempts to find some overreaching pattern on the part of women judges to make decisions in line with connection, community, or context, yet they also commonly find that in cases raising issues of gender, racial, or employment discrimination women judges may be found more often than men on the side of the claimant (Songer, Davis, and Haire 1994; Mustard 1998).

Theoretical Framework

The present study examines the possibility that identification with the goals of feminism may be more useful in understanding the behavior of women judges than either traditional judicial role theory or the newer, different-voice notion. Two main questions guide this analysis: Does traditional judicial role theory adequately capture the potentially different orientations women judges may bring to the act of judging, especially in gender-bias cases? Does feminist identification provide a more useful tool in explaining judicial decisions in gender-bias cases than political party affiliation or judicial role?

A recent study concludes that some women judges have a strong sense that part of their judicial role is to "act for" the interests of other women (Martin 1993b). That women judges, women law professors, and women attorneys are already working together to legitimate a female "counterbalance" to the perspectives embodied in a legal system dominated by men judges, men litigators, and men-dispensed law is clear.

One important example of this collective action will suffice: Spearheaded by the National Association of Women Judges, federal and state courts have created dozens of gender bias task forces. Since 1983, 39 states have established task forces on gender bias in the courts, and 34 reports are now in print (Kearney and Sellers 1997). The task forces investigate gender bias in the courtroom and in substantive law and promote the design of educational curriculums to alert both men and women judges to the presence, and danger, of gender bias. Without exception, the task force findings convincingly establish the pervasiveness of gender bias in the courtroom and under the law.

Norma Wikler (1987) and Lynn Shrafran (1993) have written extensively on the efforts of women judges and attorneys in sponsoring these task forces to document and remedy the problems of gender bias. Wikler says, "Especially in the early years, doors opened only after careful strategic planning and much negotiation and persuasion." Members of the National Association of Women Judges went home from meetings and pushed for the creation of task forces in their states (Billings 1989). They were remarkably successful in eliciting support from their judicial brothers. The National Association of Women Judges has now developed judicial education programs for gender fairness in such substantive law areas as custody and visitation, spousal and child support, and domestic violence. These materials are used in such places as the National Judicial College.

What do these activities by women judges mean for scholars who study judicial behavior? They surely mean that the time has come to rethink our notions of judicial behavior and judicial role theory developed through the study of an almost exclusively male judiciary. A necessary first step in this process is to consider whether judicial role theory ought to be modified to take into account the more complex orientations women may bring to their role as judges.

The judicial role model is fairly simple and straightforward. According to the model, "behavior is a function of the role orientation of the role occupant. These orientations are a product of role expectations" (Gibson 1981). Role expectations define for the role occupant how he or she ought to behave in the role and are derived from role alters. Role alters are mostly those involved in the courtroom process, e.g., defense lawyers and district attorneys, although some attention has been given to the influence of public opinion (e.g., Wasby 1981). Additionally, for judges, most of this model is directed not toward the *substance* of outcomes but rather toward the *process* through which outcomes are produced.

The notions of judicial role and gender role have much in common. Therefore, much of the literature on the impact of gender role expectations on the behavior of women with children, who pursue professional careers outside the home, is as relevant to women judges as to other women professionals. Much of this literature discusses the *complexity* of the role behaviors engaged in by such women in response to multiple and conflicting expectations produced by the large number of role alters in their lives (Barnett and Baruch 1985; Beutell and Greenhaus 1983; Martin and Keyes 1988; Mueller 1982; Verbrugge 1983). This literature supports the possibility that women judges may respond to a far broader range of role alters than those present in the courtroom. Women might well respond to role alters, for example, who adjure them to consider results, not merely process. Feminist jurisprudence makes a strong case that law itself is biased, having been produced by men and from a male perspective. Feminist women judges might well look beyond their courtrooms to respond to a different set of expectations from other women, from other feminists, and from feminist scholarly literature.

The Survey and Methodology

A six-page questionnaire was mailed to all women judges known to be sitting on the bench in 1987 and a random sample of men general jurisdiction trial court judges stratified by court location. Four sets of questions will be used in this analysis: those having to do with judicial role orientation, self-identification as a feminist, political party affiliation, and responses to five hypothetical cases raising issues of gender fairness.

Mailing lists for women were obtained from the National Center for State Courts, which also acts as secretariat for the National Association for Women Judges. Although there may have been women judges not on the list, it was the most complete listing available. The known universe of women judges was 1,188, and 693 women responded, for an overall response rate of 58.3 percent. Limited-jurisdiction judges had a lower response rate than higher-court judges. Women judges from all court levels were merged in the analysis. Names and addresses for 647 men judges sitting in the same court locations as women judges were randomly drawn from the *BNA's Directory of State Courts: Judges and Clerks* (King and Springberg 1988). The response rate for the men's sample was 46 percent.

The judicial role measure used in the survey is one developed by James Gibson (1978) and has been demonstrated to be as useful in predicting the sentencing behavior of trial judges as it is the decisions of appellate judges. As noted by Gibson (1981), his scale has a number of advantages: its format is closed-ended; it is a multi-item measure with considerable variation among items; it is one-dimensional; and it has generated stable response patterns across judges from different states. Respondents were almost evenly distributed into two judicial role categories: activists and non-activists. Eighty-nine respondents did not answer one or more of the items in the judicial scale and so could not be categorized. Of those remaining, there were 111 men and 309 women activists and 194 men and 371 women non-activists.

Feminism was measured by agree/disagree responses on a five-point scale to a single statement: "I consider myself a feminist." Only those respondents who agreed or agreed strongly with this statement were categorized as feminists. As Cook (1980) pointed out in an earlier study of women judges, it is an act of courage for a judge to label herself a feminist. Given the essentially conservative bias of the legal profession, this remains true today, especially for men. Thus there can be little doubt that the self-identified feminists in this study feel their feminist commitment strongly and that some "closet feminists" may be hidden among the non-feminist respondents (Carroll 1985).

Feminism as a role construct is a complex concept that is just beginning to undergo serious research. A number of researchers have struggled with the question of why more women political elites who hold feminist-leaning attitudes have not behaved more aggressively in pursuing feminist policies (Dodson, this volume). Conversely, many people look like feminists and act like feminists but claim not to be feminists. This makes it difficult to define feminism.

For purposes of this study, I have chosen to accept the respondents' own report of self-identification as a feminist. I argue that feminist self-identity includes not only a set of attitudes but also a commitment to action. In support of this contention I offer the following. Respondents were asked to agree or disagree on a five-point scale with a statement similar to one used in a nationwide *New York Times* poll. Overall, according to the *Times*, 61 percent of women and 51 percent of men in the United States support the statement, "The United States continues to need a strong women's movement to push for changes that benefit women." Self-identified feminist judges in the present study showed support for this notion far beyond that of their gender in the general population: 94 percent of men and 91 percent of women agreed or agreed strongly. Self-identified non-feminists, on the other hand, fell below their gender in the general population. Only 48 percent of both men and women non-feminists agreed or strongly agreed with the need to push for changes to benefit women. I contend that it is this perceived need for active agents of change to benefit women that separates self-identified feminists from non-feminists in this study.

Not surprisingly, the ratio of men feminists to the total number of men respondents is the reverse of the women's: 90 feminists and 218 non-feminists. Despite the disparity in the ratio of feminists to non-feminists, there were sufficient numbers of both groups to make statistical analysis possible.

Respondents were asked to state their political party affiliation. This variable was used as a substitute measure of political ideology as is common in judicial politics research. There were somewhat more women Democrats (391) than Republicans (224), and men were almost evenly divided, 138 Republicans and 149 Democrats.

Our purpose here is to test the potential impact of feminism on a narrow range of cases which raise issues related to the expansion of women's rights. The five hypothetical cases present issues of battered women's rights, abortion rights for minors, property rights for divorcing homemakers, maternity leave rights, and protection from sexual harassment on the job. Respondents were asked to choose in favor of one party: the women claimants or the opposing party (law enforcement officials, parents, spouses, or private corporations). All cases were drawn from 1987 newspaper accounts of actual decisions rendered by state court judges. At the time of the survey, the issues raised in the hypothetical cases were all unsettled law. Thus respondents were faced with refusing to make "new law" or making new law in favor of women. Decisions in favor of women claimants were coded as "pro-woman" decisions.

Respondents' decisions in the hypothetical cases are, of course, surrogates for real behavior, and must be viewed as such. Judges are, however, quite familiar with the use of hypothetical cases, as they are used extensively in legal education. Thus hypotheticals are useful for model building, although the judges in this study may never be confronted with the special issues described in the cases. Even if so confronted, they may not behave as they reported they would.

Findings

Women Judges

Logit analysis allows the researcher to estimate each independent variable's contribution to the probability that the dependent variable equals 1 (in our hypothetical cases the value of 1 signifies a pro-woman vote). Our interest in this chapter is to evaluate the potential impact of self-identified feminism on the operation of the traditional judicial role model of decision-making. This model typically uses two independent variables, political party and judicial role orientation, to predict judicial behavior. We also use these variables in our model but add the independent variable of self-identified feminism. With the logit technique we are able to estimate the probability that a feminist judge will decide a given hypothetical case in a pro-woman direction, while controlling for both judicial role and political party.

Table 10.1 summarizes five separate logit analyses of the impact of the three independent variables (feminist self-identification, political party self-identification, and judicial role orientation) on the dependent variables: women judicial respondents' decisions in each of the hypothetical cases. The independent variables were coded as follows: 1 if the respondent was a self-identified feminist and 0 if the respondent was a self-identified non-feminist; 1 if the respondent was affiliated with the Democratic Party and 0 if a Republican; 1 if categorized as an activist on the judicial role scale and 0 if categorized as a non-activist. The dependent variable was coded as 1 if the respondent supported the woman claimant and 0 if not. The coefficients in Table 10.1 show the change in the log of odds ratio for a pro-woman decision, given the respective presence of each independent variable and the absence of the other two.

Because the coefficients are not readily interpretable, the column labeled "impact" provides the estimated probability that the decision will be pro-woman when the independent variable in question is 1 and the two others are 0. The impact estimate assumes that the hypothetical vote in question otherwise has a 50 percent chance of being pro-woman.

Table 10.1. Logit Analysis of the Influence of Self-Identified Feminism, Judicial Role, and Political Party on Five Hypothetical Cases (Women Judges)

Independent Variable	Abortion	Leave	Harassment	Abuse	Divorce
Feminism	1.126***	0.896***	0.736***	0.705***	0.597
Impact	0.882	0.875	0.849	0.660	0.925
Judicial Role	0.228	−0.111	0.129	0.301	0.948**
Impact	0.753	0.719	0.754	0.415	0.945
Political Party	0.060	0.566**	0.661**	0.298	0.056
Impact	0.720	0.834	0.840	0.564	0.877
Intercept	0.886***	1.050***	0.995***	−0.042	1.192***
Model Chi square =	22.36***	19.55***	17.52***	21.41***	10.07**
n =	506	542	519	528	534

**significant at .05
***significant at .01

As is apparent from a quick glance at the top row of Table 10.1, the feminist attitudes of a woman judge play a large role in determining her decision. The variable "self-identified feminism" is statistically significant in four of the five cases. The fifth case, "divorce," approaches significance at $p = .10$. In contrast, "judicial role" is significant in only one case and "political party" in two cases.

The second row of the table, labeled "impact," shows the probability that a self-identified feminist, who is also a Republican and a nonactivist, will take a pro-woman position. The results are quite impressive.

In the case labeled "abortion," respondents were asked to decide whether an eleven-year-old girl, pregnant by her mother's boyfriend, should be granted an abortion which she wants but which her mother opposes. A decision in favor of the pregnant girl's wishes was coded as pro-woman. The only coefficient found to be statistically significant was for self-identified feminism. Thus, if a woman judge respondent is a self-identified feminist, but is not an activist and belongs to the Republican Party, then there is an 88.2 percent probability that she decided the abortion case for the pregnant girl.

The case labeled "leave" asked respondents to decide whether a woman claimant should be reinstated in her job after taking maternity leave. The company claims a decision in her favor would discriminate against men and non-pregnant women and be too costly. Both independent variables, self-identified feminism and political party, were found to be statistically significant. If a woman judge is a feminist, but is not an activist and belongs to the Republican Party, then there is an 87.5 percent probability that she decided the maternity leave case for the woman plaintiff. If a woman judge is a Democrat, but she is neither feminist nor an activist, then the probability of her deciding the maternity leave case in favor of the woman plaintiff is 83.4 percent.

The case "harassment" requires respondents to decide whether a woman claiming a job climate of intimidation through sexually suggestive remarks, jokes, and requests for sexual favors should be given money damages and job protection. Management claims she is overreacting to normal male camaraderie, is trying to cover up her own inability to adjust to a new work environment, and needs to be replaced. Two variables, self-identified feminism and political party, were statistically significant. If a woman judge is a feminist but is not an activist and belongs to the Republican Party, then there is an 84.9 percent probability that she decided the case in favor of the woman claimant.

If a woman judge is a Democrat but is neither feminist nor an activist, then the probability of her deciding this case in a pro-woman manner is 84 percent. It may be that the importance of the party variable here is related to traditional Democratic support of labor over management.

The "abuse" case involves a class-action suit against a police department by a group of battered women. Respondents are asked whether they would impose new rules of intervention in crimes of domestic violence and require officer training in the new rules. The Police Chief objects to the erosion of individual officer discretion and the increased likelihood of false-arrest suits. This particular case was probably the most problematic from the point of view of judicial restraint, as upholding the women claimants required a degree of interference with the operation of an arm of local government. That may be why the probability of a feminist, non-activist, Republican judge deciding this case in favor of the battered women's request was only 66 percent.

The final case, "divorce," involved a 55-year-old woman's suit for divorce after 37 years of marriage. She asks for no alimony and accepts half of the community property but wants half of her spouse's substantial retirement income in ten years' time, at age 65. Her spouse is willing to make a settlement based on the face value of his retirement fund but is not willing to share its future income. At the time this case was presented to respondents, a decision in favor of the woman's suit would have been groundbreaking "new" law. Interestingly, it is the only case in which feminism is not statistically significant, although it approaches significance at p = .10. It is also the only case in which the judicial role variable is statistically significant. If a woman judge is an activist but is not a feminist and belongs to the Republican Party, then there is a 94.5 percent probability that she decided this case in favor of the woman plaintiff. It may be that inequity in divorce settlements was such a common problem for women in the 1980s (Weitzman 1987), that activist women judges, feminist or not, were quite willing to break ground in the law to redress inequities.

Men and Women Judges

Table 10.2 presents the logit analyses of the same cases and variables as above but with the independent variable of gender added. Gender is coded as 1 for a woman, 0 for a man. For example, in row 1 under the case "abuse," gender is statistically significant. This means that if a judge is a woman, and she is also a non-feminist, non-activist, Republican, then there is still a 55.9 percent probability that she decided the abuse case in favor of the battered women. Gender is statistically significant in two of the cases: "divorce" and "abuse."

Interestingly, feminist identification remains statistically significant across the board, although in four of the five cases its impact is lower than in Table 10.1. Neither judicial role or political party is statistically significant in any of the cases.

The impact of the independent variable, self-identified feminism, on the probability that a given judicial respondent decided a particular case in favor of the woman plaintiff should be read in the following manner. In each case, the impact of the feminism variable refers to a judicial respondent who is a man, a non-activist, and a Republican. Although the impact is not quite as strong for such a man as it is for a similar woman (Table 10.1), the implication is clear. Self-identified feminism overrides judicial role orientation and political party.

Discussion

Two central questions guiding the present study may now be addressed with some confidence. First, does traditional judicial role theory adequately capture the potentially different orientations women judges may bring to the act of judging in gender-bias cases? The answer appears to

Table 10.2. Logit Analysis of the Influence of Gender and
Self-Identified Feminism, Judicial Role, and Political Party on Five
Hypothetical Cases (Women and Men Judges)

Independent Variable	Abortion	Leave	Harassment	Abuse	Divorce
Gender	0.166	−0.285	0.349	0.809***	0.671***
Impact	**0.679**	**0.763**	**0.762**	**0.559**	**0.876**
Feminism	0.957***	0.790***	0.712***	0.541***	0.609**
Impact	**0.844**	**0.904**	**0.822**	**0.492**	**0.869**
Judicial Role	0.362	0.084	0.220	0.154	0.487
Impact	**0.749**	**0.823**	**0.738**	**0.397**	**0.854**
Political Party	0.352	0.307	0.322	0.118	0.195
Impact	**0.747**	**0.854**	**0.757**	**0.338**	**0.812**
Intercept	0.732***	1.460***	0.816***	−0.572***	1.280***
Model Chi square =	39.08***	17.81***	29.71***	58.61***	26.31**
n =	757	799	771	786	790

**significant at .05
***significant at .01

be a qualified "no." In two of the hypothetical cases, divorce and abuse, the probability that a judge who is a woman but a non-feminist, a non-activist, and a Republican will nevertheless cast a vote in favor of the woman plaintiff is respectively 87.6 percent and 55.9 percent.

The answer to the second question, whether feminist identification provides a more useful tool in explaining judicial decisions in gender-bias cases than political party or judicial role orientation, seems more definitive. The impact of the independent variable, self-identified feminism, was statistically significant in four of the five cases for women judges and in all five cases for men judges. It should be noted, however, that the impact of feminist identification was somewhat less for men judges than for women judges.

Political scientist Judith Baer (1992) argues that the presence of enough women lawyers and judges conscious of women's interests and willing to innovate in legal and constitutional doctrine offers the possibility of achieving meaningful sexual equality in American law. The implications of the present study must be viewed with caution, because of the limited number of cases and issues considered and the artificial nature of the use of hypothetical cases. However, it would appear that Baer's argument is supported by the results above.

McGlen and O'Connor (1998, 94) contend that gender differences among judges' decisions on discrimination issues would be even greater if it were not that the very presence of women colleagues on the bench appears to make male jurists more sensitive to problems of gender bias. It is not clear that McGlen and O'Connor's contention is supported by the present study. However, certainly nothing in this study controverts their contention, and other studies support it. For example, a survey of women judges found that the most frequently mentioned type of behavior that women felt "made a difference" had to do with their efforts to raise the consciousness of their male colleagues (Martin 1993b). It is clear in the present study that once men's consciousness is raised, self-identified feminism impacts the pro-woman decisions of men judges in much the same manner as for women judges, taking into account both judicial role and political party.

There is no way to know how representative the sample is of the feminist attitudes of all judges. However, it is worth noting that two-thirds of the sample group of women (n = 460) described themselves as feminists. Even if we assume that all non-respondents were non-feminists, this still means that nearly 40 percent of women judges in 1987 were feminists. This is not an inconsiderable proportion and certainly warrants further investigation into the potential impact of feminism on judicial behavior.

Toward the Future

This study is essentially exploratory. It raises more questions than it answers. However, it does seem clear that judicial scholars must begin to rethink the concept of judicial role and the impact of personal attitudes and values on judicial decision-making as more women and feminist men join the ranks of judges. A recent text in judicial politics describes the typical state court judge as a well-educated, middle-aged, white man inclined to be a staid establishment type, recruited from private legal practice, with at least a 50-50 chance of being Republican. Stumpf (1998, 156) concludes that such judges are "likely to be oriented to the maintenance of the status quo." The overall probability that a non-feminist, non-activist, Republican, male judge in the present study will vote to support the woman plaintiff in the hypothetical cases is 52 percent. By way of contrast, a feminist, activist, Democratic woman judge has an overall 89 percent probability of voting in favor of the woman plaintiff. It seems clear that a theoretical construct that has worked well for explaining the behavior of a predominately male judiciary that is inclined to support the status quo will not work so well for a gender-mixed judiciary that may well be primed to challenge the status quo with regard to gender-fairness issues.

The research presented here shows how judicial role theory might be modified to better fit feminist attitudes. The logical next step is to determine a readily available way to identify possible feminist leanings among judges, short of the survey research conducted here. Possibly an examination of background variables such as group memberships would be useful. The research now taking place on the impact of feminism and feminist attitudes on the behavior of legislators should be instructive in this regard (Dodson, this volume).

We must also find better ways of measuring the output of trial courts. The traditional focus on sentencing severity overlooks potential gender differences in judicial behavior in cases which may not involve sentencing outcomes and are particularly relevant to women's unique experiences such as family law, reproductive issues, domestic violence, and children's rights. That these topics meet a special interest of women judges is testified to by the fact that the Women's Judges Fund for Justice budgeted $350,000 in 1990 for a project on "bioethics, family, and the law" (Nejelski 1990). The key focus is the institution of the family and how it is affected by biotechnology and the law.

The traditional study of judicial behavior as exhibited by individual judges should be expanded to take into account the collective action of judges. The gender-bias task forces described above were commonly initiated by women judges, but they could not have gone forward without the vigorous support of many dedicated men judges.

Collective action may also lessen the pressures of token status on women judges. Tokenistic behavior is a consequence of isolation and stress. Role alters in an organization such as the National Association of Women Judges may promote the courage in individual token women to defy the norms of their immediate working environment. This group identification may well relieve women judges from what might otherwise be intolerable pressures (Kessler 1983). Rowland, Carp, and Songer (1985) have examined the role of group identification in fostering cohesiveness in decision making on the federal bench among presidential-appointment cohorts. We need to know how group identification works when the judges are widely separated in different communities and did not go through the same selection processes. More than half the women judges in the United States belong to the National Association of Women Judges. What is the potential impact of this fact on women judges' behavior, broadly defined?

There is obviously far more to judicial behavior than deciding cases or issuing sentences. The judicial role constraints and the institutional forces mentioned in the introduction to this chapter are much more powerful in limiting the exercise of judicial discretion in deciding cases than in other aspects of judicial behavior. We need to explore definitions of judicial behavior that will be as complex as the role orientations judges may bring to that behavior.

Note

I would like to give special thanks to Barry Pyle for all his help with logit analysis.

References

Allen, David, and Diane Wall. 1993. "Role Orientations and Women State Supreme Court Justices." *Judicature* 77: 156–165.

Baer, Judith. 1992. "How Is Law Male? A Feminist Perspective on Constitutional Interpretation." In *Feminist Jurisprudence,* ed. Leslie Goldstein. Lanham, Md.: Rowman and Littlefield.

Barnett, R. C., and G. K. Baruch. 1985. "Women's Involvement in Multiple Roles and Psychological Distress." *Journal of Personality and Social Psychology* 49: 135–145.

Becker, Theodore. 1966. "A Survey Study of Hawaiian Judges: The Effect on Decisions of Judicial Role Variation." *American Political Science Review* 60: 677–686.

Beutell, W. J., and J. Greenhaus. 1983. "Integration of Home and Non-Home Roles: Women's Conflict and Coping Behavior." *Journal of Applied Psychology* 68: 43–48.

Billings, Judith. 1989. Panelist, "Making a Difference: Women on the Bench." National Association of Women Judges annual meeting, Washington, D.C.

Binion, Gayle. 1993. "The Nature of Feminist Jurisprudence." *Judicature* 77: 140–143.

Carp, Robert, and C. K. Rowland. 1983. *Policymaking and Politics in the Federal District Courts.* Knoxville: University of Tennessee Press.

Carroll, Susan. 1985. *Women as Candidates in American Politics.* Bloomington: Indiana University Press.

Cook, Beverly B. 1979. "Women Judges Organize: In the Footsteps of Women Lawyers." *Women Lawyers* 66 (2): 11–14.

Cook, Beverly B. 1980. "Political Culture and Selection of Women Judges to

Trial Courts." In *Women in Local Politics,* ed. Debra Stewart. Metuchen, N.J.: Scarecrow Press.

Davis, Sue. 1993. "The Voice of Sandra Day O'Connor." *Judicature* 77: 134–139.

Davis, Sue, Susan Haire, and Donald Songer. 1993. "Voting Behavior and Gender on the U.S. Courts of Appeals." *Judicature* 77: 129–132.

Epstein, Cynthia. 1970. "Encountering the Male Establishment: Sex-Status Limits on Women's Careers in the Professions." *American Journal of Sociology* 75: 965–982.

Flango, Victor, Lettie Wenner, and Manfred Wenner. 1975. "The Concept of Judicial Role: A Methodological Note." *American Journal of Political Science* 19: 277–290.

Fleming, Gregory, David Holian, and Susan Mezey. 1998. "An Integrated Model of Privacy Decision Making in State Supreme Courts." *American Politics Quarterly* 26: 36–58.

Gibson, James. 1978. "Judges' Role Orientations, Attitudes, and Decisions: An Interactive Model." *American Political Science Review* 72: 911–924.

Gibson, James. 1981. "The Role Concept in Judicial Research." *Law and Policy Quarterly* 3: 292–311.

Gilligan, Carol. 1982. *In a Different Voice.* Cambridge, Mass.: Harvard University Press.

Ginsberg, Justice Ruth Bader. 1993. "Remarks." *Judicature* 77: 126.

Goldman, Sheldon, and Elliot Slotnick. 1997. "Clinton's First Term Judiciary: Many Bridges to Cross." *Judicature* 80: 254–273.

Goldstein, Leslie. 1992. *Feminist Jurisprudence.* Lanham, Md.: Rowman and Littlefield.

Gottschall, Jon. 1983. "Carter's Judicial Appointments: The Influence of Affirmative Action and Merit Selection on Voting on the U.S. Court of Appeals." *Judicature* 67: 165–173.

Gruhl, John, Cassia Spohn, and Susan Welch. 1981. "Women as Policy Makers: The Case of Trial Judges." *American Journal of Political Science* 25: 308–322.

Howard, J. Woodford. 1977. "Role Perceptions and Behavior in Three U.S. Courts of Appeals." *The Journal of Politics* 39: 916–938.

Jackson, Vicki. 1997. "What Judges Can Learn from Gender Bias Task Force Studies." *Judicature* 81: 15–21.

Kanter, Rosabeth. 1977. *Men and Women in Corporations.* New York: Basic Books.

Kay, Herma Hill. 1989. Panelist, "Feminism: Its Impact on Judges and Judging." Annual meeting of the National Association of Women Judges, Washington, D.C.

Kearney, Richard, and Holly Taylor Sellers. 1997. "Gender Bias in Court Personnel Administration." *Judicature* 81: 8–14.

Kessler, Gladys. 1983. "NAWJ: The Value of Sisterhood on the Bench." *Trial* (August): 55.

King, Kamla, and Judith Springberg. 1988. *BNA's Directory of State Courts,*

Judges, and Clerks. 2nd ed. Washington, D.C.: The Bureau of National Affairs.

Kritzer, Herbert, and Thomas Uhlman. 1977. "Sisterhood in the Courtroom: Sex of Judge and Defendant in Criminal Case Disposition." *The Social Science Journal* 14: 77–88.

MacKinnon, Catherine. 1983. "Feminism, Marxism, Method and the State: Toward Feminist Jurisprudence." *Signs* 8: 635–658.

Martin, Elaine. 1993a. "Women on the Bench: A Different Voice." *Judicature* 77: 126–128.

Martin, Elaine. 1993b. "The Representative Role of Women Judges." *Judicature* 77: 166–173.

Martin, Elaine. 1997. "Glass Ceiling or Skylight: Women on State Supreme Courts." Presented at the annual meeting of the Southern Political Science Association, Norfolk, Virginia.

Martin, Elaine, and Barbara Keyes. 1988. "Professional Women: Role-Innovators and Sex Role Conflict: Judges and School Teachers." *Michigan Academician* 20: 139–152.

Maule, Linda, and L. K. Hague. 1997. "A Different Voice: A Longitudinal Analysis of the Minnesota State Supreme Court." Presented at the annual meeting of the Midwest Political Science Association, Chicago.

McGlen, Nancy, and Karen O'Connor. 1998. *Women, Politics, and American Society,* 2nd ed. Upper Saddle River, N.J.: Prentice-Hall.

Menkel-Meadows, Carrie. 1985. "Portia in a Different Voice." *Berkeley Women's Law Journal* 1: 39–63.

Minow, Martha. 1987. "Foreword: Justice Engendered." *Harvard Law Review* 101: 45–61.

Mueller, Carol. 1982. "Nurturance and Mastery: Competing Qualifications for Women's Access to High Public Office." Working Paper 99, Wellesley College, Center for Research on Women.

Mustard, David. 1998. "Racial, Ethnic and Gender Disparities in Sentencing: Evidence from the U.S. Federal Courts." Presented at the annual meeting of the American Political Science Association, Boston.

Nejelski, Marilyn, executive director of the Women Judges' Fund for Justice. 1990. Letter to author, June 3.

Resnik, Judith. 1988. "On the Bias: Feminist Reconsideration of the Aspirations for Our Judges." *Southern California Law Review* 61: 1877–1944.

Rhode, Deborah. 1990. *Theoretical Perspectives on Sexual Difference.* New Haven: Yale University Press.

Rowland, C. K., Robert Carp, and Ronald Songer. 1985. "The Effect of Presidential Appointment, Group Identification, and Fact-Law Ambiguity on Lower Federal Judges' Policy Judgments; the Case of Reagan and Carter Appointees." Presented at the annual meeting of the American Political Science Association, New Orleans.

Schafran, Lynn. 1993. "Gender Equality in the Courts: Still on the Judicial Agenda." *Judicature* 77: 10.

Scheb, John, Thomas Ungs, and Allison Hayes. 1988. "Judicial Role Orientations, Attitudes and Decision Making: A Research Note." *Western Political Quarterly* 41: 427–435.

Segal, Jennifer. 1997. "The Decision Making of Clinton's Nontraditional Judicial Appointees." *Judicature* 80: 279.

Songer, Donald, and Kelley Crews-Meyer. 1996. "Does Judge Gender Matter? Decision Making in State Supreme Courts." Presented at the annual meeting of the American Political Science Association, San Francisco.

Songer, Donald, Sue Davis, and Susan Haire. 1994. "A Reappraisal of Diversification in the Federal Courts: Gender Effects in the Courts of Appeals." *Journal of Politics* 56: 425–439.

Stumpf, Henry. 1997. *American Judicial Politics.* Upper Saddle River, N.J.: Prentice-Hall.

Thomas, Sue. 1994. *How Women Legislate.* New York: Oxford University Press.

Totenberg, Nina. 1986. "Women on the Bench, the Constitution, and the Reagan Administration." Address to the annual meeting of the National Association of Women Judges, Key Biscayne, Fla.

Verbrugge, L. 1983. "Multiple Roles and Physical Health of Women and Men." *Journal of Health and Social Behavior* 24: 16–30.

Walker, Thomas, and Deborah Barrow. 1985. "The Diversification of the Federal Bench: Policy and Process Ramifications." *Journal of Politics* 47: 596–616.

Wasby, Stephen. 1981. "The Supreme Court and Public Opinion." In *Courts, Law and Judicial Processes,* ed. Sidney Ulmer. New York: The Free Press.

Weitzman, Lenore J. 1987. "Judicial Perceptions and Perceptions of Judges: The Divorce Law Revolution in Practice." In *Women, the Courts, and Equality,* ed. Laura Crites and Winifred Hepperle. Newbury Park, Calif.: Sage.

Wikler, Norma. 1987. "Educating Judges about Gender Bias in the Courts." In *Women, the Courts and Equality,* ed. Laura Crites and Winifred Hepperle. Newbury Park, Calif.: Sage.

Eleven

Acting for Women
Is What Legislators Say, What They Do?

Debra L. Dodson

If representation is "the making present in some sense of something which is nevertheless not present literally or in fact" (Pitkin 1967, 89), Anita Hill's treatment by the all-male Senate Judiciary Committee during the Clarence Thomas confirmation hearings called into question whether women's experiences, perspectives, and interests can be represented in institutions composed almost exclusively of men. Pitkin's careful efforts to separate who representatives are (descriptive or "stand for" representation) from what they do (substantive or "act for" representation) in her classic work, *The Concept of Representation,* seemed irrelevant to many as the drama of the Hill-Thomas hearings held the nation spellbound one autumn weekend and inspired some women to run for Congress (Wilcox 1994). When the subsequent 1992 election cycle yielded an unprecedented increase in the number of women serving in Congress, and when that 103rd Congress passed record numbers of bills aimed at helping women and their families (Congressional Caucus for Women's Issues 1994) in a manner generally consistent with feminist perspectives, descriptive and substantive representation of women seemed clearly connected (for further discussion of the link between substantive and descriptive representation within the context of that election see Duerst-Lahti and Verstegen 1995).

However, when the 1994 elections brought a shift to the right among women (as well as men) officeholders at both the state and national levels, some questioned whether strategies aimed at increasing the number of feminists and liberals—regardless of gender—might be more useful in holding on to feminist policy gains of the past and making gains in

225

the future. This chapter uses data from a national survey of female state legislators and their male colleagues to explore how the interaction of gender and feminism influences policy attitudes and how these factors, in turn, affect the likelihood of legislators reshaping the agenda, placing on the agenda women-related legislation consistent with feminist notions of "acting for" women.

The Literature

The research presented in this volume is consistent with the findings of much other research from the 1990s that suggests that the increased presence of women in public office transforms the political agenda, with women officeholders giving greater attention than their male colleagues of the same party to women's rights as defined by the contemporary women's movement, as well as to concerns reflecting women's traditional roles as caregivers in the family and in society more generally (Dodson and Carroll 1991; Dodson et al. 1995; Mezey 1994; Saint-Germain 1989; Thomas 1994; also see Phillips 1995). Although the evidence that women officeholders bring somewhat different priorities and perspectives to the policy-making process makes a compelling case for increasing the number of women in office, this body of research has been criticized by some as essentialist, overemphasizing the commonalities among women officeholders' life experiences or shared goals while underemphasizing the differences among women that arise from race, class, ethnicity, partisanship, ideology, urbanization, or regionalism (for example, see Reingold 1998; also see Malveaux 1990; Phillips 1995). One such important and often underexplored difference is feminism (for an exception, see Martin, this volume).

The definition of "feminist" has varied over time and across cultures (Offen 1992) and is tied to a variety of conflicting ideological perspectives ranging from Marxist to liberal feminist. Consequently, those who share a commitment to judging policy through feminist lenses may be looking through very different lenses, having concern about very different conditions and differing over what constitutes gender-related injustices (Grant 1993; Spelman 1988; Tong 1989). Despite these differences among feminist perspectives and among those who may consider themselves feminists, it seems fair to expect that feminists in general should share a commitment "to ending the subordination of women" (Jaggar 1994, 2) and to focus on women (for discussion, see Randall 1994). Hence, feminist officeholders would be more inclined than nonfeminists to recognize and reject the legitimacy of gender inequities in our society that may be unnoticed or accepted by others and to work as

officeholders toward eradication of governmental policies that perpetu-
ate the subordination of women to men, that assume gender inequity
is "natural," and that deny the legitimacy of concerns of particular
importance to women, labeling them as private concerns, outside the
proper realm of the state.

Given that the women's movement has almost certainly played some
role in women's increased presence in nontraditional roles as public
officeholders (Carroll 1989; Carroll and Strimling 1983),[1] it might be
that the increased presence of feminists, rather than women per se,
might explain the gender gap among public officeholders' attitudes
about "women's issues" such as the Equal Rights Amendment and abortion (Dodson and Carroll 1991; Johnson and Carroll 1978; Leader
1977; Stanwick and Kleeman 1983) and attitudes about ostensibly "gen-
derless" issues such as the environment and economic development, social services, the death penalty, and the economy (Burns and Schumaker
1987; Dodson and Carroll 1991; Frankovic 1977; Stanwick and Kleeman 1983); and perhaps (as Dolan and Ford 1998 suggest) it could account for women's previously noted tendency to give greater priority to
women's rights, as well as to children and family issues.[2] Thus I would
make the following prediction:

Hypothesis One: Women officeholders will be more likely than men
to express attitudinal support for feminist positions on public policy
issues.

Hypothesis Two: Women officeholders will be more likely than men to
work on legislation aimed at benefiting women in particular.

Hypothesis Three: Feminist officeholders will be more likely than non-
feminists to express attitudinal support for feminist positions on public
policy issues.

Hypothesis Four: Feminist officeholders will be more likely than non-
feminists to work on legislation aimed at benefiting women in particular.

This raises two important questions. The first centers on the relevance of the feminist label. "Feminism" is a loaded word in our society,
a label that some perceive as scaring away voters, as alienating colleagues, or as just being too "extreme." How many times have we all
heard, "I'm not a feminist but . . . I support the ERA, I am for equal
pay for equal work," etc. It seems far safer in most cases for politicians
—women included—to say, "Yes, I am for government-subsidized day
care" or "Yes, I am in favor of the Equal Rights Amendment" than to
say "I am a feminist." Labels are not important, according to this line

of thought; candidates' stands on issues are what we should consider in predicting legislative actions. Are politicians' claims of support for feminist concerns and feminist agendas good indicators that they will actually act on them once in office, regardless of whether they are feminists? Will closet feminists—those who may hold attitudes consistent with major feminist organizations but be unwilling to associate themselves with feminists (Carroll 1984)—do as much for women as feminists who embrace the label?

The second question deals with whether feminism has the same meaning for men as it does for women. Some scholars suggest that no matter how sympathetic male feminists may be, they cannot experience life as women do (Klein 1984; also see Conover 1984; Gurin 1985; Phillips 1995; Sigel and Welchel 1986), and thus, no matter how sympathetic male feminists may be, their feminism is different from that of their female counterparts. According to Klein (1984), women's feminist attitudes are more likely than men's to be grounded in concrete experiences. While women's feminism is to some extent an outgrowth of abstract commitments to equality and liberalism as well, men's feminism is even more likely to be rooted in these abstract ideological beliefs (Klein 1984). Gender consciousness,[3] a realization that one's sex affects one's relationship with the political world and "embodies an identification with similar others, positive affect toward them and a feeling of interdependence with the group's fortunes" (Tolleson-Rinehart 1992, 14), may increase the saliency of feminist goals for female feminist officeholders. Thus, I hypothesize that:

Hypothesis Five: Among feminist officeholders, women will be more likely than men to express attitudinal support for feminist positions on public policy issues.

Hypothesis Six: Among feminist officeholders, women will be more likely than men to work on legislation aimed at benefiting women in particular.

Hypothesis Seven: Among feminist officeholders with comparable levels of attitudinal support for feminist policy goals, women will be more likely than men to work on legislation aimed at benefiting women in particular.

While male and female non-feminists, like feminists, differ in their life experiences, it is less clear whether women who do not consider themselves feminists will allow these gender differences in life experiences to influence their attitudes and actions on public matters.[4] If they do, then gender differences in policy attitudes and public policy actions could occur even among non-feminist legislators. Gender consciousness may provide a lens for interpreting the experiences of being women in a predominantly male institution and as such may evoke feminist attitudes and behavior even from "closet feminists" who reject the feminist label. (See Carroll 1984 and Conover 1984 for pertinent discussions.) Alternatively, non-feminist women who lack gender consciousness may nevertheless have a "female consciousness," which accepts the sexual division of labor and manifests with a vengeance the concern with preserving life (Kaplan 1982), leading these women to behave differently from their male counterparts, even as they diverge from their female feminist colleagues as well (Dolan and Ford 1998). Therefore, assuming that for any one of a number of reasons gender differences in life experiences will affect the attitudes and actions of non-feminists, it is predicted that:

Hypothesis Eight: Among non-feminist officeholders, women will be more likely than men to express attitudinal support for feminist positions on public policy issues.

Hypothesis Nine: Among non-feminist officeholders, women will be more likely than men to work on legislation aimed at benefiting women in particular.

Hypothesis Ten: Among non-feminist officeholders with similar levels of attitudinal commitment to feminist policy goals, women will be more likely than men to work on legislation aimed at benefiting women in particular.

Given that we have thus far predicted that both feminism and being female will be important factors contributing to attitudinal support for feminist policies and increasing the likelihood of "acting for" women by working on bills aimed at helping them, it seems fairly safe to expect that feminist women will do far more than non-feminist men to support feminist goals as measured by both their attitudes and actions. What is less clear is whether feminist men or non-feminist women will be more supportive of feminist goals through their attitudes and actions. Given Klein's assertion that men come to their feminism largely through their liberal ideology, it seems reasonable to predict that:

Hypothesis Eleven: Male feminist officeholders will be more likely than female non-feminist officeholders to express attitudinal support for feminist positions on public policy issues.

The more difficult matter is actions. Hannah Pitkin's care in separating descriptive from substantive representation of any group's concerns has been challenged by Phillips (1995), for example, who asserts that a politics of ideas, advocated by Pitkin and others, should be replaced by a politics of presence. Central to Phillips' arguments for a politics of presence is an assumption that previously excluded classes, such as women, who have in recent years demanded a seat at the table, have a better chance of getting their ideas on the agenda if they themselves, rather than someone else (i.e., a man) who has not walked in their shoes, is present to speak for them. As Phillips explains, recognizing that

> the shared experience of women as women can only ever figure as a promise of shared concerns . . . changing the gender composition of elected assemblies is largely an enabling condition. . . . It is, in some sense, a shot in the dark: far more likely to reach its target than when those shooting are predominately male, but still open to all kinds of accident. (1995, 83).

Although this might suggest that any woman on average would be better than any man on average in acting for women, and thus a non-feminist woman would do a better job than a feminist man in acting for women, that is an oversimplification. Phillips, while arguing for a politics of presence, acknowledges that the relationship between gender and policy action is imperfect. Given that the question is whether the relatively rare feminist man will do more to advance feminist policy goals than non-feminist women, it seems reasonable to predict that:

Hypothesis Twelve: Feminist men will be more likely than non-feminist women officeholders to work on legislation aimed at benefiting women in particular.

Methodology

This chapter uses data from a nationwide survey of women state legislators and their male colleagues conducted by the Center for the American Woman and Politics during the summer of 1988. Four samples of legislators were drawn: (1) the population of women state senators (n = 228), (2) a systematic sample of one-half of women state representatives (n = 474), (3) a systematic sample of male state senators, stratified by state and sampled in proportion to the number of women from each state in our sample of women senators (n = 228), and (4) a systematic sample of male state representatives, stratified by state and sampled in proportion to the number of women from each state in our sample of women state representatives (n = 474). A telephone interview of approximately one half-hour was attempted with each of the legislators in the sample, resulting in the following response rates: women senators, 86 percent; women representatives, 87 percent; men senators, 60 percent; men representatives, 73 percent.[5] This analysis combines the two samples of women and the two samples of men, weighting them to reflect the population of female legislators and their male colleagues serving in the summer of 1988.[6]

Attitudinal support for feminist policies is measured by responses to five questions asked of all respondents about issues of concern to groups associated with the women's movement. These include questions about the ERA, minors' access to abortion, an abortion ban, state-subsidized child care, and raising taxes to fund increased social services.[7] Feminist policy attitudes serve as both dependent variables and independent variables predicting "feminist policy action," the indicator used in this chapter of acting for women based on whether the legislator had worked in the most recent session on at least one bill aimed at helping women.[8] While there are admittedly other ways that legislators could act for women, certainly the willingness to put women-focused matters on the agenda or work on such bills is an important aspect of acting for. Finally, feminist identification is determined by whether respondents did or did not say that they considered themselves to be feminists.[9]

Findings

Table 11.1 shows that self-identified feminists were significantly more likely than non-feminists to express attitudinal support for feminist policy positions on all five policy questions of special relevance to the women's movement: the ERA, minors' access to abortion, attitudes toward banning abortion, state-subsidized child care, and raising taxes to fund increased social services. In addition, women were more supportive than men of feminist positions in three of the five cases as well.

Feminists and women not only expressed greater attitudinal support for feminist policy positions but were also more likely to act for women. Feminists were more likely than non-feminists (67% versus 39%) and women more likely than men (59% versus 36%) to have worked during the most recent session on a bill aimed at helping women. Thus, the data support Hypotheses One through Four, showing that women and feminists were generally more likely than men and non-feminists to hold policy attitudes consistent with those of the women's movement and to act for women, as evidenced by their work on legislation focused on women.

What these data do not reveal is how the intersection of feminist

Table 11.1. Proportion Supporting Feminist Positions on Policy Questions among Self-Identified Feminists, Non-feminists, Women, and Men

Policy Questions	Feminists	Non-feminists	Phi	Women	Men	Phi
Oppose parental consent for abortion	78% (351)	31% (681)	.45***	57% (590)	33% (462)	.24***
Support ERA	97% (354)	58% (687)	.41***	79% (594)	61% (467)	.21***
Oppose abortion ban	89% (354)	57% (684)	.33***	74% (589)	61% (467)	.14***
Support gov't-subsidized child care	83% (353)	62% (685)	21***	71% (585)	68% (473)	.03
Support increased taxes for social services	79% (350)	51% (678)	.27***	61% (583)	59% (462)	.02

*p ≤ .05   **p ≤ .01   ***p ≤ .001

Note: Figures in parentheses are the total numbers of cases on which the adjacent percentages are based.

identification and gender affected policy attitudes and actions. Table 11.2 confirms that, at least on some feminist policy issues, gender differences emerged among feminist, as well as non-feminist, legislators, providing support for Hypotheses Five and Eight. Feminist women, and to a lesser extent non-feminist women, were significantly more inclined than their male counterparts to support feminist views on abortion and ERA. While gender differences did not occur among either feminists or non-feminists on raising taxes to increase social services funding or government-subsidized child care—matters that require government take a more activist role in providing resources for ostensibly "private" needs in order to ensure equality—the results suggest an undercurrent of feminism that is manifested in the views of women reluctant to label themselves as feminists. However, they also suggest that feminist self-identification has meaning for men, for, as predicted in Hypothesis Eleven, feminist men were substantially more likely than non-feminist women to express policy attitudes consistent with the goals of the contemporary women's movement.

No matter how vocal politicians may be in their support for women's

Acting for Women

Table 11.2. Proportion Supporting Feminist Positions on Policy
Questions among Self-Identified Feminist and Non-feminist
Legislators

Policy Questions	Feminists			Non-feminists		
	Male	Female	Phi	Male	Female	Phi
Oppose parental consent for abortion	69% (91)	81% (260)	.14**	24% (365)	38% (318)	.15***
Support ERA	91% (91)	99% (263)	.19***	53% (369)	64% (318)	.11*
Oppose abortion ban	82% (91)	92% (262)	.14*	55% (368)	60% (316)	.05
Support gov't-subsidized child care	88% (92)	81% (261)	.07	63% (374)	61% (313)	.03
Support increased taxes for social services	81% (92)	78% (258)	−.03	54% (364)	48% (315)	.06

*p ≤ .05   **p ≤ .01   ***p ≤ .001

Note: Figures in parentheses are the total numbers of cases on which the adjacent percentages are based.

concerns and feminist policies, what really matters is whether they follow their words with action. Attitudinal support for feminist policy issues is only evidence of the potential for feminist policy actions; it is no guarantee that legislators actually will translate their attitudes into action (cf. Fazio and Zanna 1981; Nisbett and Ross 1980). Indeed, when it comes to action, not all feminists (or non-feminists) are equal. As predicted in Hypothesis Six, feminist women were significantly more likely than feminist men to have worked in the most recent session on a bill aimed at helping women (73% versus 49%). Hypothesis Nine is supported as well, for among non-feminists, more women than men reported working on a bill aimed at helping women (46% versus 34%).

Feminist women, not surprisingly, were most likely and non-feminist men least likely to have worked on a bill aimed at helping women. What was surprising was that feminist men, who were significantly more likely than non-feminist women to express attitudinal support for feminist policies, were not more likely than non-feminist women to have worked on a bill aimed at helping women. While I can only specu-late about the gap between feminist men's attitudes and actions and the reasons that Hypothesis Twelve was not supported, it may be that the commitment of feminist men's attitudinal support for women's rights policies fails to run deeply enough to be converted into action when time, resources, and energy are required. Conversely, when non-feminist women have the opportunity to define their policy priorities and personal agendas in their own terms, their apparent rejection of feminism erodes as they find ways to act for women consistent with the goals of the contemporary women's movement.

To explore the effects of issue attitudes, feminism and gender on the likelihood of acting for women, the five feminist policy attitude questions are used to construct an additive index, the Feminist Policy Attitude Index.[10] Table 11.3 shows that both gender and feminist self-identification are important intervening variables in the relationship be-tween issue positions and legislative action aimed at helping women. As predicted in Hypothesis Seven, among feminists who scored high on the Feminist Policy Attitude Index, women were significantly more likely than their male counterparts to have worked on a bill targeted toward women. (Although the gender gap is almost as large among self-identified feminists who express only a moderate level of support for feminist policy goals, the smaller number of cases in those cells keeps it from attaining statistical significance at the .05 level.) The same pat-tern holds among non-feminists as well, providing support for Hy-pothesis Ten and suggesting that even among non-feminists, women do make a difference. Indeed, at each point on the Feminist Policy Attitude Index, non-feminist women tend to be somewhat more likely than their non-feminist male colleagues to work on a bill aimed at helping women; however, the differences are statistically significant only among those with moderate levels of support for feminist policies.

Overall, the data suggest that both being female and feminist self-identification increase the likelihood of acting for women. The tendency for female self-identified feminists to be the most likely, and male non-feminists the least likely, to have worked on a bill aimed at helping women continued even among those who shared equal levels of attitudi-nal support for feminist policies. More importantly, there was no addi-tional evidence that would allow us to accept Hypothesis Twelve, for even among those with similar levels of attitudinal support for feminist policies, self-identified feminist men and non-feminist women tied for second place, with the men being no more likely than the women to act for women. And willingness to accept the feminist label counts among women as well, for even among those women with similar views on

Table 11.3. Percentage Working on Bill Aimed at Helping Women, Controlling for Gender, Feminist Identification, and Feminist Policy Attitudinal Support Scores

Feminist	Feminist Policy Attitudinal Support Score		
	Low	Medium	High
Men	*a*	44% (17)	54% (68)
Women	*a*	62% (45)	75% (214)
		Phi = .16	Phi = .20***
Non-feminist			
Men	24% (n = 96)	32% (186)	48% (83)
Women	34% (n = 92)	48% (118)	55% (108)
	Phi = .10	Phi = .15**	Phi = −.07

*p ≤ .05   **p ≤ .01   ***p ≤ .001

Note: Figures in parentheses are the total numbers of cases on which the adjacent percentages are based. An *a* denotes a number of cases insufficient for computation.

feminist policy issues, feminists were more likely than non-feminists to have acted for women by working on a bill aimed at helping women. It may well be that the same factors that affect women's comfort with the feminist label also affect the willingness of women to act for women, even when they are equally supportive of policies central to the agenda of the women's movement. At the same time, the life experiences of women can make even female non-feminists as focused on matters of concern to women as male feminists who lack the direct personal experiences.

Conclusion

The results of this study do suggest that increased descriptive representation will lead to improvements in substantive representation of women consistent with the goals of the women's movement. But as Anne Phillips (1995) cautions in her discussion of the politics of presence, efforts to ensure group members a seat at the table in policymaking provide only the potential that the group's concerns and perspectives will be included on the political agenda.

Feminist women demonstrated the greatest commitment to putting women on the legislative radar screen. Not only were they the most likely to express policy attitudes consistent with those generally supported by the feminist movement, feminist women were by far the most likely to report that they had worked on a bill aimed at helping women in the most recent session. If the choice is between a feminist woman and a feminist man who share equally high levels of attitudinal support for feminist policy goals, the chances are better that the woman, rather than the man, will act for women.

Similarly, there is little doubt that if a non-feminist is going to be elected, substantive representation of women is more likely to be furthered by the election of women than men. Non-feminist women may have been only slightly more feminist than non-feminist men on abortion and the Equal Rights Amendment, but they were substantially more likely than their male colleagues to report working on a bill aimed at helping women. These tendencies held even after taking into account their attitudes about feminist public policy issues.

The more difficult issue is whether substantive representation of women is likely to be furthered by the election of more women if the choice is between a feminist man and a non-feminist woman. At first glance, when the focus was on public policy attitudes, the male feminists (who were only about 20 percent of the male legislators surveyed) seemed the more likely to increase the substantive representation of women as defined by feminists, for they were substantially more likely than non-feminist women to support abortion rights, the ERA, greater access to child care, and increased taxes to provide for increased social services. Yet the picture became far more cloudy when the focus shifted from attitudes to actions, for feminist men and non-feminist women were about equally likely to report having worked on at least one bill aimed at helping women. While the feminist men may be important allies in floor votes and (to a lesser extent) working on legislation aimed at helping women (and certainly as a group are a better source of support than non-feminist women on votes dealing with pro-choice legislation, the ERA, and other matters that have been high-profile feminist policy concerns), it is also clear that non-feminist women may nevertheless contribute (albeit at a lower level than feminist women) to efforts to make sure that concerns of particular importance to women are on the political agenda and that women's lives are considered in the policy process. What they say about support for feminist policies is not necessarily what they do. Non-feminist women are more inclined to act for women, and feminist men less inclined to act for women, than we might expect from their attitudes about major policy issues of concern to the contemporary women's movement.

Feminist women are clearly more dedicated to seeing that government pays attention to women's needs than is true on average for feminist men who may express abstract support for the same types of policies. In other words, what they say is what they do when it comes to pushing legislation through the legislative process. But until feminist women are a majority of legislators (which does not seem likely any time soon), they need support from other legislators sympathetic to their concerns. Feminist men's support for feminist policies and willingness to work on bills that benefit women (even though not at the same high level as feminist women's) makes them potentially sympathetic and valuable allies.

Yet what may sometimes be overlooked is that women who do not self-identify as feminists, but who show at least a moderate level of attitudinal support for feminist policies, may be equally important in at least some legislative efforts to place women's concerns on the legislative agenda. The impact of non-feminist women is apparent once they are allowed to define the type of women's policy on which they wish to work, rather than being confined to a narrow range of feminist "litmus" issues. When feminist issues are broadly defined, the female non-feminists are just as likely as male feminists to engage in efforts aimed at helping women consistent with feminist policy goals.

Notes

1. For example, the proportion of women state legislators has increased more than fivefold, rising from 4 percent in 1969 to 22.5 percent in 2000 (Center for American Women and Politics 2000b). Similar increases have occurred at other—although not all—levels of government (Center for American Women and Politics 2000a).

2. For related discussion at the mass level, see Conover 1988.

3. No consensus exists in the literature on the appropriate definition of this concept (cf. Gurin 1985; Conover 1984; Sigel and Welchel 1986; Tolleson Rinehart 1992). For some, gender consciousness (or concepts with different labels but similar meanings such as minority consciousness or female consciousness) can occur only among feminists (e.g., Gurin 1985), while for others gender consciousness either is not explicitly feminist (Conover 1984) or is explicitly not feminist (Kaplan 1982). The assumption in this chapter is that gender consciousness potentially may occur among feminists and non-feminists, but the nature of this consciousness could differ for feminists and non-feminists.

4. Gender difference explanations that may be applicable to assessing the impact of non-feminists include the greater saliency of the private sphere in

women's lives (Hartman 1981; Elshtain 1982; Sapiro 1982; Kaplan 1982), the greater connection between the public and private spheres for women (Ackelsberg 1984; Flammang 1984), and the greater importance women assign to relationships and caring for others (Chodorow 1985; Gilligan 1985).

5. Respondents and non-respondents did not differ substantially from one another with regard to party affiliation, the one variable for which we have data for all lawmakers sampled.

6. Since all women senators but only one-half of women representatives were surveyed, we statistically weighted the data to ensure that our findings were representative of the population. The resulting women's sample and men's sample are weighted to reflect the population of women state legislators and to provide a comparable sample of men. The weights are as follows: women senators, 0.5; women representatives, 1.23; men senators, 0.57; men representatives, 1.17.

7. Respondents were asked to agree strongly, agree somewhat, disagree somewhat or disagree strongly with a battery of questions that included the following:

Government should provide child care services to all parents who need them, with fees charged according to ability to pay.

Minors should be able to obtain a legal abortion without parental consent.

State and local taxes should be raised to help make up for some of the decrease in federal funding for social services.

The Equal Rights Amendment should be passed by Congress and ratified by the states.

I personally think abortion should be prohibited in all or most circumstances.

Throughout this chapter, feminist positions and feminist policy actions are defined as those endorsed by the major national feminist organizations such as the National Organization for Women or the National Women's Political Caucus.

8. Legislators were asked whether they had worked on a bill during the most recent session where the bill itself or specific provisions of the bill were intended to help women in particular. If respondents answered "yes" to the initial question but did not describe what the bill did for women, they were recoded as "no," as were those responding "don't know" and those refusing to answer the initial question. This meant that responses of 2.6 percent of the women and 4.8 percent of the men were recoded as "no." Bills or bill provisions mentioned that did not obviously relate to women (e.g., bills aimed specifically at children or the elderly) were considered invalid and the responses were recoded as "no." About 5.6 percent of women's and 5.4 percent of men's responses were recoded as no on these grounds. In addition, we also excluded anti-feminist bills from this category, but only

1.4 percent of women and 1.2 percent of men mentioned these. The reclassification had little impact on the relative likelihood that various subgroups had worked on a women's rights bill, although it slightly reduced the number reporting such activities. The measure, of course, does not reflect differences in the number of such bills they worked on, but it can reveal whether they worked on at least one. Examples of qualifying bills included: establishing greater equity in dividing marital property in divorce or assessing alimony; custody and child support; teen pregnancy prevention; domestic violence prevention; pay equity; parental leave; day care; prenatal care or health care for women; Medicaid funding of abortion; sex equity in education; displaced homemakers' assistance; emergency room protocol for rape victims; increased penalty for rape; funding for rape crisis centers; insurance coverage for mammograms; providing services for elderly women; equal pay for equal work; pro-choice legislation; equal treatment in insurance; prohibiting sexual harassment; and regulation of judges' instructions to juries in rape cases.

9. Respondents were asked whether they did or did not identify with a variety of labels, one of which was "feminist." Those who did identify with the label "feminist" were classified as feminists and others as non-feminists. About 20 percent of the men and 45 percent of the women identified themselves as feminists.

10. The "Feminist Policy Attitude Index" is an additive index based on the number of feminist answers given to the five policy issues deemed particularly relevant to the women's movement. Creating an index that can be used for both women and men presented some problems. When all five issue items were factor analyzed, two factors emerged for the men (one factor relating to abortion and a second relating to issues other than abortion), while only one factor emerged for women.

References

Ackelsberg, Martha. 1984. "Women's Collaborative Activities and City Life: Politics and Policy." In *Political Women: Current Roles in State and Local Government,* ed. Janet A. Flammang. Beverly Hills: Sage.

Burns, Nancy Elizabeth, and Paul Schumaker. 1987. "Gender Differences in Attitudes about the Role of Local Government." *Social Sciences Quarterly* 68: 138–147.

Carroll, Susan. 1984. "Women Candidates and Support for Feminist Concerns: The Closet Feminist Syndrome." *Western Political Quarterly* 37: 307–323.

Carroll, Susan J. 1988. "Women's Autonomy and the Gender Gap: 1980 and 1982." In *The Politics of the Gender Gap,* ed. Carol M. Mueller. Beverly Hills: Sage.

Carroll, Susan J. 1989. "Gender Politics and the Socializing Impact of the Women's Movement." In *Political Learning in Adulthood: A Sourcebook of*

Theory and Research, ed. Roberta S. Siegel. Chicago: University of Chicago Press.

Carroll, Susan J., and Wendy Strimling. 1983. *Women's Routes to Elective Office: A Comparison with Men's.* New Brunswick, N.J.: Center for the American Woman and Politics.

Center for American Women and Politics. 2000a. "Women in Elective Office 2000." Fact Sheet.

Center for American Women and Politics. 2000b. "Women in State Legislatures 2000." Fact Sheet.

Chodorow, Nancy. 1985. "Gender Relation and Difference in Psychoanalytic Perspective." In *The Future of Difference,* ed. Hester Eisenstein and Alice Jardine. New Brunswick, N.J.: Rutgers University Press.

Congressional Caucus for Women's Issues. 1994. "Funding of Women's Programs Continues to Rise in FY95." *Update* (September/October).

Conover, Pamela Johnston. 1984. "The Influence of Group Identification on Political Perception and Evaluation." *Journal of Politics* 46: 760–785.

Conover, Pamela Johnston. 1988. "Feminists and the Gender Gap." *Journal of Politics* 50: 985–1010.

Dodson, Debra L., and Susan J. Carroll. 1991. *Reshaping the Agenda: Women in State Legislatures.* New Brunswick, N.J.: Center for the American Woman and Politics.

Dodson, Debra L., Susan J. Carroll, Ruth B. Mandel, Katherine E. Kleeman, Ronnee Schreiber, and Debra Liebowitz. 1995. *Voices, Views, Votes: The Impact of Women in the 103rd Congress.* New Brunswick, N.J.: Center for the American Woman and Politics.

Dolan, Kathleen, and Lynn E. Ford. 1998. "Are All Women State Legislators Alike?" In *Women and Elective Office: Past, Present, and Future,* ed. Sue Thomas and Clyde Wilcox. New York: Oxford University Press.

Duerst-Lahti, Georgia, and Dayna Verstegen. 1995. "Making Something of Absence: The 'Year of the Woman' and Women's Representation." In *Gender Power, Leadership and Governance,* ed. Georgia Duerst-Lahti and Rita Mae Kelly. Ann Arbor: University of Michigan Press.

Elshtain, Jean Bethke. 1982. "Feminism, Family, and Community." *Dissent* 29: 442–449.

Fazio, Russell H., and Mark P. Zanna. 1981. "Direct Experience and Attitude-Behavior Consistency." In *Advances in Experimental Social Psychology,* vol. 14, ed. L. Berkowitz. New York: Academic Press.

Flammang, Janet A. 1984. "Introduction: A Reflection on Themes of a 'Women's Politics.'" In *Political Women: Current Roles in State and Local Government,* ed. Janet Flammang. Beverly Hills: Sage.

Frankovic, Kathleen. 1977. "Sex and Voting in the U.S. House of Representatives: 1961–1975." *American Politics Quarterly* 5: 315–330.

Gilligan, Carol. 1985. "In a Different Voice: Women's Conceptions of Self and Morality." In *The Future of Difference,* ed. Hester Eisenstein and Alice Jardine. New Brunswick, N.J.: Rutgers University Press.

Grant, Judith. 1993. *Fundamental Feminism: Contesting the Core Concepts of Feminist Theory.* New York: Routledge.

Gurin, Patricia. 1985. "Women's Gender Consciousness." *Public Opinion Quarterly* 49: 143–163.

Jaggar, Alison M. 1994. "Introduction: Living with Contradictions." In *Living with Contradictions: Controversies in Feminist Ethics,* ed. Alison M. Jaggar. Boulder, Colo.: Westview Press.

Johnson, Marilyn, and Susan Carroll. 1978. "Statistical Report: Profile of Women Holding Public Office, 1977." In *Women in Public Office: A Biographical Directory and Statistical Analysis,* ed. Kathy Stanwick and Marilyn Johnson. Metuchen, N.J.: Scarecrow.

Kaplan, Temma. 1982. "Female Consciousness and Collective Action: The Case of Barcelona, 1910–1918." *Signs: Journal of Women in Culture and Society* 7: 545–566.

Klein, Ethel. 1984. *Gender Politics.* Cambridge, Mass.: Harvard University Press.

Leader, Shelah G. 1977. "The Policy Impact of Elected Women Officials." In *The Impact of the Electoral Process,* ed. Louis Maisel and Joseph Cooper. Beverly Hills: Sage.

Malveaux, Julianne. 1990. "Gender Difference and Beyond: An Economic Perspective on Diversity and Commonality among Women." In *Theoretical Perspectives on Sexual Difference,* ed. Deborah L. Rhode. New Haven: Yale University Press.

Mezey, Susan Gluck. 1994. "Increasing the Number of Women in Office: Does It Matter?" In *The Year of the Woman: Myths and Realities,* ed. Elizabeth Adell Cook, Sue Thomas, and Clyde Wilcox. Boulder, Colo.: Westview Press.

Nisbett, Richard, and Lee Ross. 1980. *Human Inference: Strategies and Shortcomings of Social Judgement.* Englewood Cliffs, N.J.: Prentice-Hall.

Offen, Karen. 1992. "Defining Feminism: A Comparative Historical Perspective." In *Beyond Equality and Difference,* ed. Gisela Bock and Susan James. New York: Routledge.

Phillips, Anne. 1995. *The Politics of Presence.* Oxford: Oxford University Press.

Pitkin, Hannah. 1967. *The Concept of Representation.* Berkeley: University of California Press.

Randall, Vicky. 1994. "Feminism and Political Analysis." In *Different Roles, Different Voices: Women and Politics in the United States and Europe,* ed. Marianne Githens, Pippa Norris, and Joni Lovenduski. New York: Harper Collins College Publishers.

Reingold, Beth. 1998. "Making a Difference: Legislative Behavior and the Meaning of Women's Political Representation." Presented at the annual meeting of the American Political Science Association, Boston.

Saint-Germain, Michelle. 1989. "Does Their Difference Make a Difference? The Impact of Women on Public Policy in the Arizona Legislature." *Social Science Quarterly* 70: 956–968.

Sapiro, Virginia. 1982. "Private Costs of Public Commitments or Public Costs of Private Commitments? Family Roles Versus Political Ambition." *American Journal of Political Science* 26: 265–279.

Sigel, Roberta S., and Nancy L. Welchel. 1986. "Assessing the Past and Looking toward the Future: Perceptions of Change in the Status of Women." Presented at the annual meeting of the American Political Science Association, Chicago.

Spelman, Elizabeth V. 1988. *Inessential Woman: Problems of Exclusion in Feminist Thought*. Boston: Beacon Press.

Stanwick, Kathy A., and Katherine E. Kleeman. 1983. *Women Make a Difference*. New Brunswick, N.J.: Center for the American Woman and Politics.

Thomas, Sue. 1994. *How Women Legislate*. New York: Oxford University Press.

Tolleson-Rinehart, Sue. 1992. *Gender Consciousness and Politics*. New York: Routledge.

Tong, Rosemarie. 1989. *Feminist Thought*. Boulder, Colo.: Westview Press.

Wilcox, Clyde. 1994. "Why Was 1992 the 'Year of the Woman'? Explaining Women's Gains in 1992." In *The Year of the Woman: Myths and Realities*, ed. Elizabeth Adell Cook, Sue Thomas, and Clyde Wilcox. Boulder, Colo.: Westview Press.

Contributors

Edith J. Barrett is Associate Professor in the School of Urban and Public Affairs at the University of Texas at Arlington. She is co-author of *Support for the American Welfare State* (1992) as well as articles on welfare policy and the intersection between gender and race/ethnicity issues. Her current research focuses on the political development of urban low-income minority adolescents.

Susan Abrams Beck is Associate Professor at Fordham University. She has published articles on the American presidency and women in politics, including "Gender and the Politics of Affordable Housing," in Judith A. Garber and Robyne S. Turner, eds,. *Gender in Urban Research* (1995). Her most recent research is on the role of Eleanor Roosevelt in support of women's rights at the framing of the U.N. Declaration of Human Rights in 1948.

Janet K. Boles is Professor of Political Science at Marquette University. She is the author of *The Politics of the Equal Rights Amendment* (1979) and is co-editor of the forthcoming *Women of Color: Hearing the Voices, Raising the Issues*. She and her co-author are preparing a second edition of their *Historical Dictionary of Feminism*.

Susan J. Carroll is Professor of Political Science at Rutgers University and Senior Research Associate at the Center for American Women and Politics (CAWP) of the Eagleton Institute of Politics. She is the author of numerous works on women's political participation, including *Women* *as Candidates in American Politics* (Indiana University Press, 2nd ed., 1994). Her current research focuses on the impact of women in Congress, media coverage of women voters and candidates, and the effect of term limits on the representation of women in state legislatures.

Debra L. Dodson is Senior Research Associate at Rutgers University's Eagleton Institute of Politics. Her work focuses on women's impact in public office and reproductive rights policy. She is writing a book about gender and representation in the United States Congress.

Lyn Kathlene is Associate Professor of Political Science and Director of the Public Policy Analysis Program at the University of Nebraska–Lincoln. Her work centers on the question of underrepresented voices in the policy process and has been published in the *American Political Science Review*, the *Journal of Politics*, the *Journal of Policy Analysis and Management*, and various edited volumes.

Elaine Martin is Professor of Political Science at Eastern Michigan University. She has been a pioneer in the study of gender and the judiciary and has published many articles and book chapters on various aspects of that subject. She is completing a book, *Women Judges and Justices: Voices from the Bench*.

Nancy E. McGlen is Dean of Arts and Sciences and Professor of Political Science at Niagara University. She is the co-author of *Women, Politics and American Society* (1998), *Women and Foreign Policy: The Insiders* (1993), and other publications on women in foreign policy. Her current research examines the changing nature of academia as it impacts on women professors.

Meredith Reid Sarkees is Visiting Professor of Political Science at DePaul University. She is co-author with Nancy E. McGlen of *Women in Foreign Policy: The Insiders* (1993) and several articles concerning the status of women in political science. Her most recent work with J. David Singer focuses upon interstate and intrastate war.

Janann Sherman is Assistant Professor of History at the University of Memphis. She is the author of *No Place for a Woman: A Life of Senator Margaret Chase Smith* (2000) and co-author of *The Perfect 36: Tennessee Delivers Woman Suffrage* (1998).

Sue Thomas is Associate Professor of Government at Georgetown University. She specializes in the study of women officeholders, and her books on this subject include *Women in Elective Office: Past, Present, and Future* (1998) and *How Women Legislate* (1994).

Sue Tolleson-Rinehart is the Program Administrator of the UNC Program on Health Outcomes at the University of North Carolina at Chapel Hill, where she oversees research, education, and service activities. She is the co-editor of *Gender and American Politics* (2000), to which she contributed a chapter on gender, health politics, and health policy; the author of *Gender Consciousness and Politics* (1992); and co-author, with Jeanie R. Stanley, of *Claytie and the Lady: Ann Richards, Gender, and Politics in Texas* (1994).

Susan Welch is Professor of Political Science at The Pennsylvania State University where she is also Dean of the College of the Liberal Arts. She is the author of numerous articles on women and politics and a co-author, with Robert Darcy and Janet Clark, of *Women, Elections, and Representation* (2nd ed., 1994). She is completing a co-authored book on race and American cities.

Index